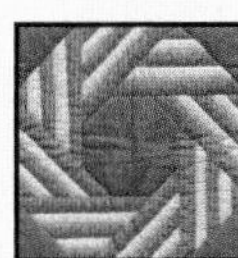

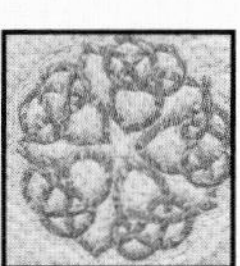

The Essential Sampler Quilt

Contents

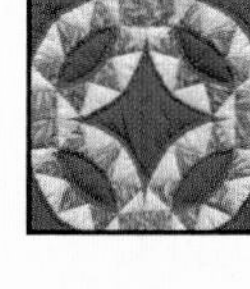

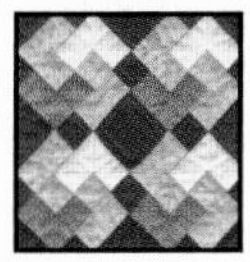

Introduction

What draws the likes of you and me to patchwork and quilting primarily? I'd hazard a guess that I began for the same reasons that you did too: the endless and universal attraction for women of handling fabrics, the incessant urge to put needle into fabric and the desire to discover new and exciting ways to create pattern and fill our lives with colour.

When I began to make patchwork, many years ago and before I gave any thought to making an actual quilt, I worked in hexagons – I thought that was what patchwork was all about. Soft clutch balls for babies and scrappy cushion-covers were all stitched by hand over papers while my family was still young – when the children were at the toddler stage, it was great fun to get out the 'making bag' on a rainy day. Besides playing with the usual empty yoghurt pots and tubes of glitter, I let my children choose and cut their patches of fabrics and see how they could then be joined together.

All patchwork is creative, but when I discovered block patchwork (as in quiltmaking), I found that it filled a creative need in me that hadn't been met by other forms of needlework or art. I began by making several small sampler quilts – these were invaluable for working through new techniques by trial and error while achieving realistic goals. Motivation gathered momentum, and I experienced a sense of achievement as these smaller projects were finished fairly quickly.

As I began on my first small quilts, I learnt the basics of various different skills. I worked through many traditional blocks, at the same time covering numerous techniques. During this time I tried and tested many techniques, and I don't mind admitting that some were more successful than others. No patchwork block comes with any guarantees – there'll inevitably be some that you like and some that you won't touch again with the proverbial bargepole – but at least if you have a go at something new, you'll be pushing the boundaries of your knowledge just that little bit more. You may also find that you quite like that next stage: there's nothing wrong with setting yourself a personal challenge now and again. If you then decide that a specific technique is not right for you (at this stage in your quiltmaking, anyway), at least you can give an informed opinion on the whys and wherefores of that particular skill. And who knows; it just might come in handy one day when you're least expecting it to. In a nutshell: you may not use what you've learnt immediately or on a big scale, but at least you'll have learnt how to do it.

Whether you're making a quilt to go on your bed to keep you warm, a smaller lap quilt to snuggle under while watching TV, or a quilted piece to be hung as a work of art on the wall, sampler quilts provide an invaluable learning curve, while at the same time becoming an heirloom work in their own right. I look back on my quilt *Constant Inspiration*, which forms the basis for this book, almost as my apprenticeship into the art of quilt making (and it is an art); I hope that it will last for many years and be appreciated by others along the way.

The making of the quilt

My very first sampler quilts were made by piecing the entire quilt top first of all, then layering and tacking (or basting) the three quilt layers together in the traditional way. For *Constant Inspiration* I used the 'quilt as you go' method of construction, and I found the method invaluable for this larger quilt. For one thing it meant that I worked on manageable and portable sections for the majority of the time I was actually quilting, before I joined up the different sections to create the whole quilt. As a result, the end product was certainly far more densely quilted than it would have been if I'd made a 'three-layer' quilt and then had the task of quilting from the centre and working outwards.

The quilt as you go technique can be useful for constructing any large quilt which involves a design that can be broken down into smaller sections – for instance sampler quilts, medallion quilts, group quilts etc. The individual sections can be quilted first then assembled later. When you're working a large quilt top for a double- or king/queen-sized bed, then layering this into a fabric sandwich which you then have to quilt from the centre

outwards, the logistics can be daunting to say the least. With quilt as you go, you'll have more convenient, transportable and easy-to-handle sections in the first stages of construction, and by the time you're ready to put the design together, you'll find that the majority of your quilting has been stitched.

I feel that a true sampler quilt ought to include a good number of differing techniques – a proper *sample* of each. If you're new to quiltmaking, you'll find that the blocks I've given in this book will provide you with a good grounding in a selection of traditional blocks and styles: British and American patchwork based on both regular and irregular grids: the use of symmetrical and asymmetrical shapes and mirror-imaging: various aspects of appliqué, and so on. If you're a more adventurous and/or advanced quilter, you may choose to replace some of the blocks I've given with others that you prefer, but I can guarantee that most of the blocks I've given here will challenge you in one way or another.

You could also include patterns of your own design – once you're used to recognising the various grids that most block patchwork is based on, get out your pencil, ruler and coloured pencils and see what you can come up with yourself.

When deciding on blocks to add to your sampler quilt, try to visualise the quilt as a whole – the complete picture – and aim to achieve a good balance of techniques and dimensions along with visual harmony. You may find it easier to achieve this if you draw up your own quilt plan to work from. It need not necessarily be to scale, (although this does have its own benefits); a roughly-sketched quilt plan can often be better than nothing. Do remember that this is *your* quilt, though, and no-one else's (even if it's handed over to a lucky recipient afterwards, it's still your work while it's in the making). So if you prefer to work a sampler quilt consisting of block patchwork only, for instance, or appliqué only, remember: the choice is yours.

I've selected the blocks in this particular quilt to suit most levels of ability. They've also been chosen for their adaptability for hand and/or machine-stitchers. The patchwork blocks I've included are based on traditional template-making and are designed so that they can be used by any quiltmaker, whether or not they own rotary cutting equipment.

My aim with this book is to offer you a good grounding in patchwork and quilting techniques; the quilt isn't designed to be a 'speedy' project to have completed in a weekend, a week or even a month. Of course if you want a short-term project (perhaps even while you're working on the large quilt), you can always use one or several of the blocks for smaller items such as cushion covers or a cot quilt. Remind yourself now and again that quilt making is (usually) a marathon and not a sprint – take your time making your own version of my quilt and enjoy the hours spent on making your very own heirloom quilt.

Before you begin

Planning your time

If you're planning to make this quilt for a special occasion, either for yourself or for someone else, and you really need to work to a deadline, it may be useful to set yourself what I call a 'working diary'.

List your weeks, beginning with the week you're starting the quilt and ending with the week **before** it has to be finished (a small but valuable allowance for unforeseeable problems). Against each week, list what you hope to have achieved (ie, don't allow only one day for attaching binding or only one week for constructing your quilt centre).

Make your diary realistic – if you have a busy lifestyle, set achievable goals that you know you can meet in the time you have available to devote to your sewing. If you then find that you're ahead of yourself at any stage of your 'working diary,' you'll find that your achievements are really motivating. If, on the other hand, you fall a little behind your expectations at any stage, you can then set aside extra time during another week to catch up.

START QUILT SEPT 1st	Choose fabrics and colours. Plan quilt. Draw up diary . . .
week 1	Prepare fabrics. Cut all backing fabric and wadding squares.
week 2	Block No1: construct, layer, quilt. Choose colours for blocks 2 and 3.
week 3	Construct and layer blocks 2 and 3, ready for quilting on holiday.
FINAL WEEK	Remove all tacking. Make and attach label. Take photo!

Tools and equipment

You'll find that some of the items listed in this section are already to be found in your household or in your sewing-box. These are essential items that you'll benefit from collecting together before you begin making this quilt project.

Sewing equipment: essential

- scissors for fabric cutting (patchwork or fabric shears)
- scissors for thread snipping (small, sharp embroidery scissors)
- scissors for cutting paper/card/ plastic (or craft knife and board)
- pins
- a selection of all-purpose sewing threads to blend with your fabric colours
- quilting thread/s
- all-purpose sewing needles
- quilting needles
- fabric marking pen/pencil and a selection of quilting stencils
- PLUS an A4 (approx) sheet of medium-grade sandpaper, glued to a sheet of card

Sewing equipment: optional

- sewing-machine

Most of the patchwork and appliqué blocks I've provided for this quilt can be sewn either by hand or by machine. The exceptions are:

I recommend hand-sewing for Dresden Plate (see p18), Celtic Knot (see 26) and Hawaiian Hearts (see p36).

I recommend machine-sewing if you're going to piece the striped fabric for Basketweave (see p22), and for easy, split-colour spikes on Mariner's Compass (see p48).

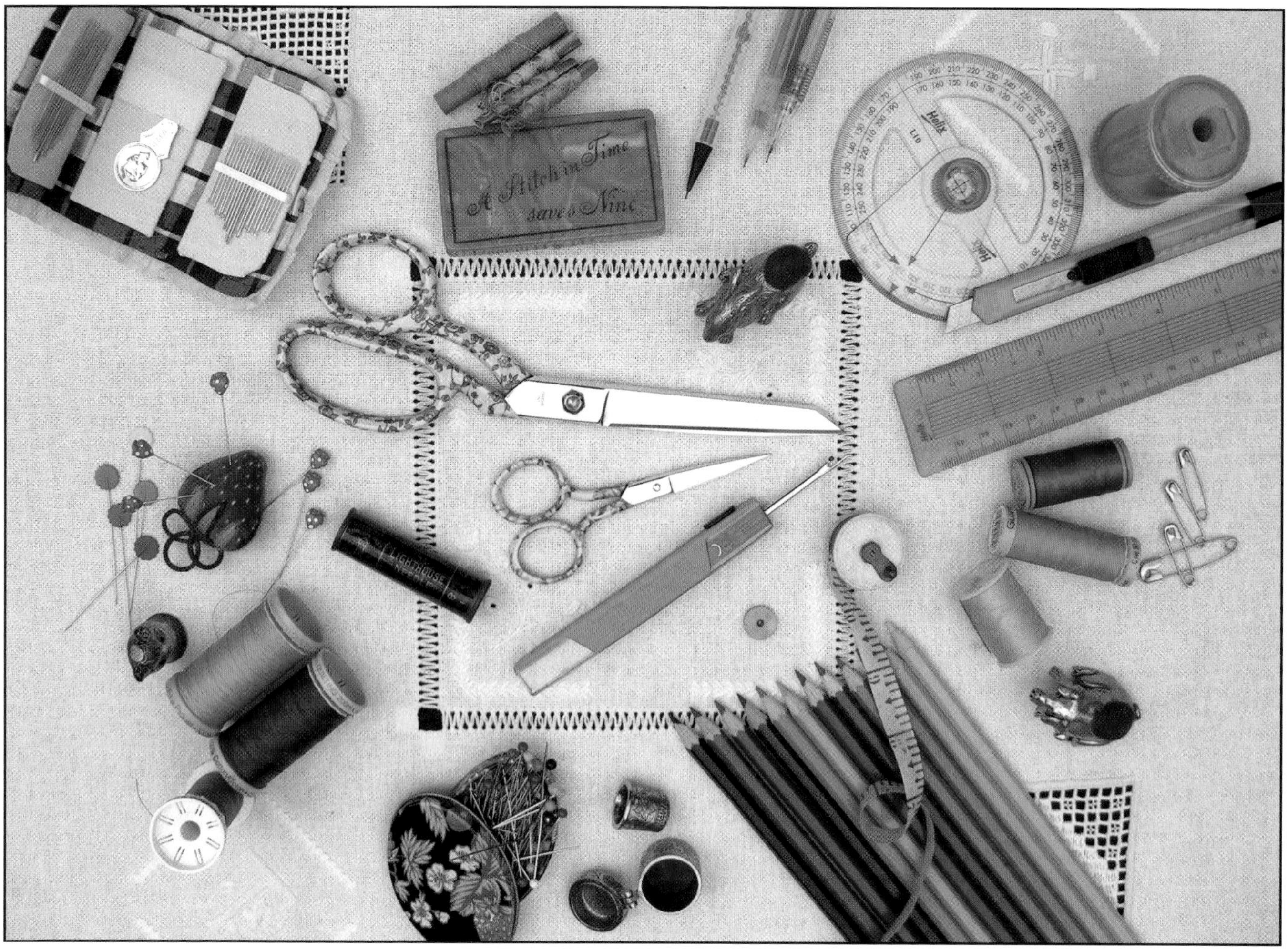

- rotary cutting board/cutter/ safety ruler

Throughout this book I'm presuming that you don't have rotary cutting equipment – and it certainly isn't essential for creating any of the blocks. However, if you do have this useful equipment and you'd prefer to speed up your fabric cutting just a little, then simply align your drawn template shapes on the relevant fabrics so that you can rotary-cut between the shapes quickly and easily in straight lines.

Supplies for making templates

This is an optional stage; if you do decide to create your own templates, you'll find that the process provides a useful learning curve. If you prefer, you can simply trace or photocopy the templates provided and glue them to card –in which case you won't need the template plastic.

- sheet of card or template plastic
- ruler (measuring 18in/46cm) and a sharp pencil
- card/paper-cutting scissors, or a craft knife and board
- glue stick for use on paper/card
- tracing paper (if you're not photocopying)

Supplies for drafting blocks:

This is another optional stage; if you'd like to draft the patterns to create blocks that are either larger or smaller than the ones I've used, you'll find full instructions and requirements on pages 96-108.

Fabrics and waddings

Before you choose ...

The quilt as you go method of quilt construction requires some major decision-making at the outset where fabric and wadding is concerned. Therefore, on the following pages I've listed the supplies that you'll need to buy into different sections; this will enable you to pinpoint which part of the quilt you're buying for, and you can then choose to buy everything at the same time, or separately. You will, though, need to buy all of your backing fabric and choose your wadding at the very beginning of the project (unless you decide to back each of the blocks with a different fabric, which will produce a chequerboard effect or a random squared pattern on the reverse of your quilt). Choosing a busy print for your

4 Join the shorter strips to the sides of the large AA square (**e**), making sure that the small triangles of one colour are next to the large triangle of the contrasting colour.

e

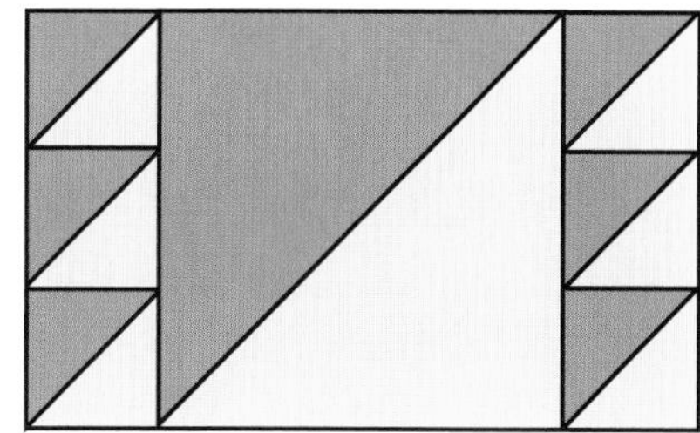

5 Join the longer strips to the top and bottom of the central unit in the same way (**f**) to complete the block (**g**).

f

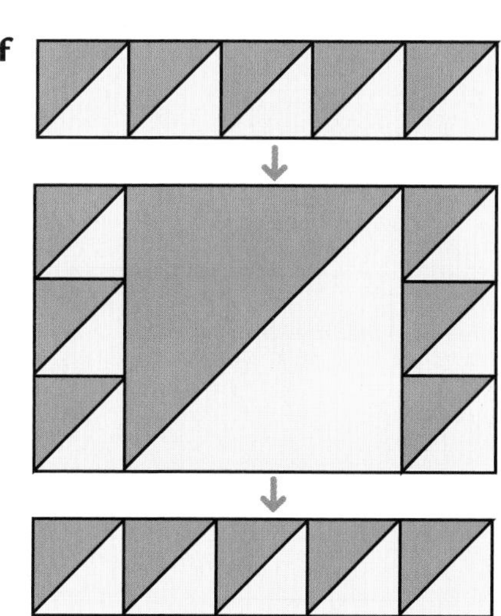

g

◆ **TIPS** ◆

If you choose a simple colour-scheme of two strongly contrasting fabrics or tonal values, this will create good definition in your finished block.

Make sure that you place the templates correctly on the straight grain of the fabric, using the SG arrows as guidelines – and handle the bias edges (the longer sides) of the triangles with care.

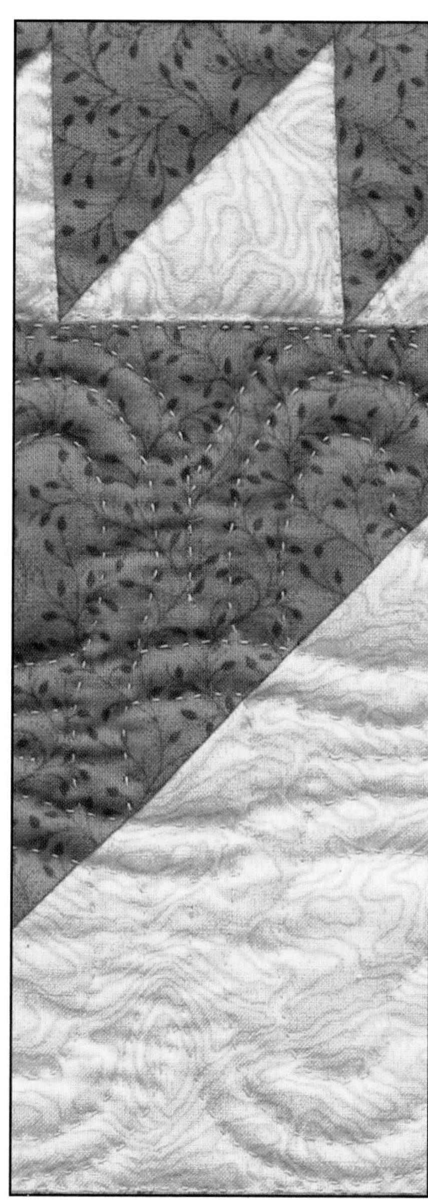

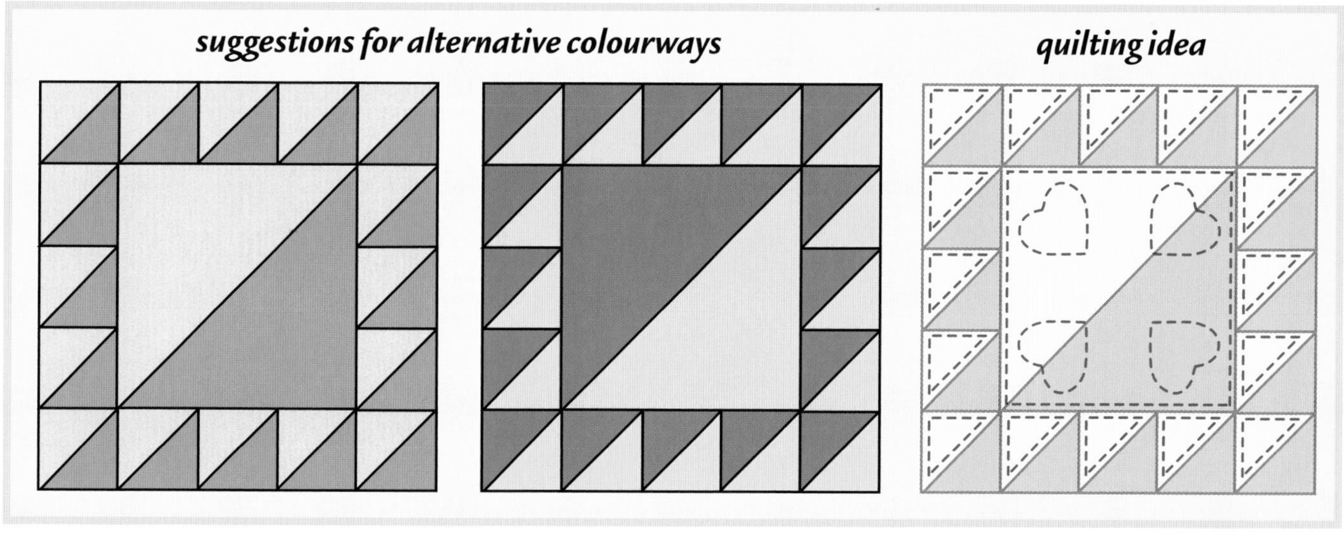

▪ BLOCK 2 ▪
Dresden Plate

Dresden Plate is one of our more traditional appliqué patterns; the individual 'petals' are joined to form the circular 'plate' before being applied to the background fabric.

You may like to choose 20 different fabrics from your scraps bag, or you might find that you can add a lot of visual interest to the petals by using just one fabric with an interesting print.

■ **Grid**

this block is based on a 2 x 2 grid

■ **Technique**

◆ hand-sewn appliqué over freezer paper (see Appliqué on pp13-14)

■ **What you will need**

◆ basic supplies *(all-purpose sewing thread; needles; fabric scissors and thread-snipping scissors; pins; pencil)*

◆ freezer paper

◆ tacking thread and needle

◆ paper-cutting scissors

■ **Fabrics:** minimum 3

As a background for the design, you'll need a 10in (25cm) square of fabric with seam allowances added on all sides.

■ **Templates:** 2

you'll find the *Dresden Plate* templates A and B on p75

■ Constructing the block

1 Follow the instructions on page 14 to create the freezer paper petals and cover them with the appropriate fabric(s). Join the petals in pairs (**a**),

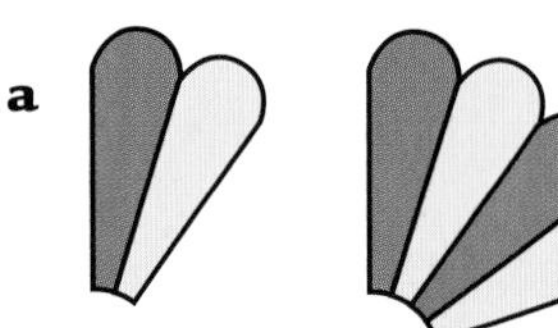

then join all the pairs into fours (**b**). Complete the plate by joining all the sections (**c**) to form a circle (**d**).

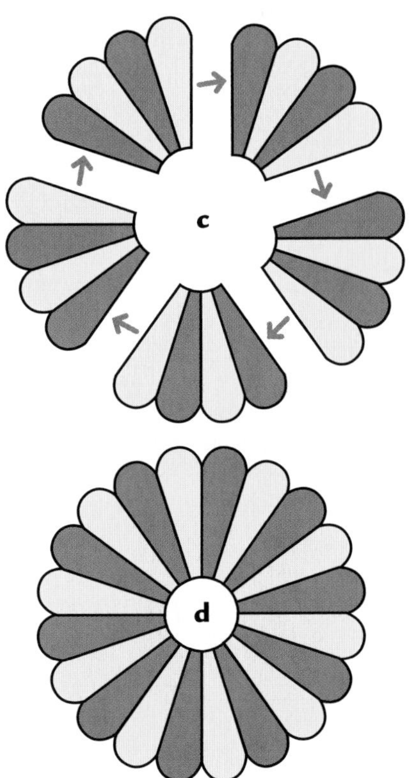

2 Once you've joined the complete circle of petals, pin/tack it to the square of background fabric and use appliqué stitch all around the ***outer edge only*** of the ring of petals (**e**).

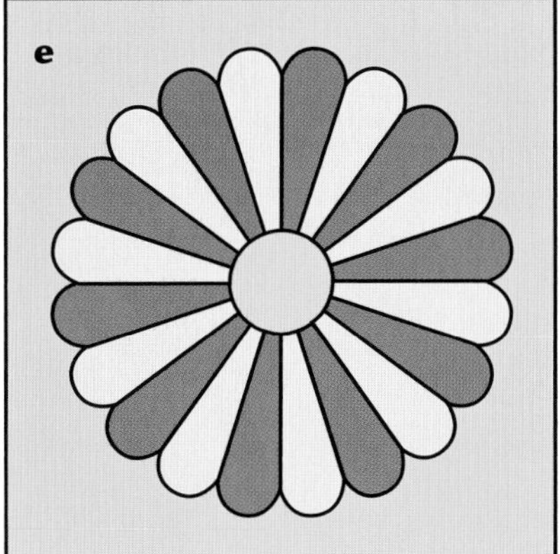

3 Place the central circle in position and stitch the edge of it to the petal fabrics (**f**). Follow the instructions on page 14 for removing the freezer paper shapes.

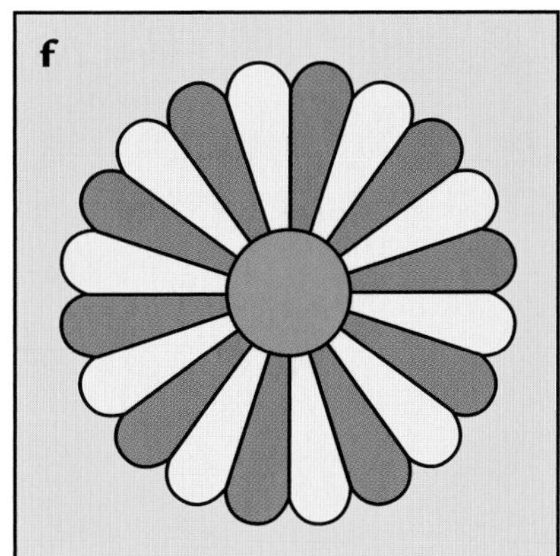

◆ TIPS ◆

When you're drawing round the templates onto the freezer paper, always use a sharp pencil and ensure that you hold the pencil tightly up against the edge of the template. Cut out the freezer paper shapes directly on the pencil line.

Similarly, when you're folding the fabric around the paper shapes, ensure that the fabric is folded tightly up against the edge of the paper. This will ensure that you're not enlarging the petals at any stage – if they become wider during construction they won't lie in a flat circle.

suggestions for alternative colourways

quilting idea

▪ BLOCK 3 ▪

Storm at Sea

Storm at Sea is a simple yet effective block, based on a recognisable grid, and introduces mirror-image shapes. Try joining multiple copies of this block together to see the wonderful wavy lines that the design produces when it's repeated across an entire quilt top.

■ **Grid**
this block is based on a 4 x 4 grid

■ **Techniques**
- triangles, diamonds and squares (see Piecing Your Patchwork on p12)
- mirror-image shapes (see p12)

■ **What you will need**
- basic supplies *(all-purpose sewing thread; needles or sewing machine; fabric scissors and thread-snipping scissors; pins; pencil)*

■ **Fabrics:** minimum 2
A simple colour-scheme works well for this block – the central square could be the same fabric as the outside squares and diamonds to simplify it further.

■ **Templates:** 7
you'll find the *Storm at Sea* templates A-G on p76

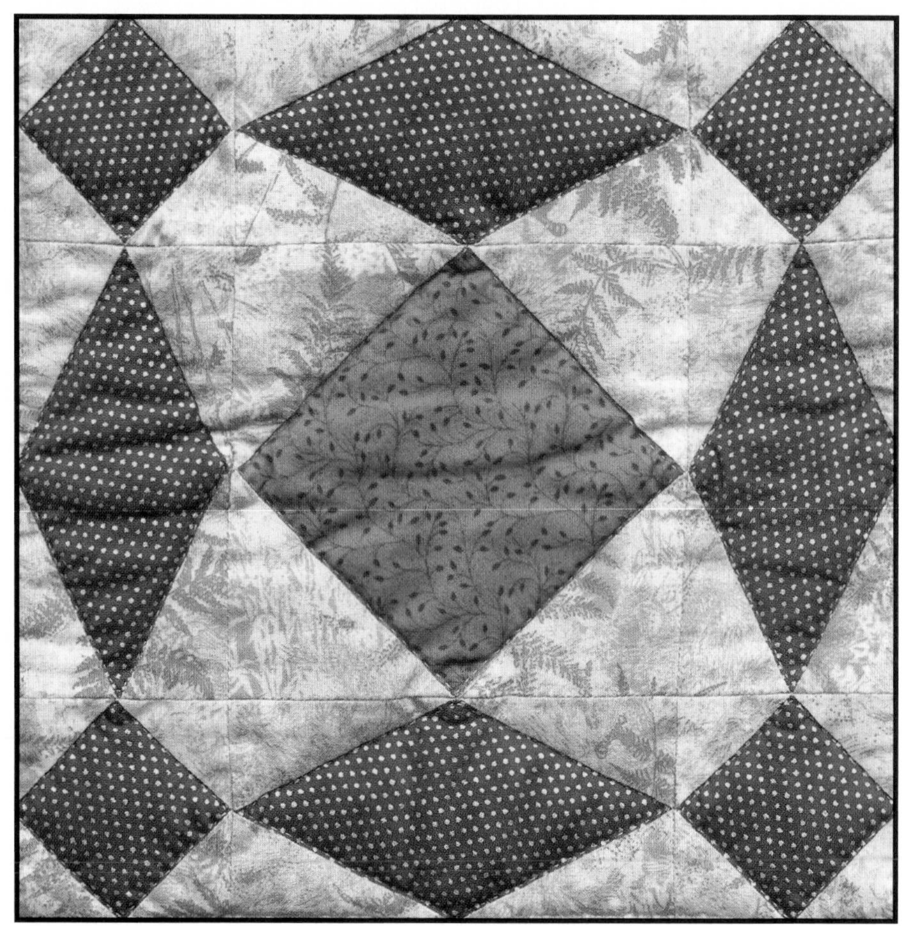

■ Constructing the block

1 Join the long sides of the B triangles to the edges of the large A square (**a**).

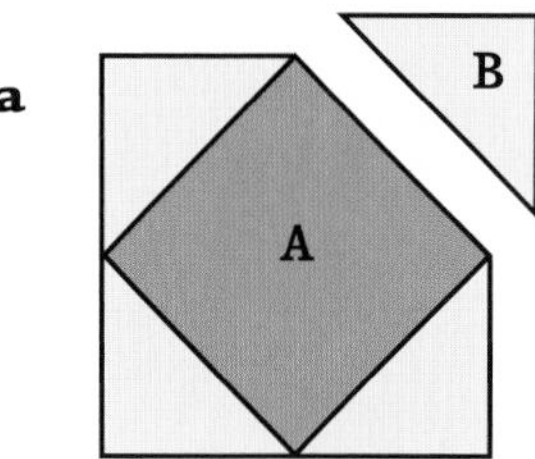

2 Join the long edges of two D triangles to opposite sides of the diamond shape C (**b**), then join two E triangles to the remaining two sides (**c**). Create four units in this way.

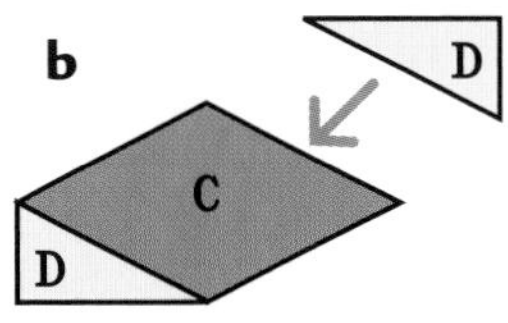

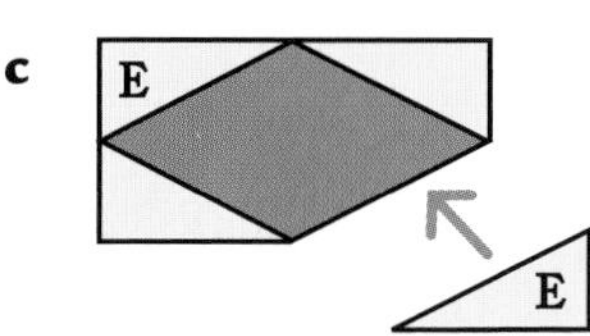

3 Join the long sides of four G triangles to the edges of one small F square (**d**). Create four units in this way.

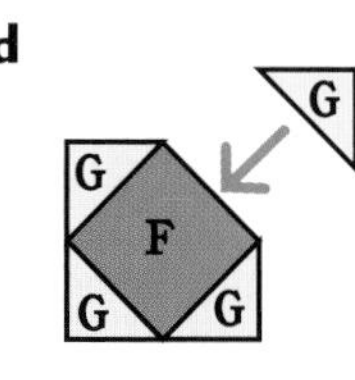

4 Join one FG unit to each end of a CDE unit as shown (**e**);

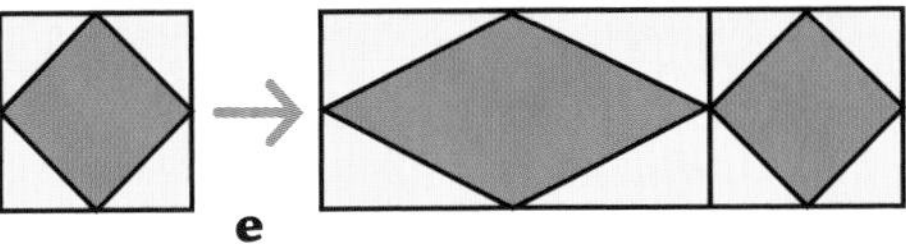

e

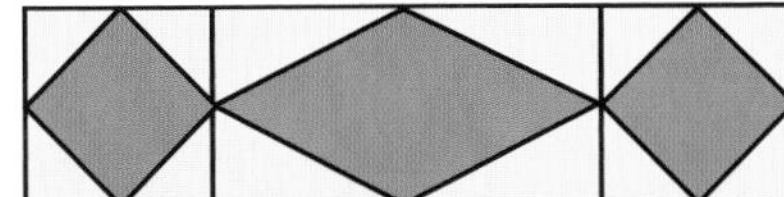

make two units in this way. Add the remaining CDE unit to each side of the central square (**f** and **g**) to create the central row of the block.

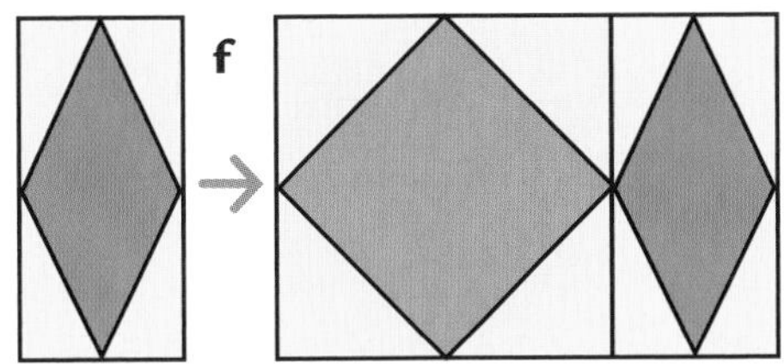

f

g

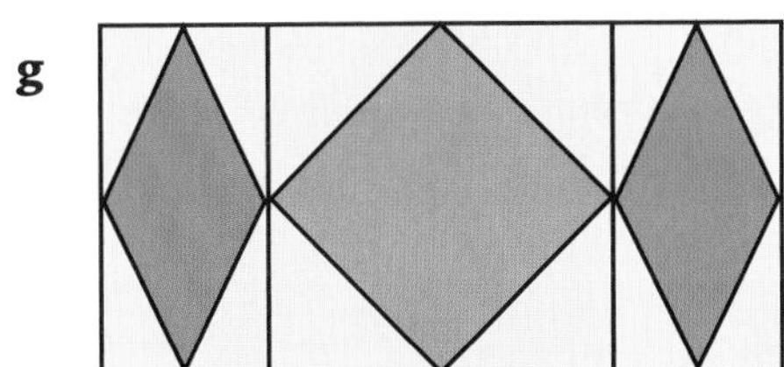

Join the rows (**h**) to complete the block (**i**).

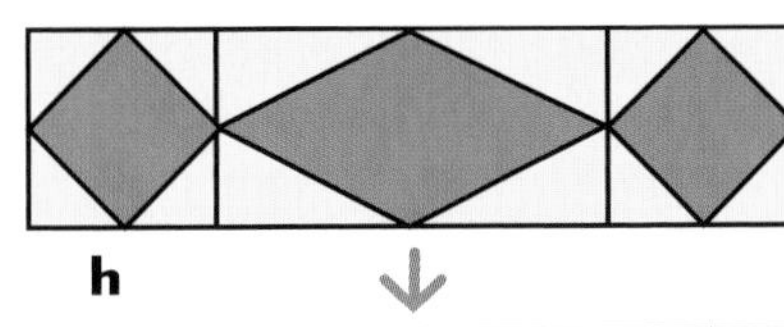

h

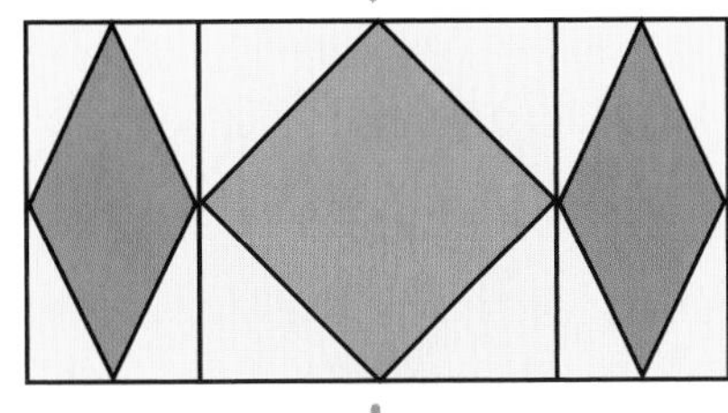

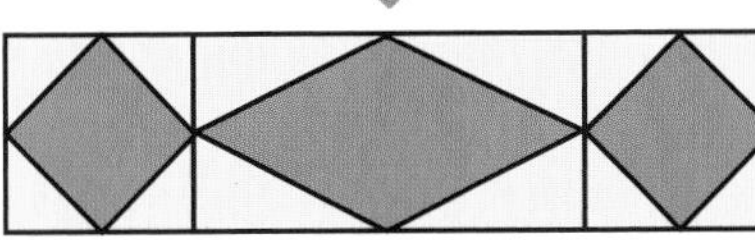

i

> **◆ TIP ◆**
>
> The wavy effect is created by mixing the angles of the diamonds and the squares. By cutting the diamond shape with the straight grain of fabric on at least one set of parallel lines, you'll help to stabilise what could otherwise be a difficult shape to handle.

quilting idea

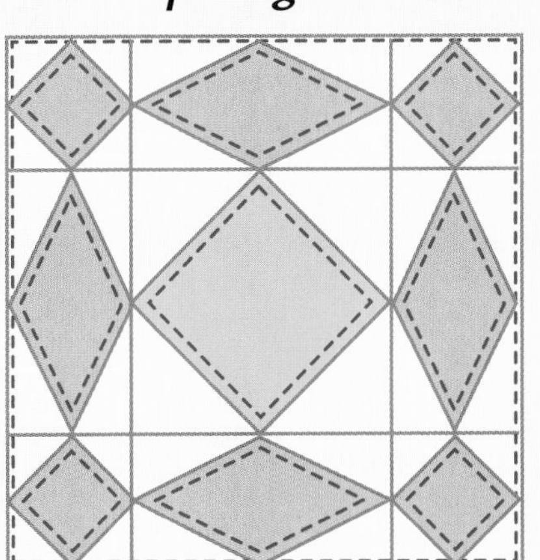

▪ BLOCK 4 ▪

Basketweave

This fascinating block will introduce you to a technique called partial seaming, which will help in the construction. It's great fun to make your own striped fabric by machining strips of material together to form a 'college scarf' effect. As you eventually have to cut across these sewn strips, if you're a hand-stitcher I suggest using a boldly striped, pre-printed fabric.

■ **Grid**
this block is based on a 2 x 2 grid

■ **Techniques**
- partial seaming (see p13)
- strip-piecing (machine-stitching only)
- triangles (see Piecing Your Patchwork on p12)

■ **What you will need**
- basic supplies *(all-purpose sewing thread; needles or sewing machine; fabric scissors and thread-snipping scissors; pins; pencil)*

■ **Fabrics:** minimum 2 (hand-sewing), or 3 (machine-sewing)

■ **Templates:** 3
you'll find the *Basketweave* templates A-C on p78

■ Constructing the block

1 If you're piecing your own 'college scarf,' do this first. Then use template B to cut eight patches from your pieced or printed striped fabric. If your striped fabric consists of even stripes, beginning and ending with the same colour, you'll be able to cut the shapes by laying the template as shown in (**a**); remember to leave enough space between the shapes for the seam allowances. If the striped fabric won't work in this way, cut all the triangles by laying the template in the same direction each time (**b**).

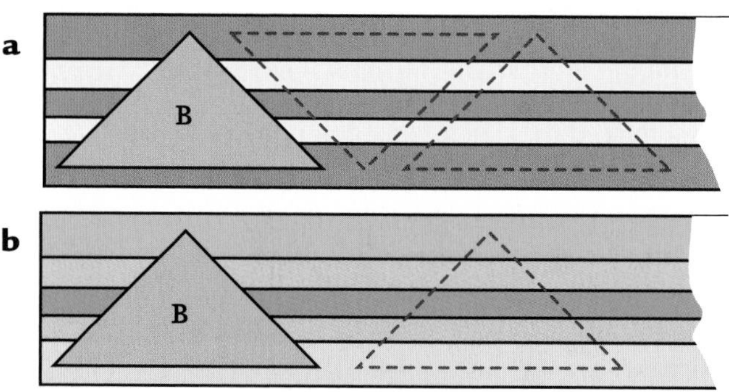

2 Stitch a partial seam, between the two asterisks marked on the diagram, to join part of one B triangle to the central octagon (**c**).

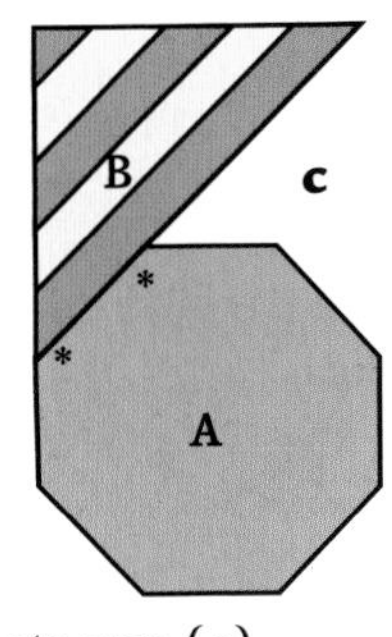

3 Working anticlockwise (counterclockwise) round the octagon, add a second B triangle to the next edge of the octagon plus the existing triangle (**d**).

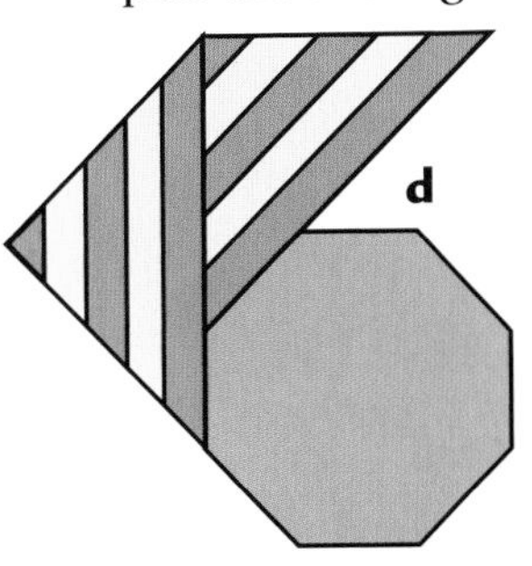

Continue adding triangles around the shape to create a large octagon. When the final triangle is in place, complete the seam between the asterisks (**e**).

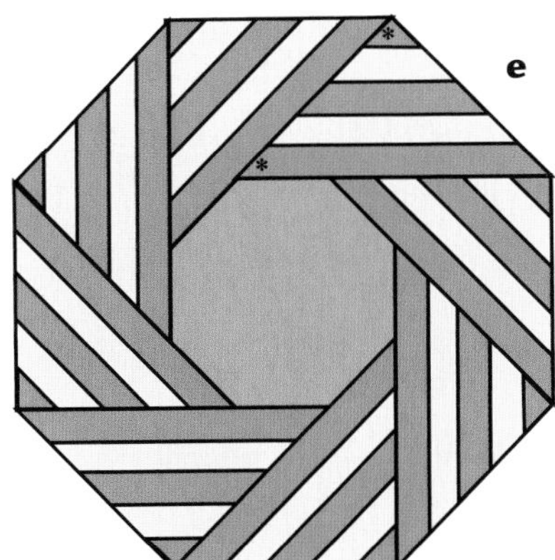

4 Add a C triangle to each corner of the new octagon (**f**) to complete the block (**g**).

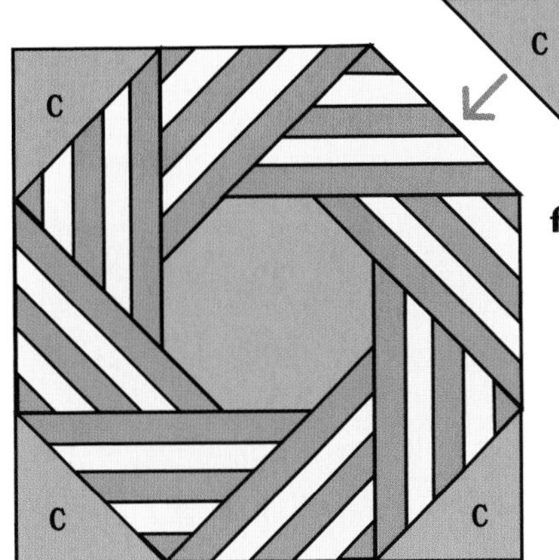

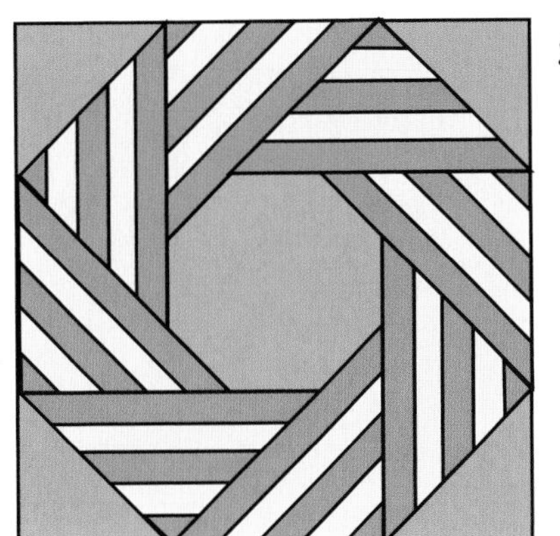

◆ TIP ◆

If you're machine-sewing a 'college scarf' made up of strips of different fabrics, try different widths for the stripes and possibly different combinations of tonal values for a varied effect. It's easier, quicker and certainly cheaper to try this out using coloured pencils on paper before experimenting with your fabrics.

suggestions for alternative colourways

quilting idea

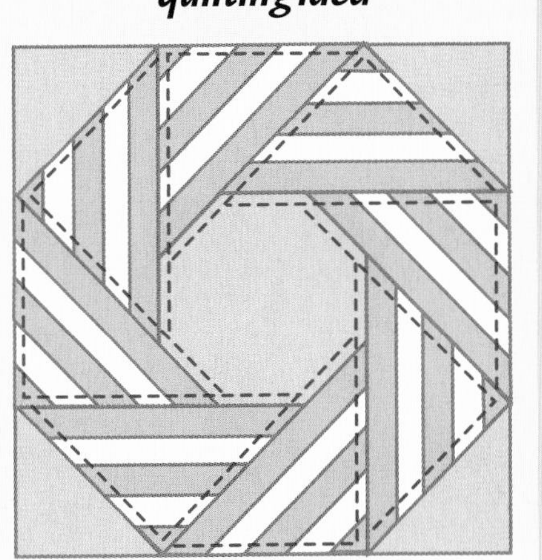

■ BLOCK 5 ■

Bear's Paw

Take a closer look at this block and you'll begin to see the bear's paw in each quarter, with the sharp triangles representing the claws. This is another good block to repeat across an entire quilt top – without sashing in between, you'll find that secondary patterns emerge where the blocks join.

■ **Grid**

this block is based on a 7 x 7 grid

■ **Techniques**

◆ triangles, squares and rectangles (see Piecing Your Patchwork on p12)

■ **What you will need**

◆ basic supplies *(all-purpose sewing thread; needles or sewing machine; fabric scissors and thread-snipping scissors; pins; pencil)*

■ **Fabrics:** Minimum 3

■ **Templates:** 4

you'll find the *Bear's Paw* templates A-D on p77

■ Constructing the block

1 Join the D triangles in pairs as shown (**a**) to make 16 small DD squares.

a

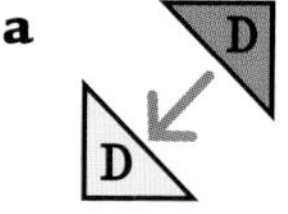

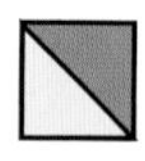

2 Make a strip of one corner C square and two DD squares, joining them in the arrangement shown (**b**).

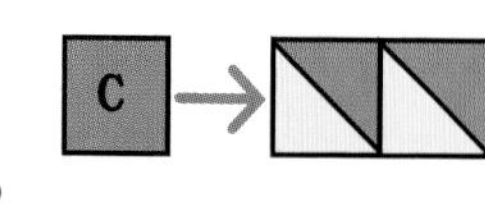

b

Make two strips this way, and two strips as shown in (**c**).

c

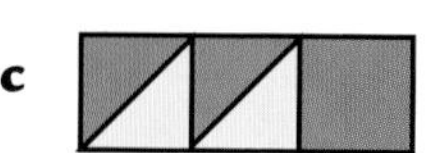

3 Make two shorter strips with two DD squares positioned as shown (**d**), and two as shown in (**e**).

d **e**

4 Add one shorter strip to the side of one large A square (**f**), then join a longer one

f

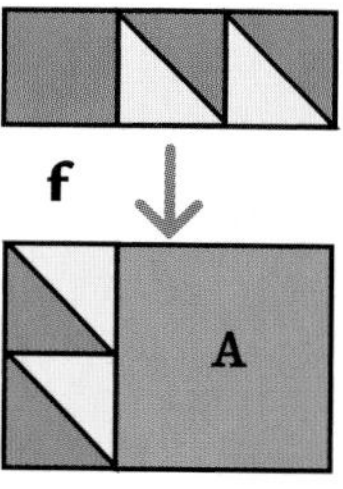

to the top as shown (**g**). Add the remaining strips to the remaining A squares to create four large square units. (Make sure that you add the strips with the triangles in the correct direction, so that the large units all have the same layout.)

5 Join two of the large units to the long sides of one B rectangle (**h**); create two units in this way.

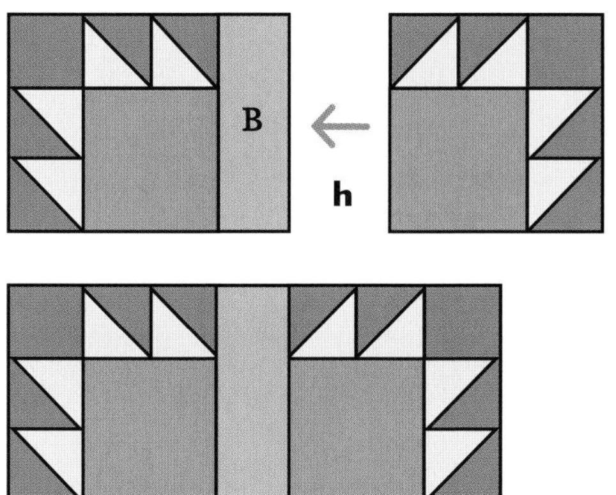

Join the other B shapes to the sides of the remaining C square, then join these rows (**i**) to complete the block (**j**).

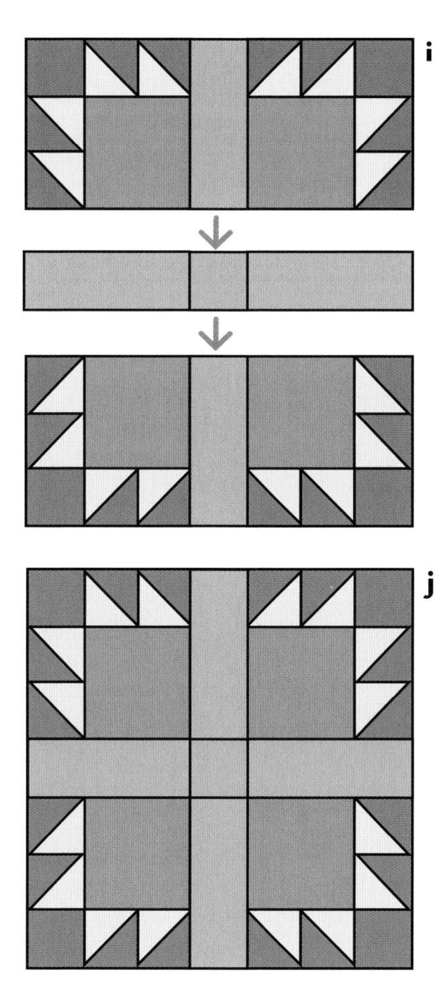

◆ **TIPS** ◆

Joining the smallest components first (that is, piecing the triangles into squares and then strips) makes them easier to handle. When you're sewing the triangles together, refer to the diagrams to ensure that each one faces in the direction that it should – it's easy to make a mistake at this stage.

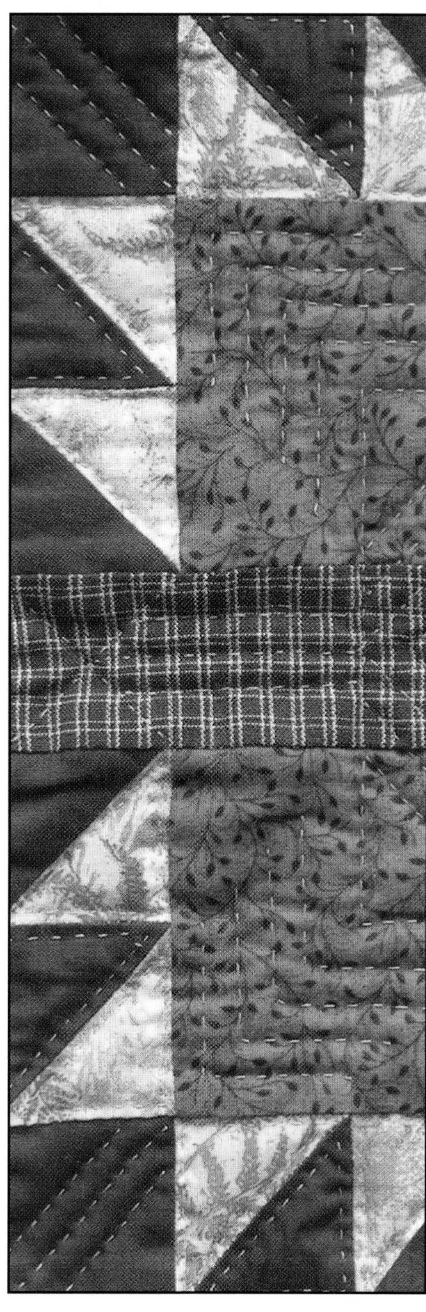

suggestions for alternative colourways

quilting idea

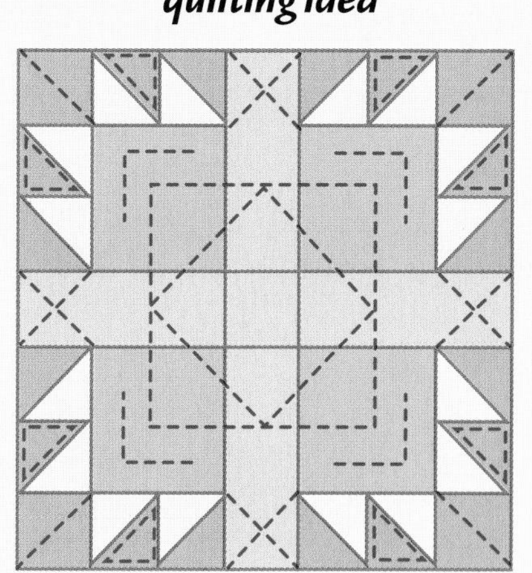

■ BLOCK 6 ■

Celtic Knot

Celtic knotwork has been around for many years and can be found in stonework and masonry, furnishings and art. Traditionally, Celtic knotwork is based on an intricate mathematical sequence using curves and circles. For this block I've used a single knot design created in bias binding.

■ **Grid**
there is no grid for this block

■ **Technique**
- hand-sewn bias strip appliqué (see Appliqué on p13)

■ **What you will need**
- basic supplies *(all-purpose sewing thread; needles; fabric scissors and thread-snipping scissors; pins; pencil)*
- tacking thread and needle
- lightbox, or a window in daylight plus masking tape
- clear tape
- rotary-cutting board, mat and ruler (optional)

■ **Fabrics:** 2
As a background for the design, you'll need a 10in (25cm) square of fabric with seam allowances added on all sides.

■ **Templates:** you need a copy of both parts of the design (see pages 80 and 81); join the sections with clear tape.

■ Constructing the block

1 Choose the finished width of your bias strip (eg, 1/4in/6mm). Cut the strip of fabric for the binding across the full diagonal of the fabric so that the strip is 'on the bias' (at approximately a 45° angle), as shown in (**a**).

a

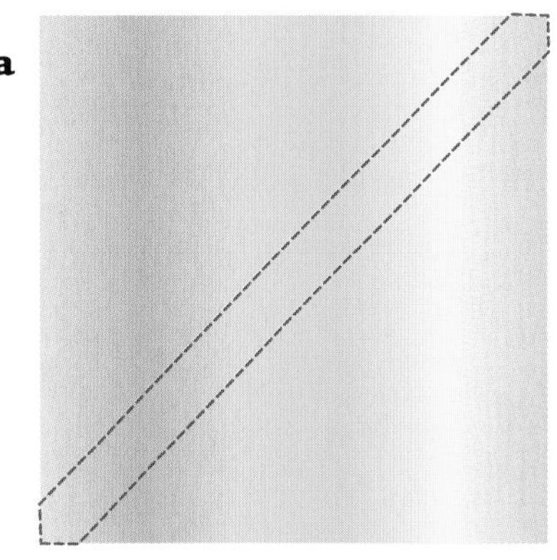

The width of the strip needs to be three times the finished size required; so, if you'd like your finished binding to be 1/4in (6mm), cut the fabric strip 3/4in (18mm) wide.

2 Fold and press inwards one third of the fabric strip along its length (**b**).

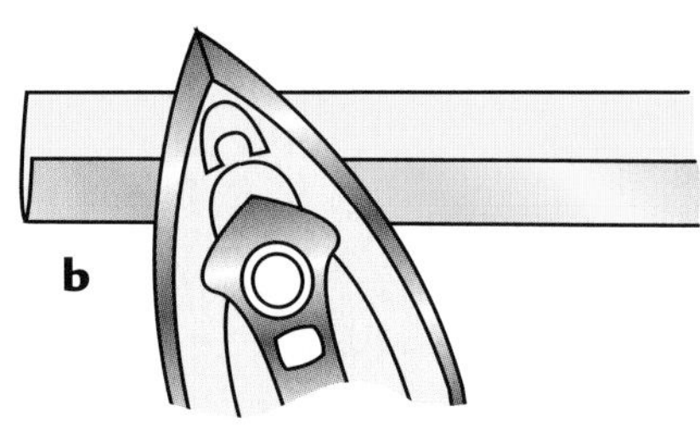
b

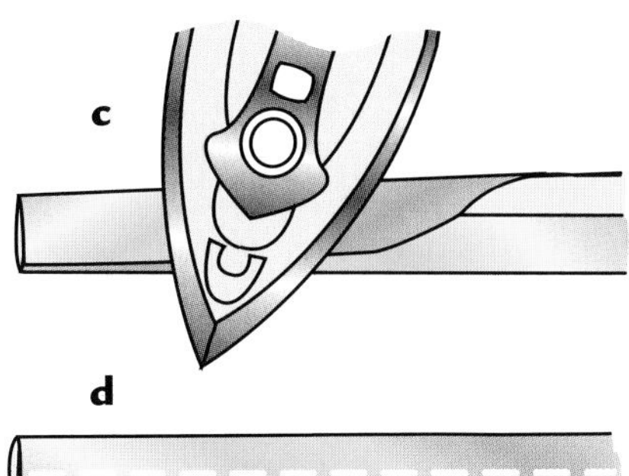

Fold and press under the opposite edge (**c**), then tack the three layers together (**d**).

3 Lay the complete design on a lightbox (or use masking tape and tape the design to a window in daylight). Position/ tape the square of background fabric over the design, centring the design, and trace the lines in pencil (**e**).

4 Starting with an 'under' junction in the design, begin laying the strip of bias binding over the design, pinning and tacking as you go (**f**).

Remove the pins as the tacking progresses. Ensure that each 'over' junction (**g**) is followed by an 'under' junction (**h**).

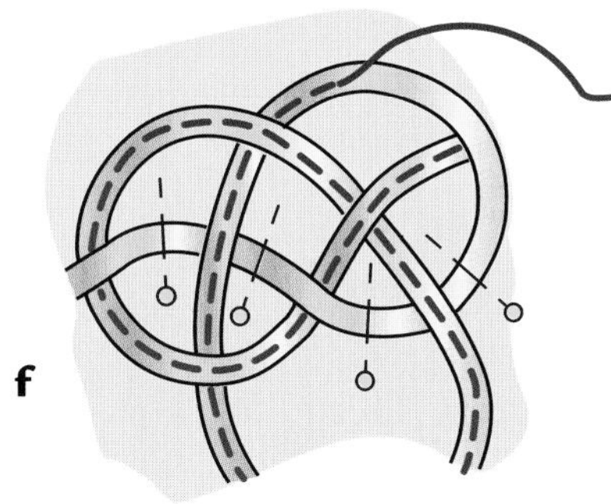
f

g

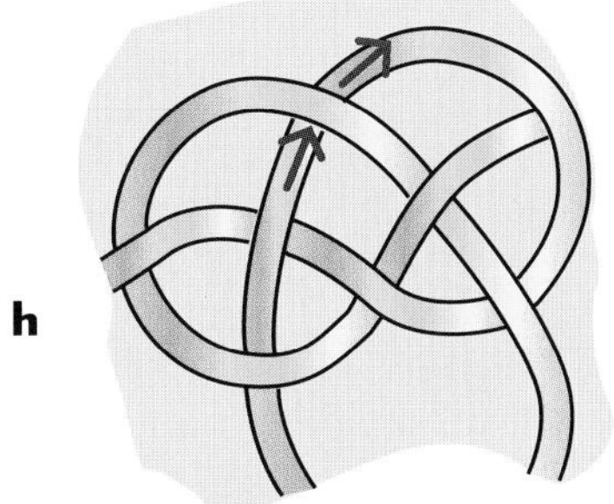
h

5 Once the complete design is tacked in place, sew the bias strip fabric to the background fabric using appliqué stitch to complete the block (**i**).

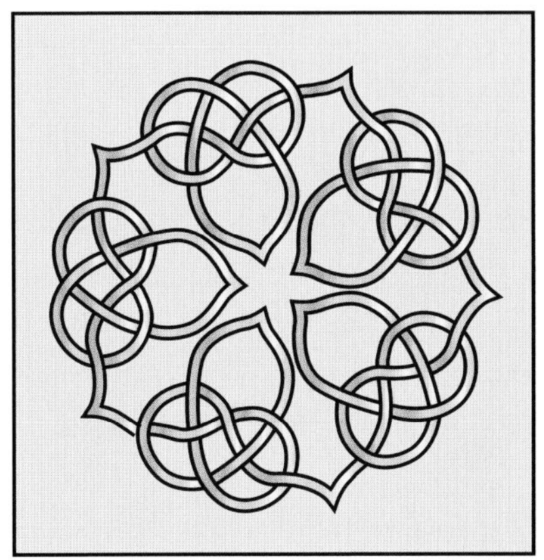
i

◆ **TIPS** ◆

A genuine Celtic knot should show an alternating sequence of 'overs' and 'unders' throughout the design (see the pattern on pages 80 and 81). Use your 'unders' to hide the raw edges of fabric where you have to start and stop a bias strip.

Use plenty of pins to secure your bias strip in place, and gently ease the stretchy bias-cut fabric to form nicely-rounded curves.

quilting idea

▪ BLOCK 7 ▪

Snail Trail

Even though it's constructed from triangles and straight lines, this block cleverly creates an optical illusion of curves and spirals. You could achieve an even stronger end result by using just two contrasting fabrics.

- **Grid**
  this block is based on a 2 x 2 grid

- **Technique**
  - triangles (see Piecing Your Patchwork on p12)

- **What you will need**
  - basic supplies *(all-purpose sewing thread; needles or sewing machine; fabric scissors and thread-snipping scissors; pins; pencil)*

- **Fabrics:** minimum 2

- **Templates:** 6
  you'll find the *Snail Trail* templates A-F on p79

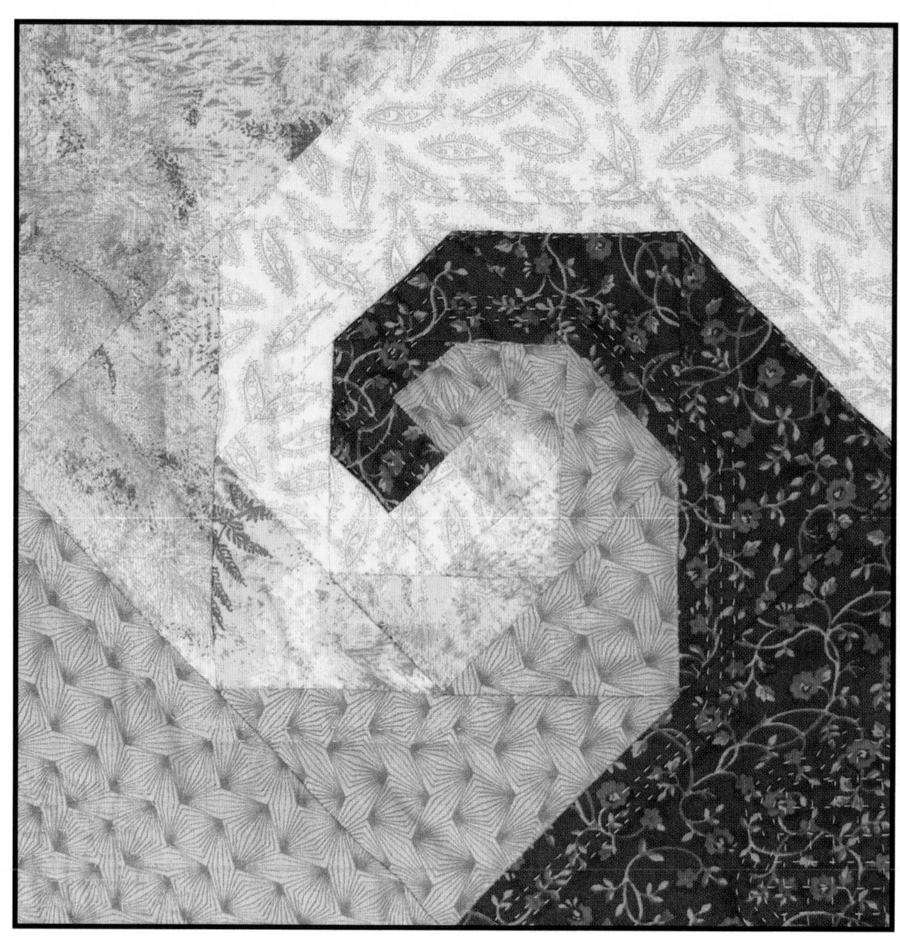

Constructing the block

1 Join the central A squares in pairs (**a**), then join the pairs to form a square (**b**).

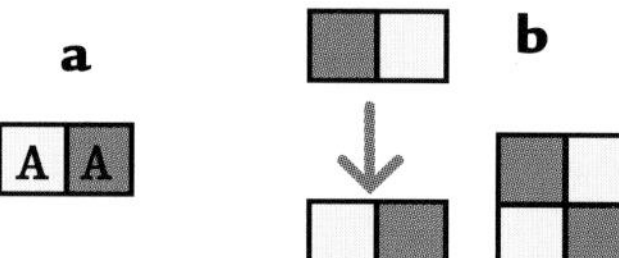

2 Add two B triangles to opposite sides of the square (**c**), then add the remaining B triangles (**d**).

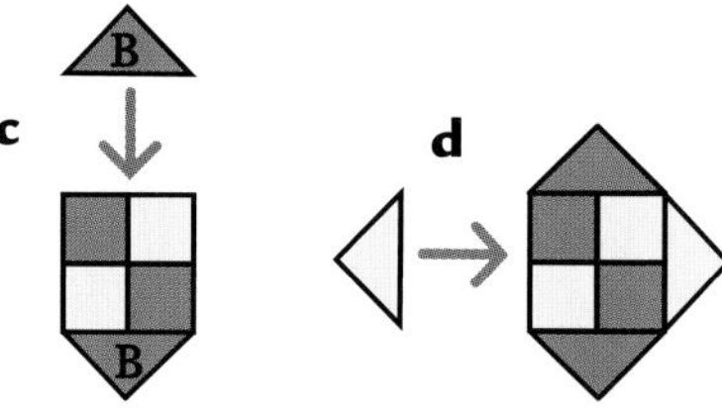

3 Add the four C triangles in the same way (**e**), then the D triangles (**f**).

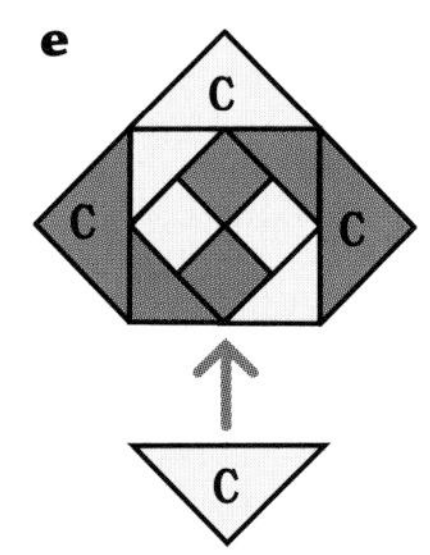

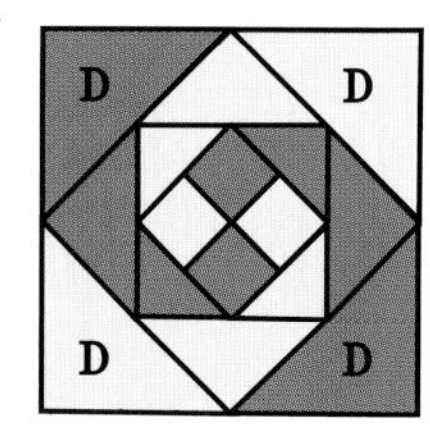

g

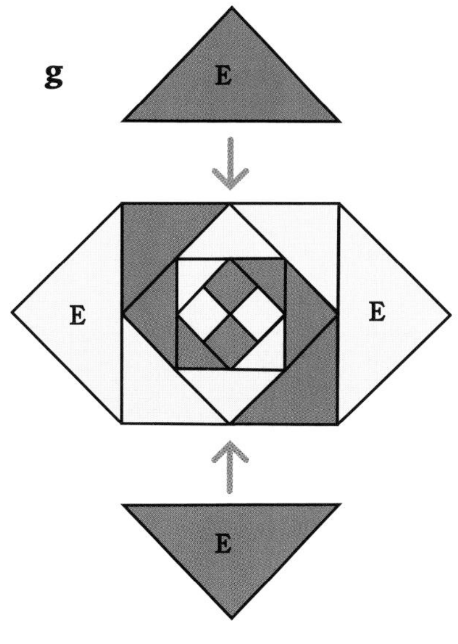

4 Use the same principle to join the E triangles to the shape (**g** and **h**).

h

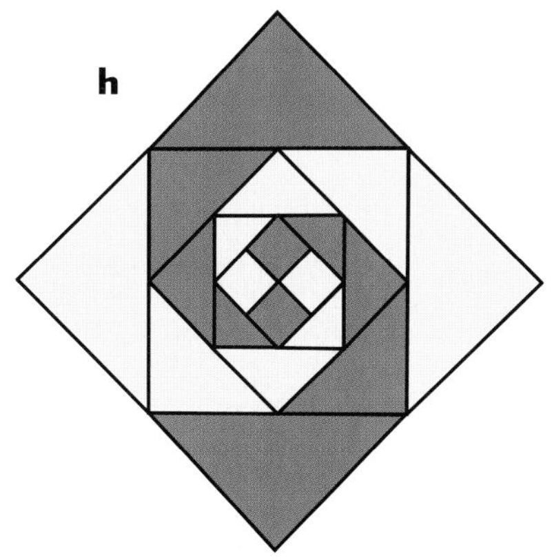

5 Finally, add the F triangles (**i** and **j**) to complete the block (**k**).

i

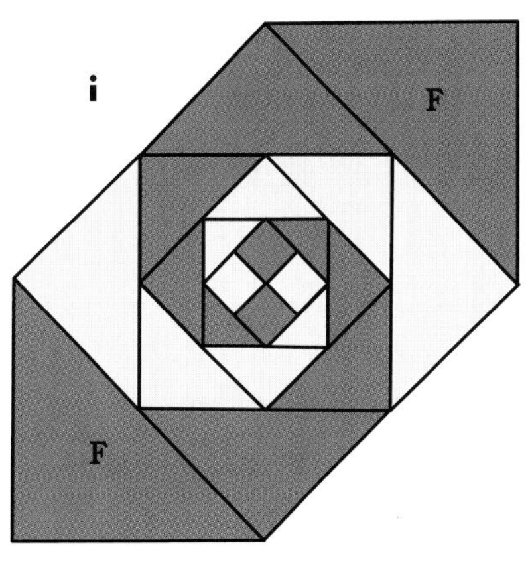

j

F

F

k

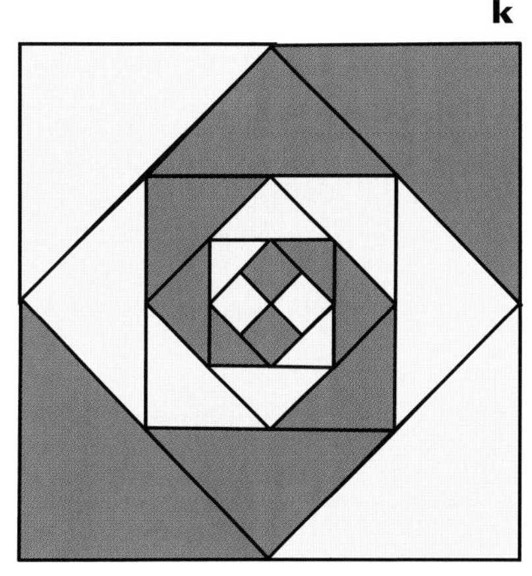

> **◆ TIP ◆**
>
> When you're adding each circuit of four triangles, stitch two opposite triangles first, then add the remaining two.

quilting idea

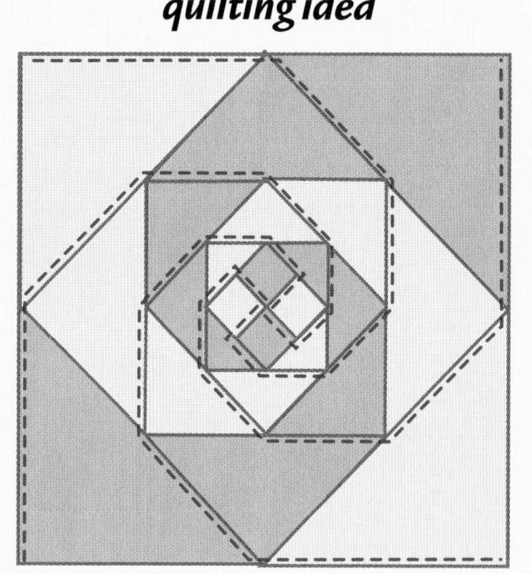

▪ BLOCK 8 ▪

Trip Around the World

The patches of different colours, fabrics and tonal values in the *Trip Around the World* block are arranged in diamonds radiating out from the centre. This pattern can often be seen covering complete quilt tops in work produced by the Amish community, the simplicity of the squares contrasting with the movement of the radiating design and the vivid colours used.

■ **Grid**
this block is based on an 11 x 11 grid (or any alternative grid of odd numbers)

■ **Technique**
◆ squares (see Piecing Your Patchwork on p12)

■ **What you will need**
◆ basic supplies *(all-purpose sewing thread; needles or sewing machine; fabric scissors and thread-snipping scissors; pins; pencil)*

■ **Fabrics:** minimum 3

■ **Templates:** 1
you'll find the *Trip Around the World* template on p76

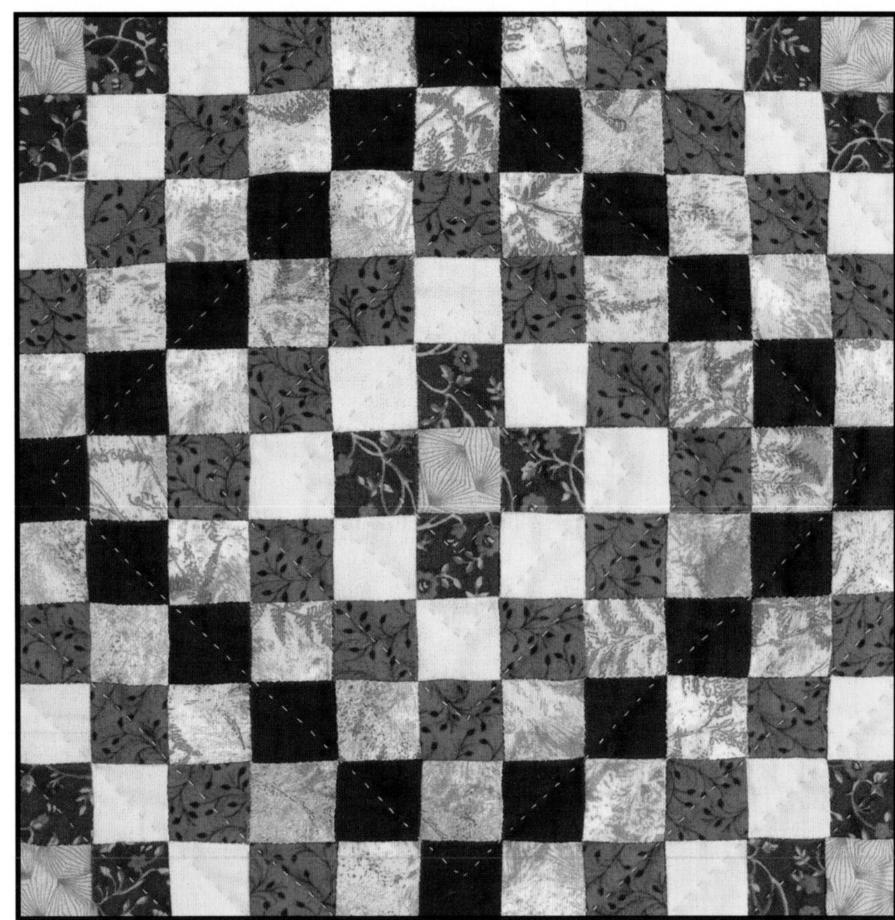

■ Constructing the block

1 Following your construction sequence carefully, piece the adjoining squares for rows 1 and 2 in pairs (**a**). Do the same with the squares for rows 3 and 4, 8 and 9, and 10 and 11. Piece the adjoining squares for rows 5, 6 and 7 into threes (**b**).

2 Join the pairs of squares in the correct sequence to create the first two complete rows of the block (**c** and **d**). Join the squares for the other rows in the same way (you'll have a unit of three rows for the centre, as shown in **e**).

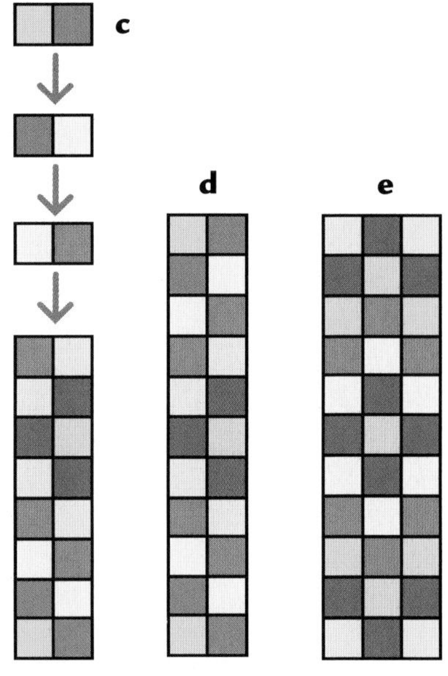

3 Join the units in the correct order as shown (**f**) to complete the block (**g**).

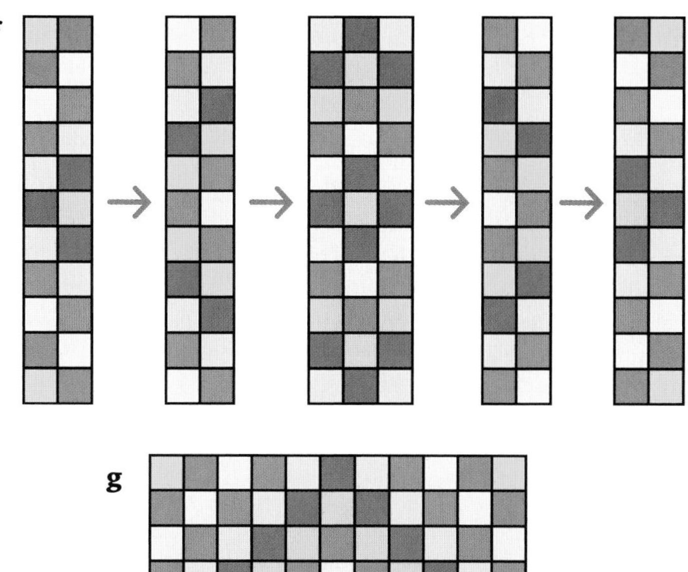

◆ TIP ◆

Check the construction sequence carefully – it's easier to handle these small squares when they are joined in pairs – and keep an eye on your colour scheme all the time. To get a preview of how your block could look, make a mock-up of a quarter of the block (including the central 'odd' square) either in fabric scraps or using coloured pencils and squared paper, then use two mirrors at right angles to create the impression of the complete design. At this stage you can see if your design is working, and if not you can change the colours accordingly.

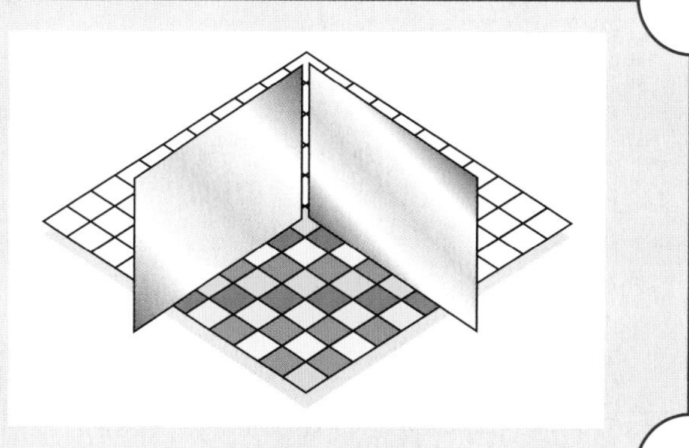

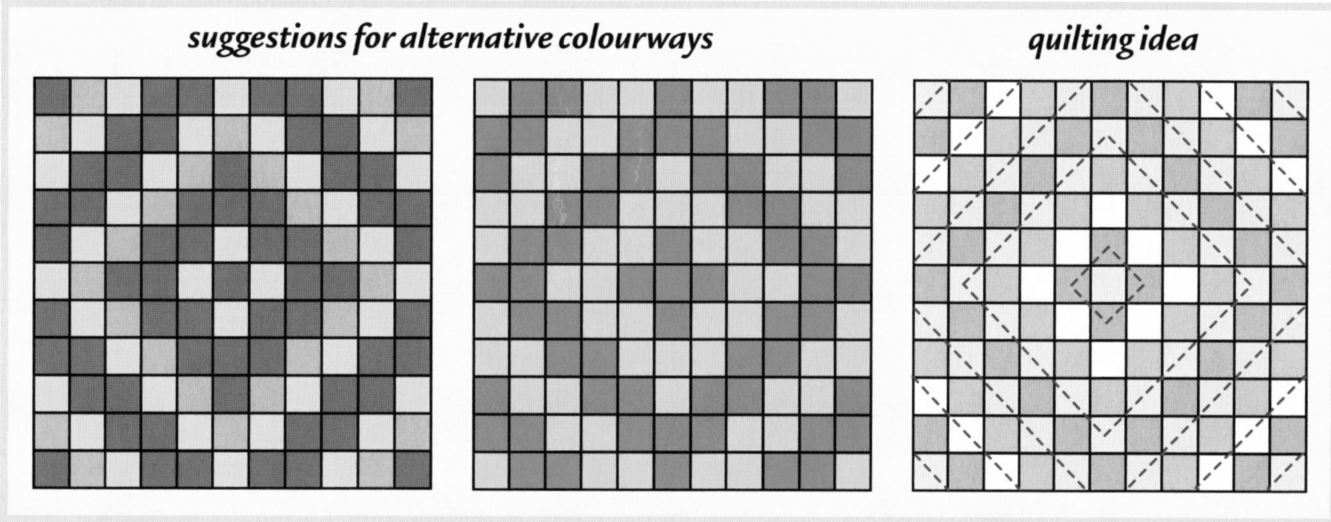

▪ BLOCK 9 ▪

Mohawk Trail

Drunkard's Path blocks, and the variation shown here (*Mohawk Trail*), both use squares which include a curved seam; the curved shape helps the design to meander throughout the block. The extra segmentation of the quarter-circle used in *Mohawk Trail* allows you to experiment with a wider variety of fabrics, colours and tonal values. As you can see, I've pieced each quarter-circle from three different tones of the same basic colour.

■ **Grid**
this block is based on a 4 x 4 grid

■ **Technique**
- curved seam patchwork (see Piecing Your Patchwork on p12)

■ **What you will need**
- basic supplies *(all-purpose sewing thread; needles or sewing machine; fabric scissors and thread-snipping scissors; pins; pencil)*

■ **Fabrics:** minimum 4

■ **Templates:** 3
you'll find the *Mohawk Trail* templates A-C on p77

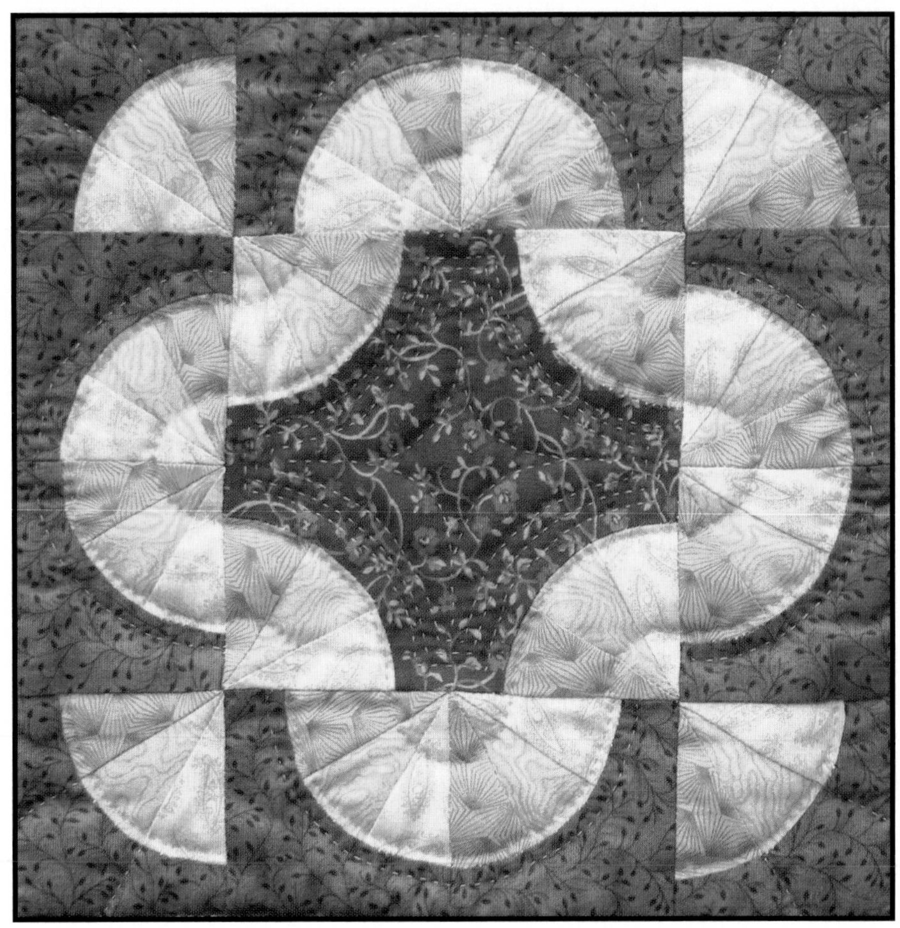

■ Constructing the block

1 Join the B segments in threes so that each quarter-circle contains one segment of each colour (**a**); make sure that the middle segment is marked with the centre point (shown as an asterisk). Make twelve units with the colours shading from light to dark as shown (**b**), and four with the colours shading the opposite way (**c**).

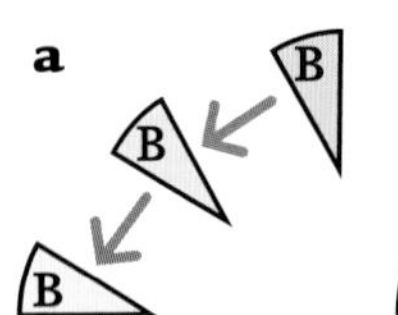

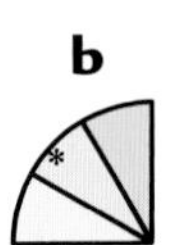

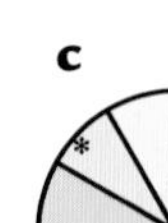

2 Join one of the twelve similar quarter-circles to the curved edge of one C shape, matching the centre points (**d**). Make twelve units this way.

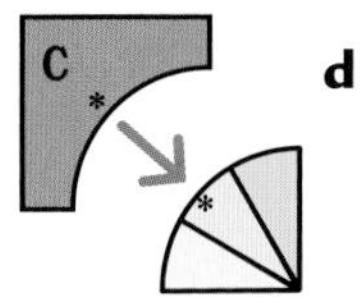

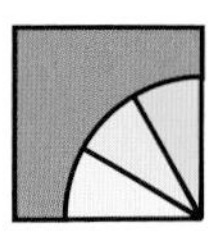

3 Add the remaining quarter-circle shapes to the curved edges of shape A, matching the centre points (**e**).

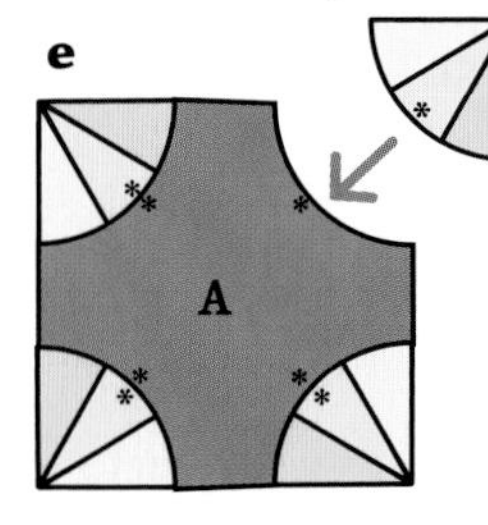

f

4 Join four of the smaller squares in the order shown to create a long unit (**f**); make two strips this way. Join the remaining smaller squares in pairs as shown (**g**), then join these pairs to the edges of the large central square unit (**h**).

g

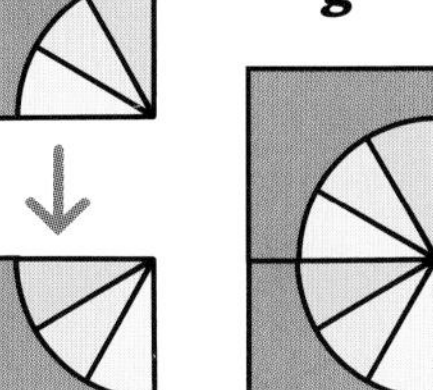

h

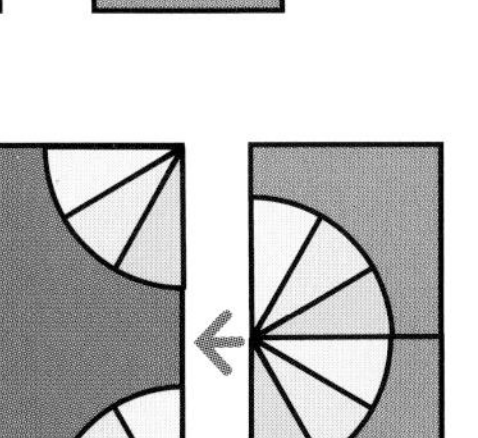

5 Join the rows of the block as shown (**i**) to produce the finished block (**j**).

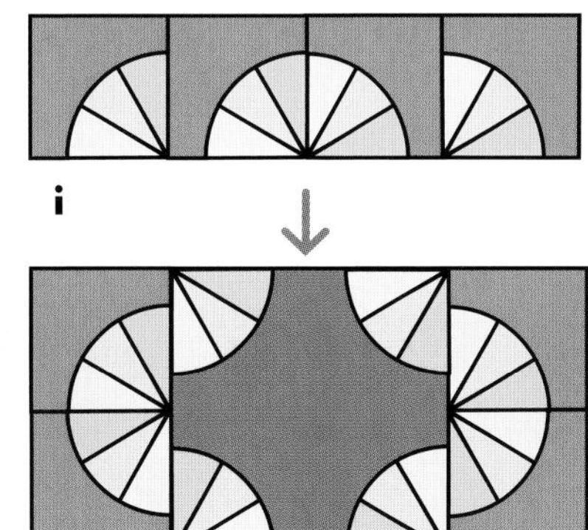

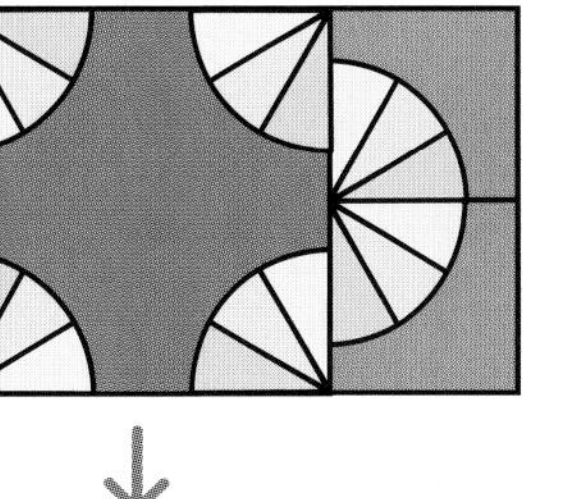

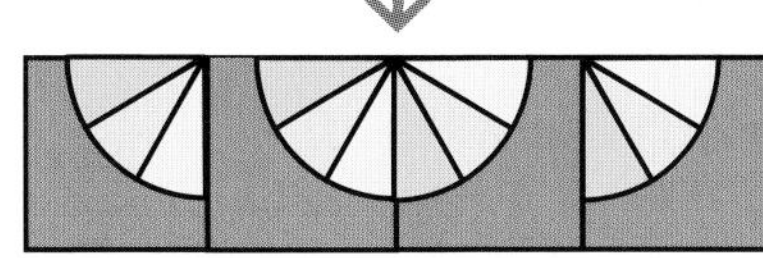

i

j

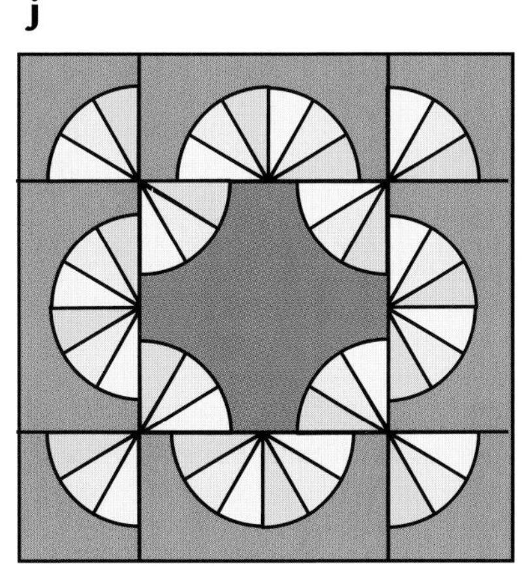

◆ TIPS ◆

You may prefer to construct the central section from four of the squares, rather than making an extra template (ie, make 16 small pieced squares instead of 12 plus the centre shape).

When you're planning and piecing the coloured patches for the Mohawk Trail segments, make sure that you put the correct colour in the correct place if you want each section of your 'trail' to follow on from the previous one.

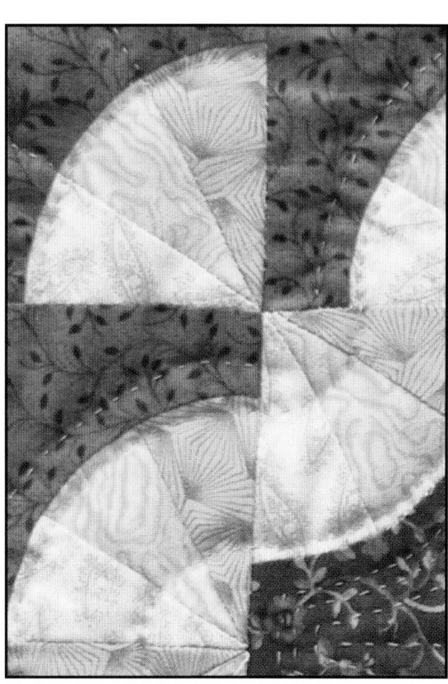

suggestions for alternative colourways

quilting idea

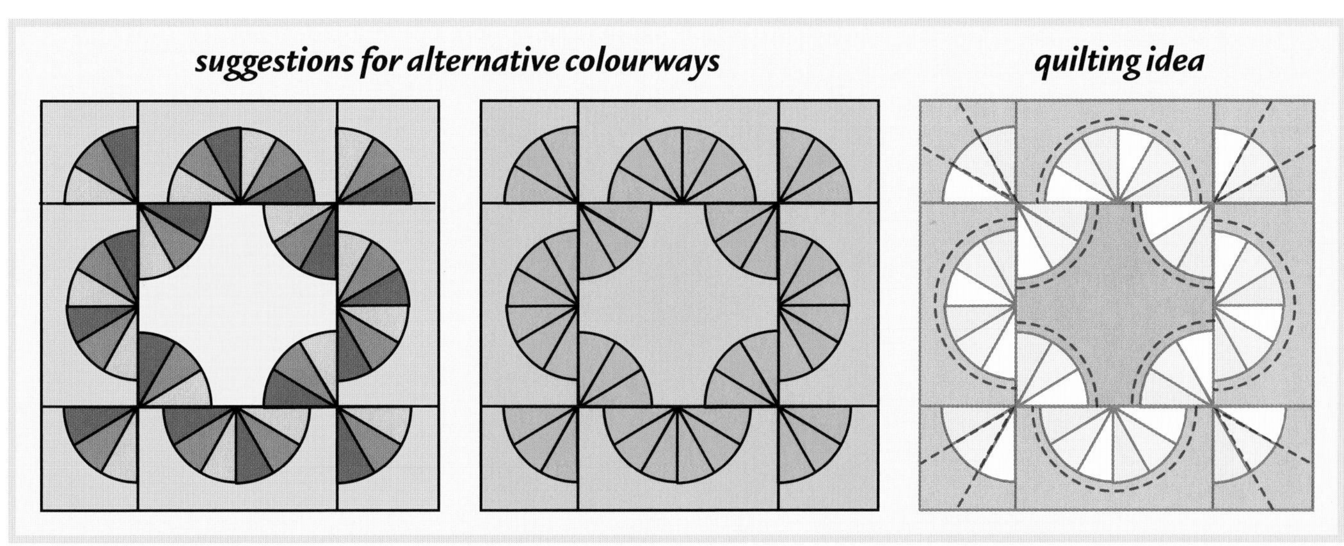

■ BLOCK 10 ■

Medallion Log Cabin

The design used for this block creates the optical illusion of two interlaced Log Cabins. If you want to alter the illusion, use one colour scheme for the central Log Cabin and a completely different one for the outer parts of the design; the colours will create the appearance of one block laid on top of another.

■ **Grid**
this block is based on a 2 x 2 grid

■ **Techniques**
- piecing (see Piecing Your Patchwork on p12)
- asymmetric shapes (see p12)

■ **What you will need**
- basic supplies *(all-purpose sewing thread; needles or sewing machine; fabric scissors and thread-snipping scissors; pins; pencil)*

■ **Fabrics:** minimum 3 (central fabric and two halves of a Log Cabin)

■ **Templates:** 17
you'll find the *Medallion Log Cabin* templates A-Q on pp84 and 85

■ Constructing the block

1 Join the short strip B to one side of the A square (**a**); working anticlockwise (counterclockwise) around the block, add the C strip in the same colour (**b**), the C strip in the alternate colour (**c**), and the first D strip (**d**) to complete the first circuit of the block (**e**).

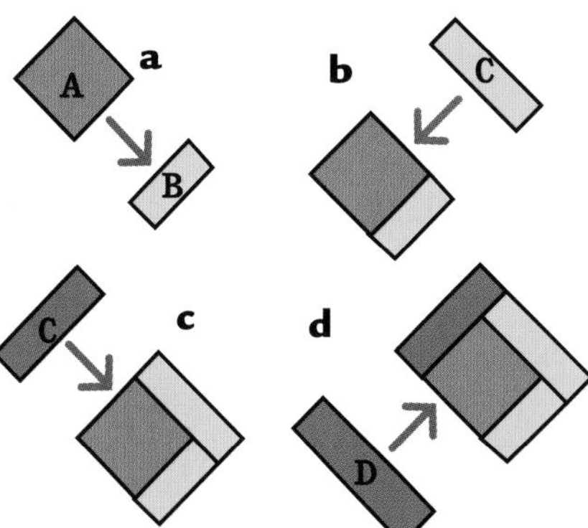

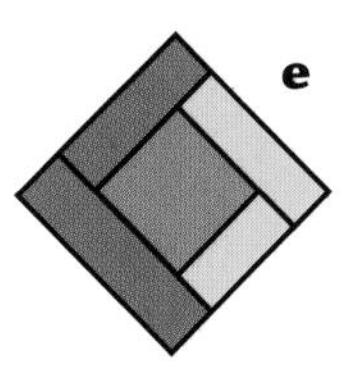

2 Continue working round the block in circuits in the same way until the central square is complete (**f**);

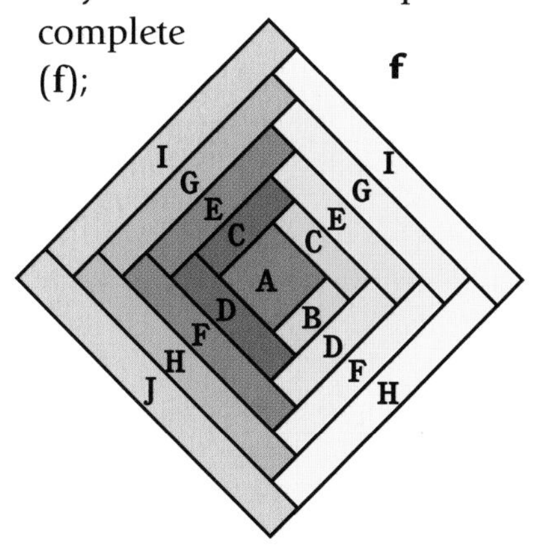

make sure on each circuit that you're adding the correct shape in the correct colour.

3 Use the same technique, but this time working just along two sides of the central triangle, to build up two pale corners (**g**) and two darker corners (**h**).

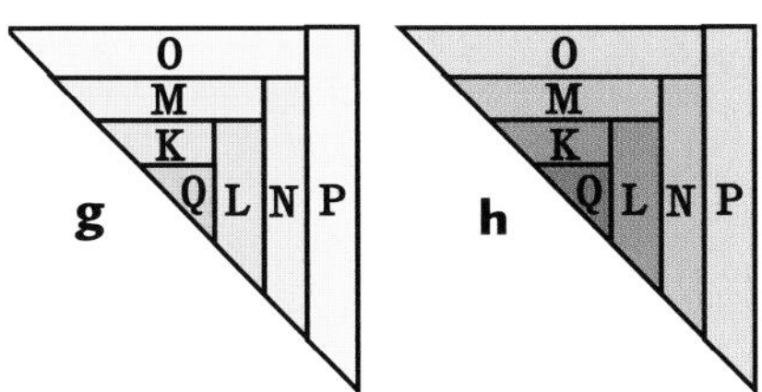

4 Join one pale and one dark triangle to opposite sides of the central block (**i**),

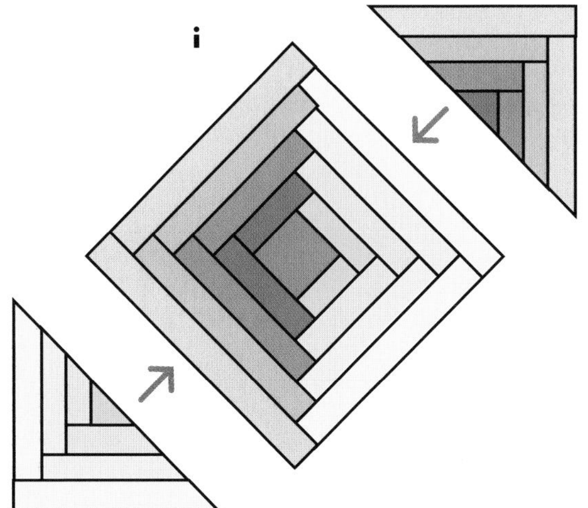

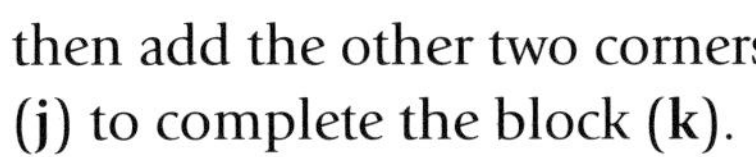

then add the other two corners (**j**) to complete the block (**k**).

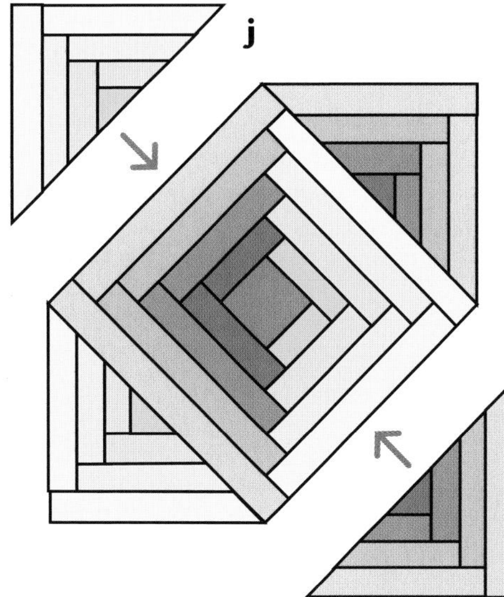

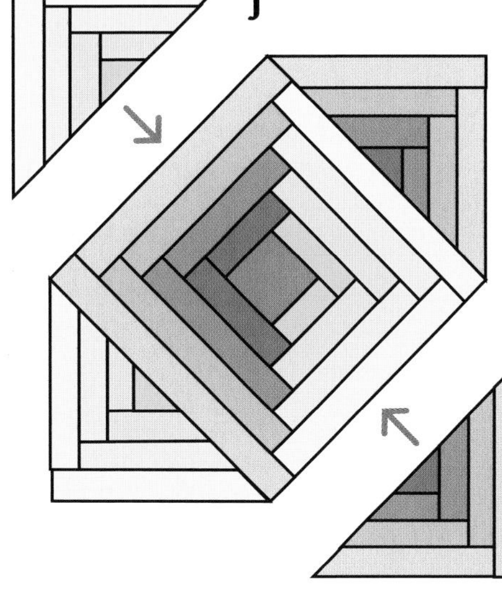

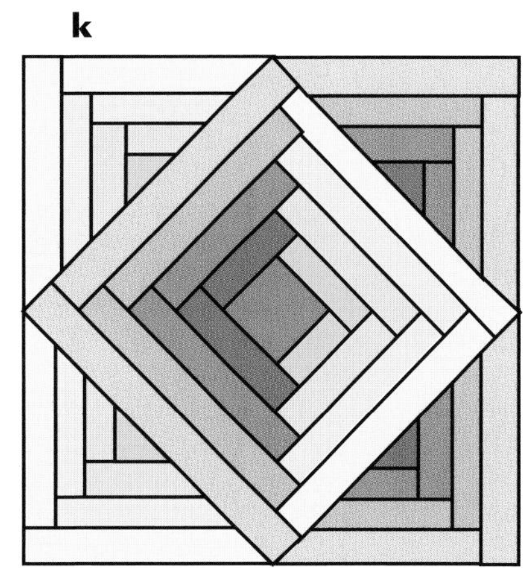

◆ TIPS ◆

Traditionally Log Cabin relies heavily on a darker side and a lighter side – use the tonal values of your fabrics carefully, as well as the colours. A strong and contrasting fabric for the central square adds a focal point to this design.

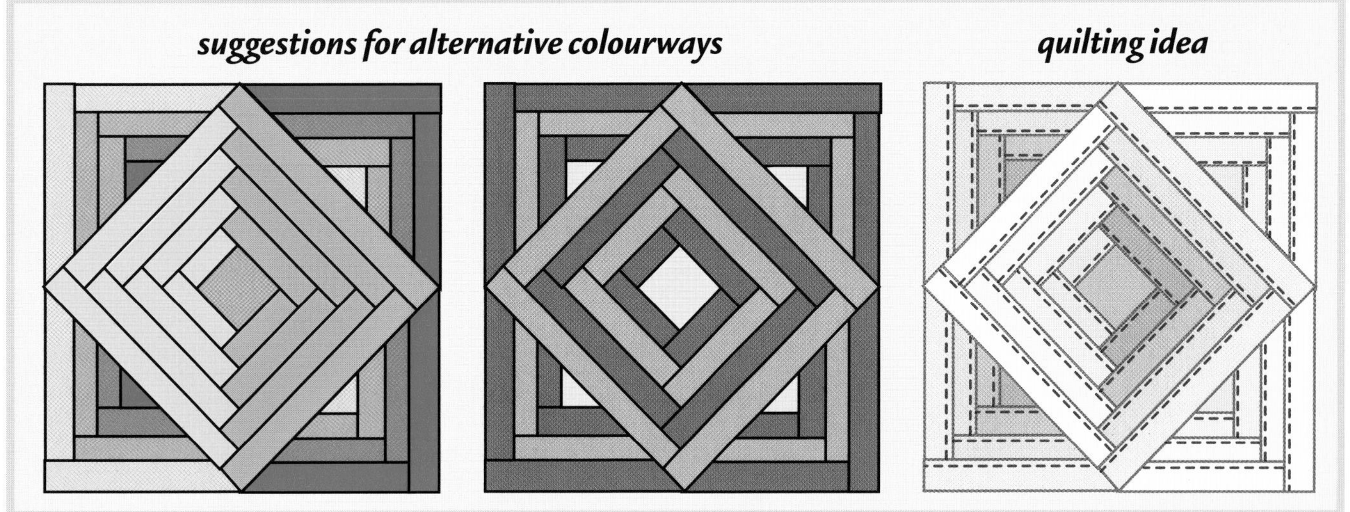

▪ BLOCK 11 ▪

Hawaiian Hearts

Hawaiian appliqué patterns are instantly recognisable because of their symmetry. The patterns and designs are many and varied, and are akin to the little snowflake cutouts that schoolchildren have fun producing. Once you've mastered the technique, it's just one more easy step forward to creating your very own, individual designs.

■ **Grid**

this block is based on a square folded into eighths diagonally

■ **Technique**

- hand-sewn appliqué (see Appliqué on p13)

■ **What you will need**

- basic supplies *(all-purpose sewing thread; needles; fabric scissors and thread-snipping scissors; pins; pencil)*
- tacking thread and needle
- paper and card
- paper-cutting scissors

■ **Fabrics:** 2

Choose two contrasting fabrics. You'll need a square of the appliqué fabric the size of your finished block, and you'll be constructing the design on a 10in (25cm) square of background fabric with seam allowances added on all sides.

■ **Templates:** 1

you'll find the *Hawaiian Hearts* template on p79

■ Constructing the block

1 Trace or photocopy the design on page 79, cut it out, and glue it to card. Cut around the shape on the card to make the template.

2 Lay the squares of fabric right side up and fold each one into halves (**a**), then quarters (**b**), then diagonally into eighths (**c**); press the creases into the fabric. Use the larger fabric square (including seam allowances) as

a

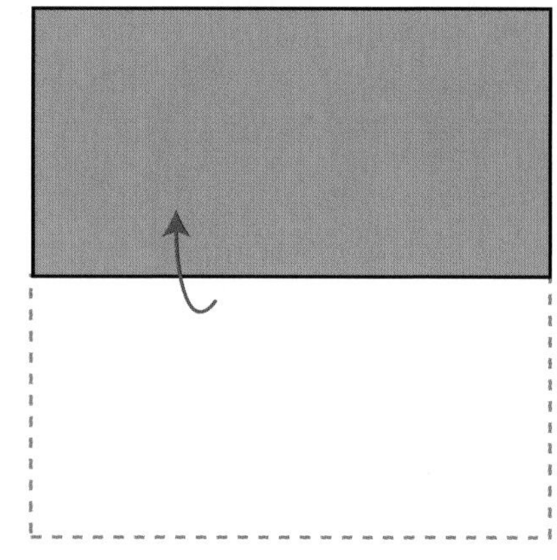

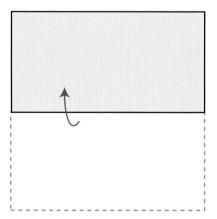

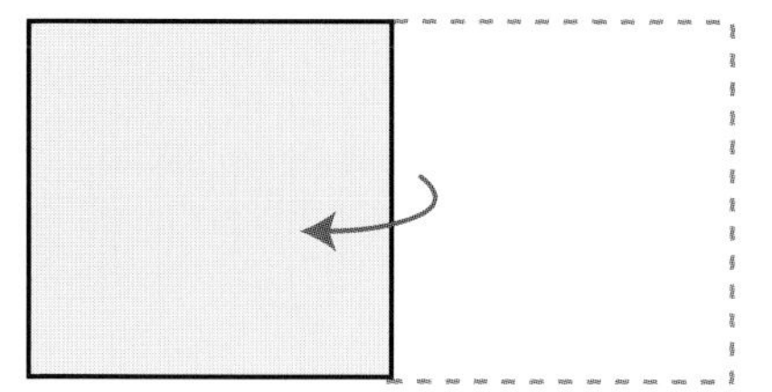

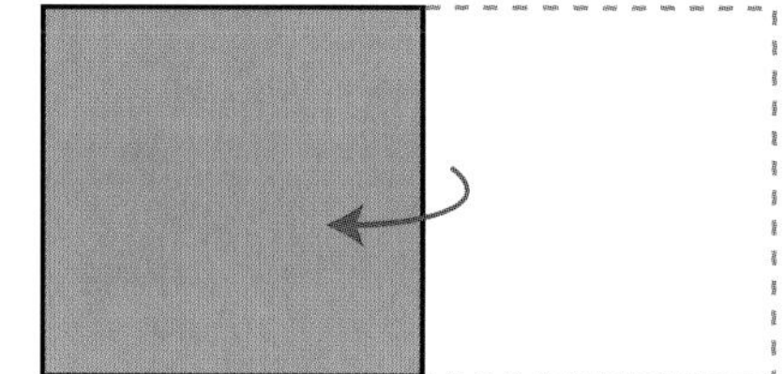

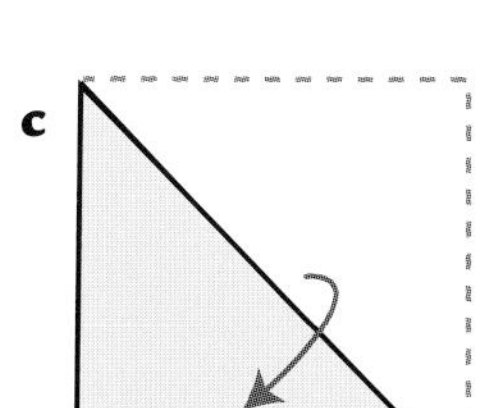

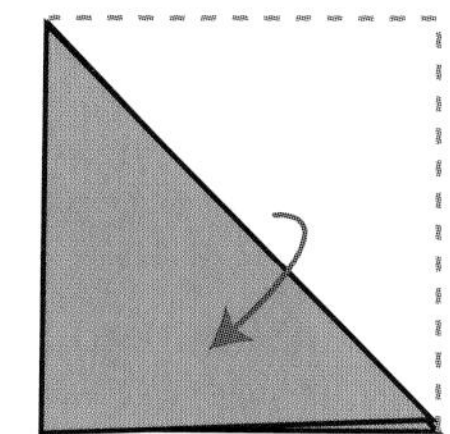

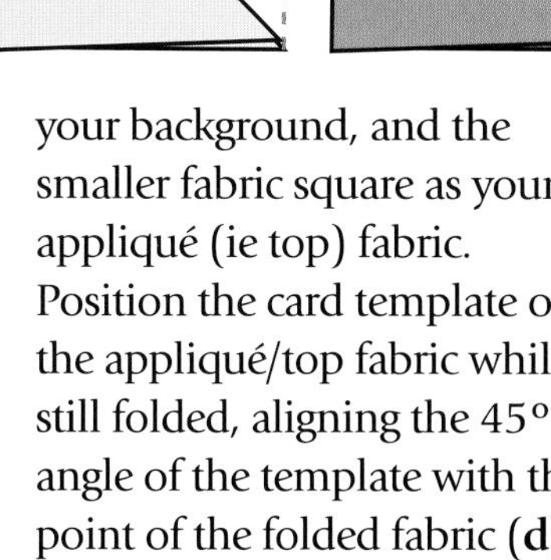

your background, and the smaller fabric square as your appliqué (ie top) fabric. Position the card template on the appliqué/top fabric while it's still folded, aligning the 45° angle of the template with the point of the folded fabric (**d**), and draw round the template with a pencil. Still keeping the fabric folded, cut out the design ***plus*** a scant quarter-inch seam allowance (**e**).

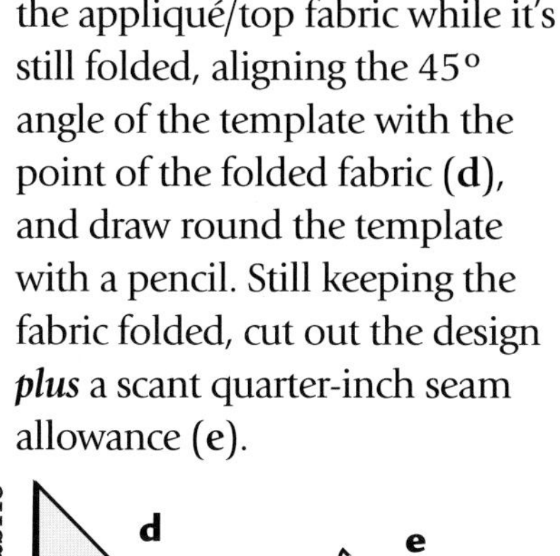

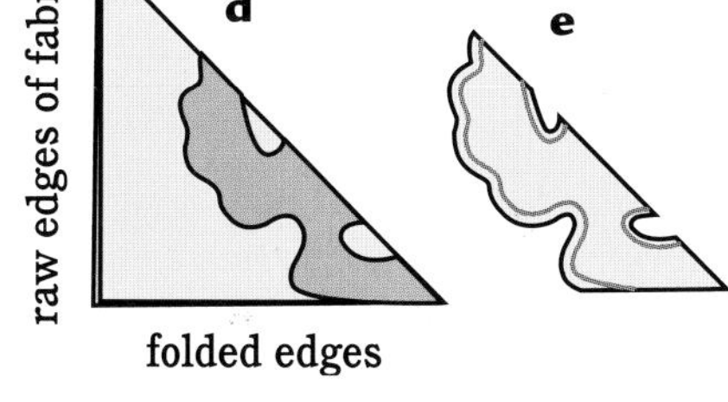

3 Unfold the background fabric square and lay it right side up on a flat surface. Place the folded triangle of appliqué/ top fabric in the matching section on the background fabric (**f**), and unfold it so that the folds of the two fabrics match (**g**).

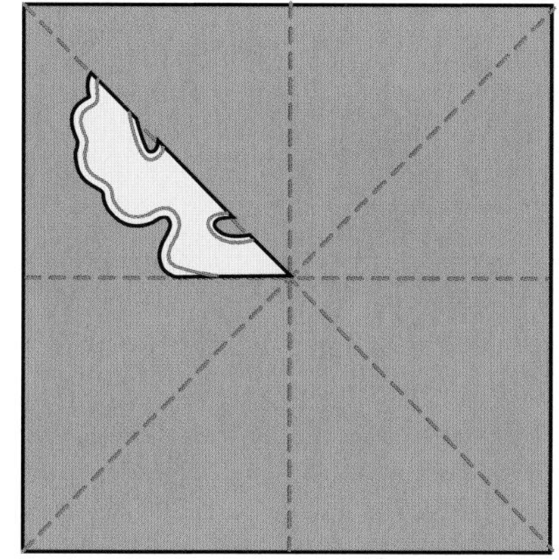

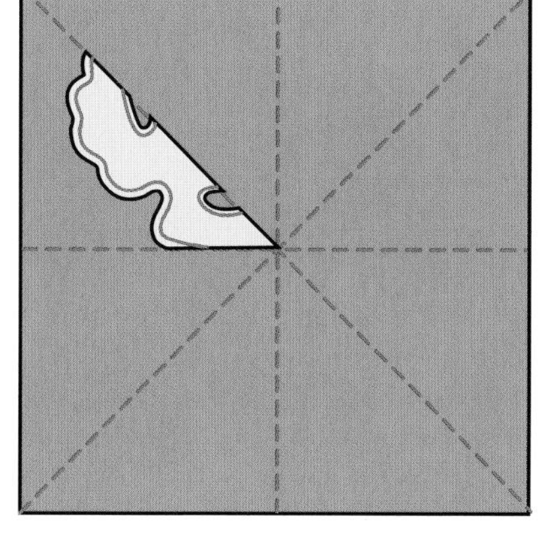

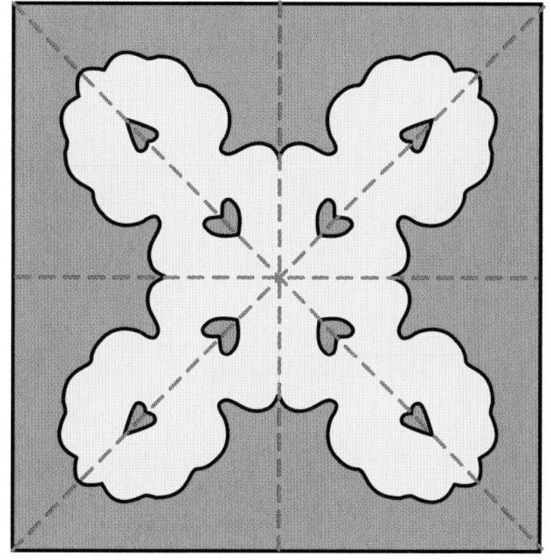

4 Tack the appliqué fabric in place, stitching around the complete outer edge of the design and the edges of the hearts, just over a quarter-inch (6mm) in from the raw edge of fabric. Use an appliqué stitch (see p13) to sew the design to the background fabric – use the point of your needle to tuck the raw edge of fabric under as you go. Once the design is completely sewn (**h**), remove the tacking.

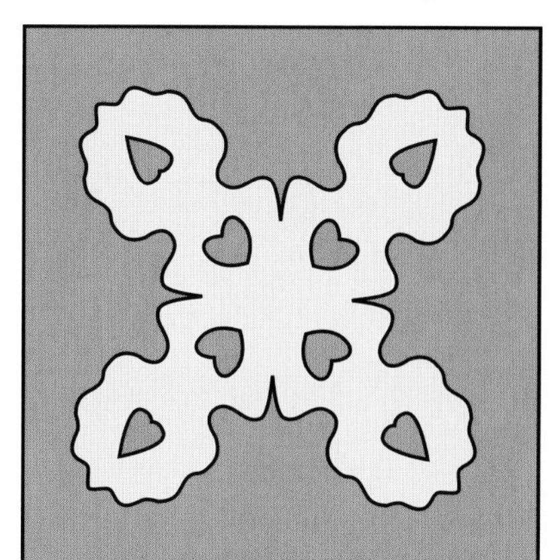

◆ **TIP** ◆

If you're making your own patterns, begin by drawing and cutting designs that have gentle curves before moving on to more complex designs incorporating sharp valleys and points. Sometimes the simpler designs work better than those that are more intricate or complicated.

suggestions for alternative colourways

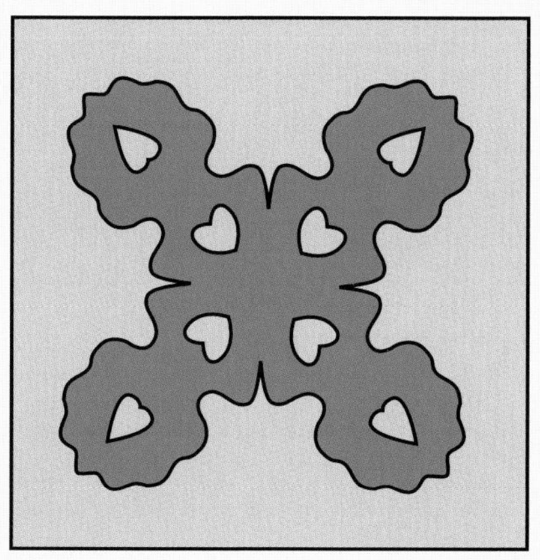

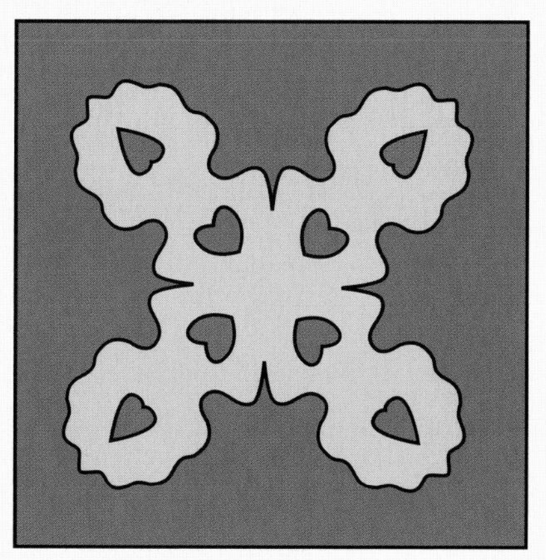

quilting idea

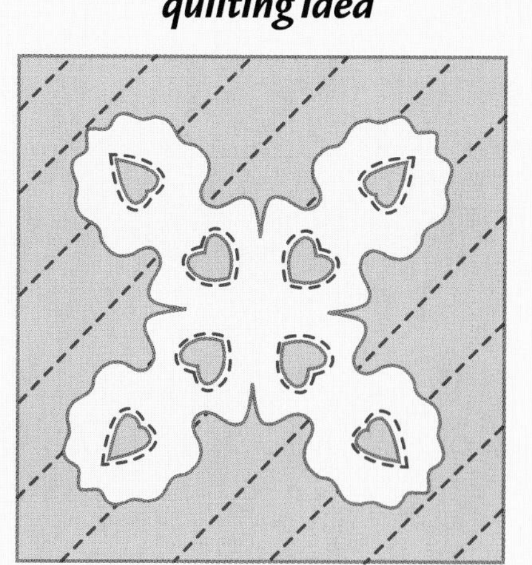

▪ BLOCK 12 ▪

Castle Keep

Castle Keep is an intriguing block, and looks quite complex. Its appearance can vary enormously depending on the fabrics, colours and tonal values of the fabrics you choose, and it can appear strikingly three-dimensional. It has a distinct flavour of castle parapets, fortresses and armour.

Grid

this block is based on a 2 x 2 grid

Techniques

- squares and triangles (see Piecing Your Patchwork on p12)
- mirror-image shapes (see p12)

What you will need

- basic supplies *(all-purpose sewing thread; needles or sewing machine; fabric scissors and thread-snipping scissors; pins; pencil)*

Fabrics: minimum 4

Templates: 7
you'll find the *Castle Keep* templates A-G on p83

Constructing the block

1 Join the eight A triangles first into pairs and then into fours as shown, then join the fours into an octagon, alternating the colours (**a** and **b**).

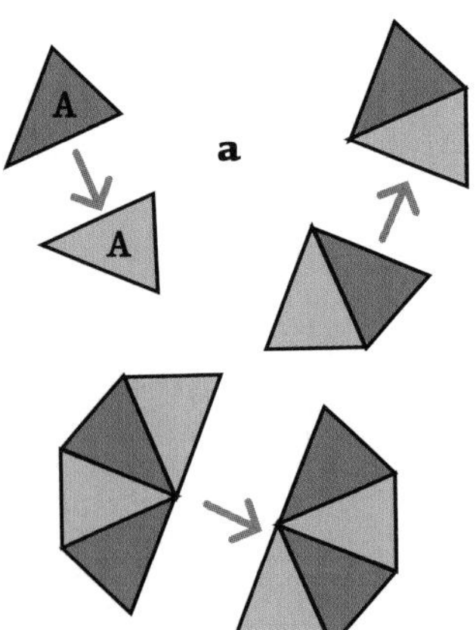

Add a small B triangle to each corner of the octagon (**c**).

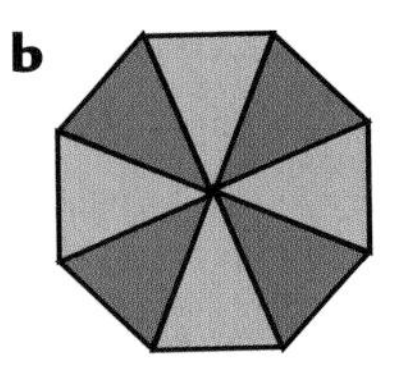

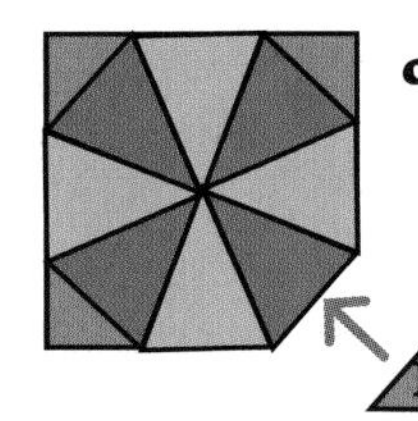

2 Join a C triangle, a D patch and an E triangle to form a square (**d**); make four units in this way. These will become the corner patches of the block.

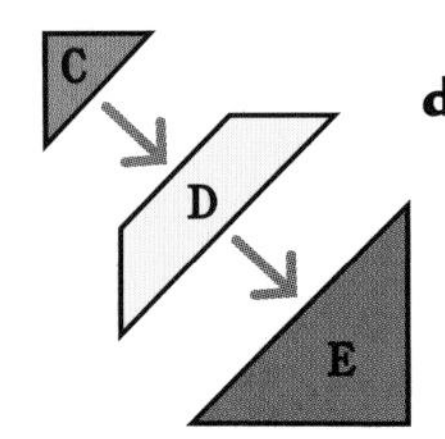

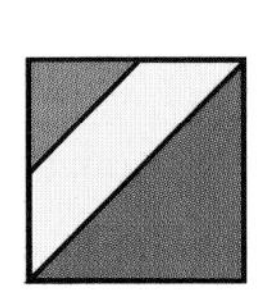

3 Join all the F and G triangles together in pairs to create kite shapes (**e**). Add a small B triangle to the edge of one pair (make sure that you add it to the correct side!); make four units this way (**f**).

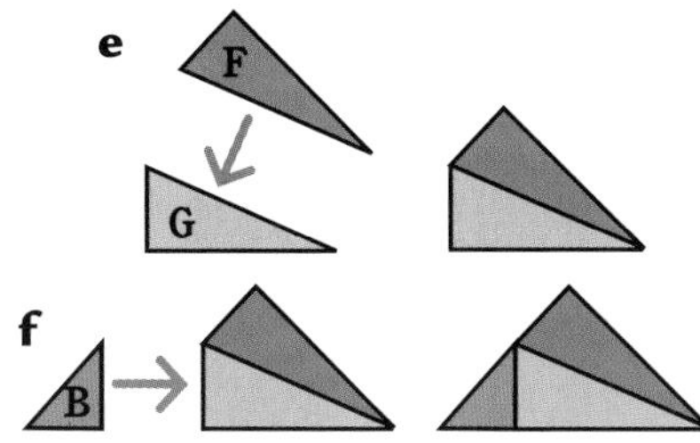

4 Join a small C triangle to a D shape (**g**); make four units this way, then join each one to an FG kite shape as shown (**h**).

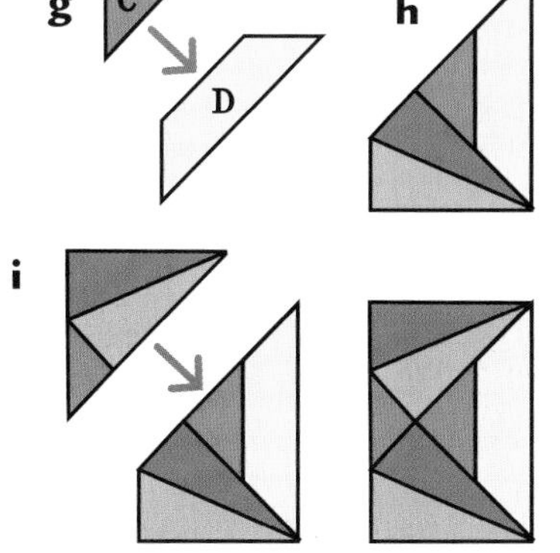

5 Join one of the units from step 3 to one of the units from step 4 as shown (**i**); create four rectangles this way, which will become the side units of the block.

6 Join two square corner patches to a side unit in the order shown to create a long strip (**j**); make two strips in this way. Join the remaining side strips to the large pieced

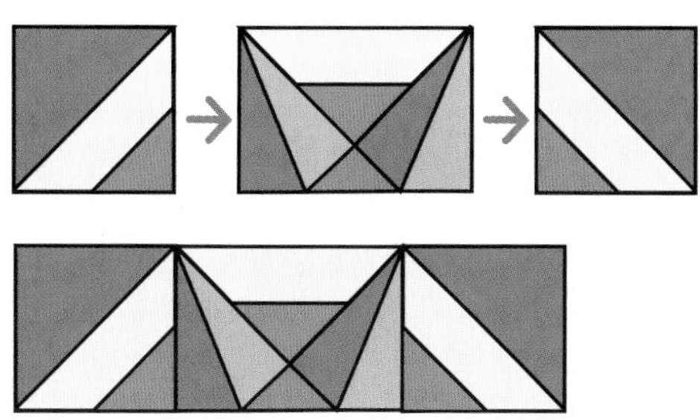

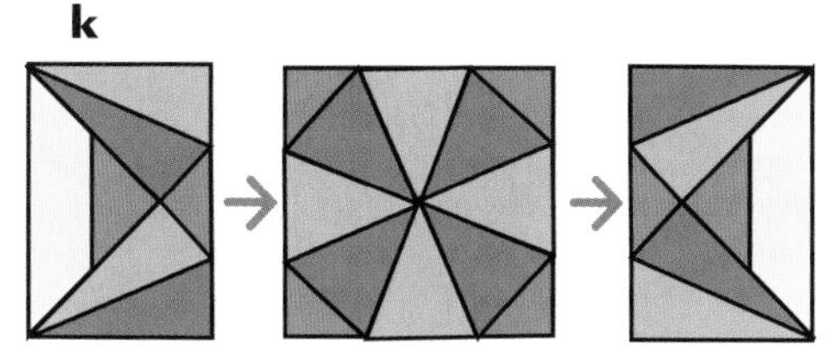

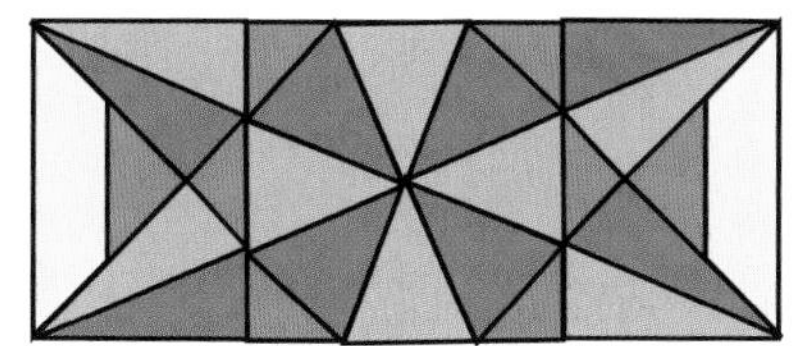

central square (**k**); check the orientation of the side blocks carefully to ensure that you put the small triangle next to the central square.

7 Join the rows in the order shown (**l**) to complete the block (**m**).

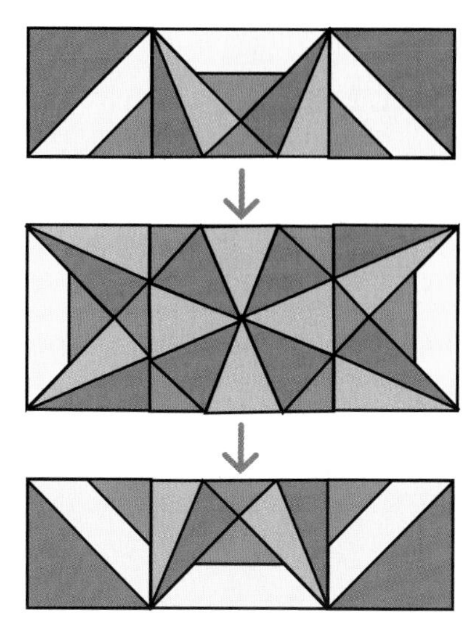

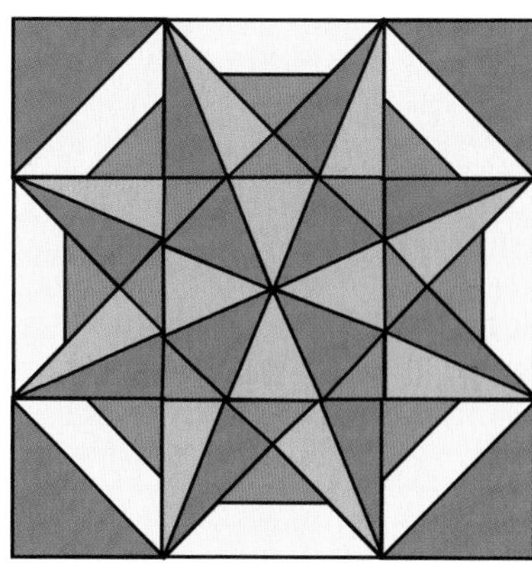

◆ **TIP** ◆

At first glance, this block looks as though it's based on a traditional 9-patch (3 x 3) grid. On closer inspection, though, you'll see that the central section on each side of the square is larger than the outer two sections (see p102, in the section on Drafting Your Own Blocks).

suggestions for alternative colourways

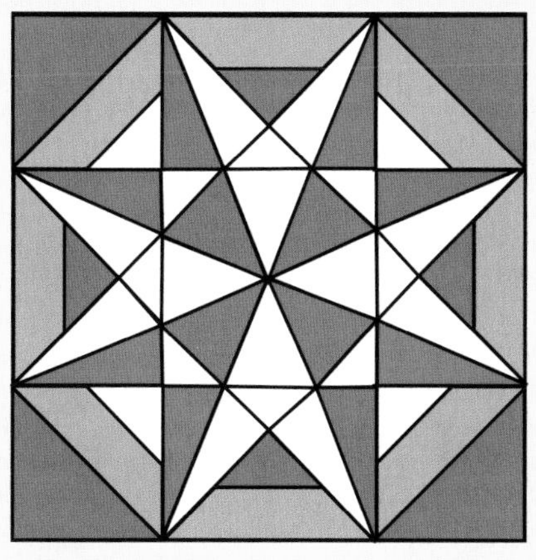

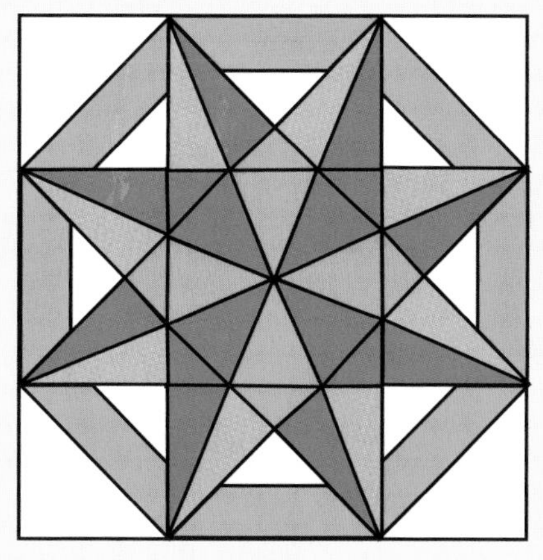

quilting idea

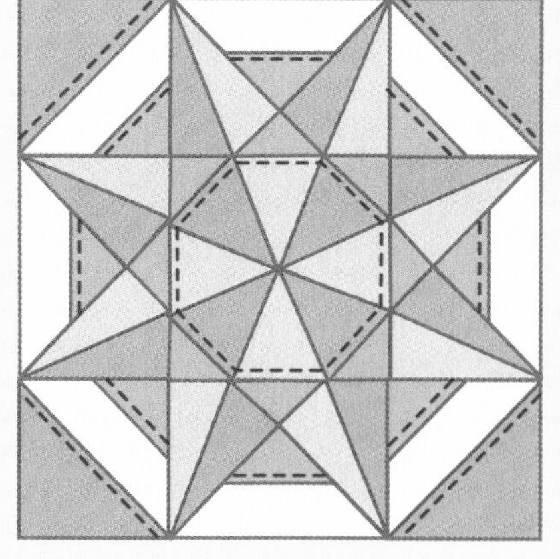

▪ BLOCK 13 ▪

Eccentric Star

Eccentric Star lives up to its name by creating the appearance of a star whirling around like a windmill. Highlighting the spikes of the star with a bolder colour strengthens the illusion of movement.

■ **Grid**

this block is based on a 3 x 3 grid (traditional 9-patch)

■ **Techniques**

- piecing (see Piecing Your Patchwork on p12)
- partial seaming (see p13)
- asymmetric shapes (see p12)

■ **What you will need**

- basic supplies *(all-purpose sewing thread; needles or sewing machine; fabric scissors and thread-snipping scissors; pins; pencil)*

■ **Fabrics:** minimum 3

■ **Templates:** 6

you'll find the *Eccentric Star* templates A-F on p82

■ Constructing the block

1 Join the B triangles to the outsides of the A square (**a**) to create the central unit (**b**). Add the C squares to the outside of this unit (**c** and **d**).

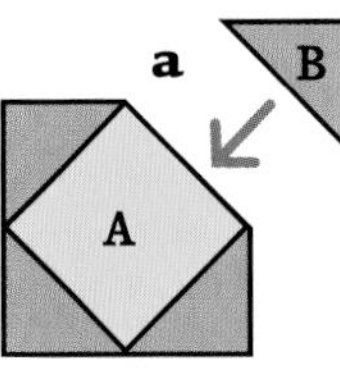

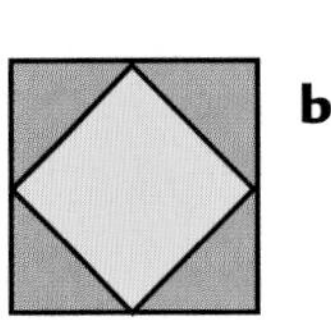

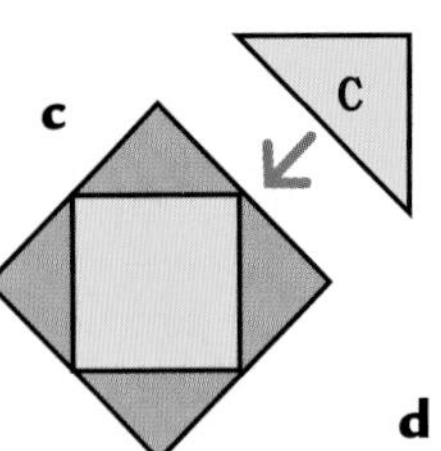

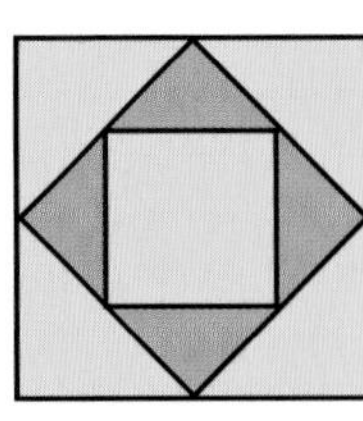

2 Join one D, one E and one F shape as shown (**e** and **f**) to create a new unit; make four units in this way.

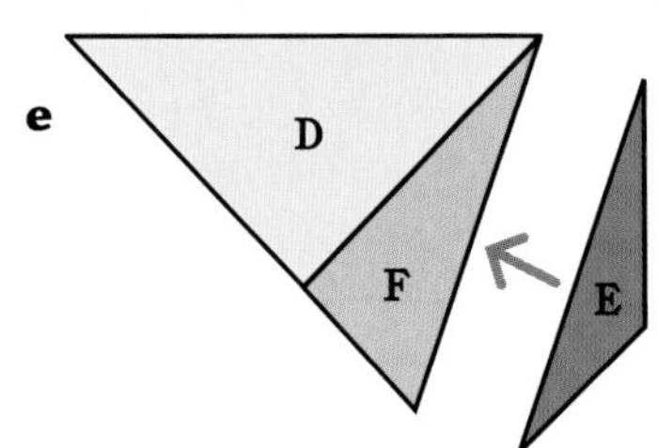

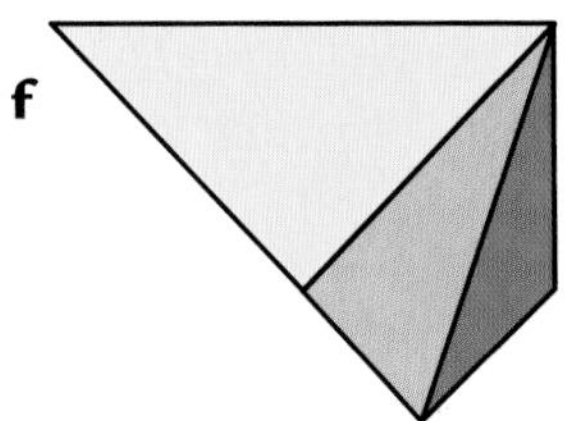

3 Use the partial seaming technique to stitch part of one DEF unit to the central square (**g**); stitch between the points marked by the asterisks.

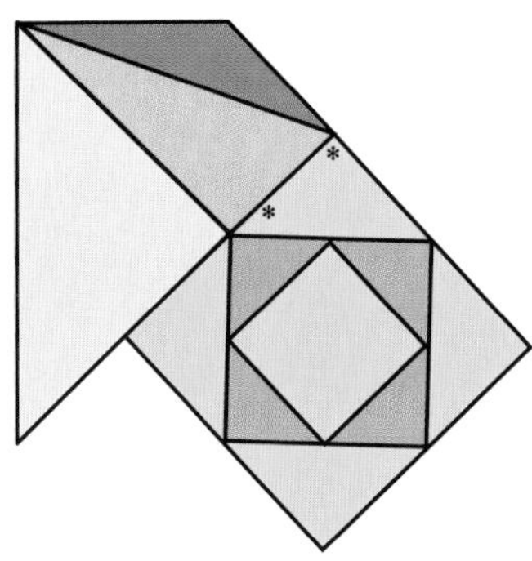

Carry on adding the DEF units, working in a clockwise direction round the edge of the square (**h** and **i**); when you've added the final unit, finish off the partial seam to complete the block (**j**).

h

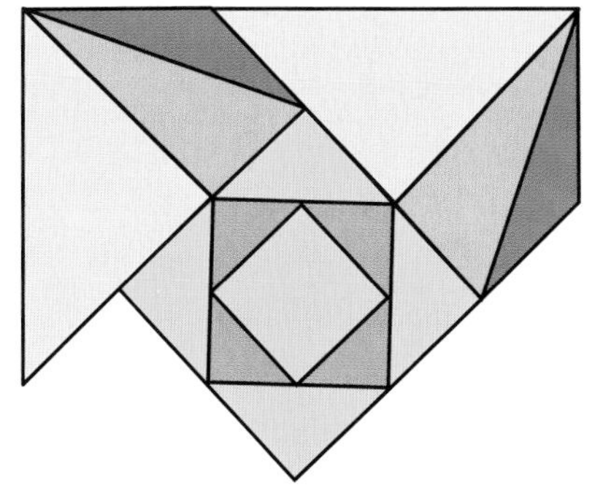

i

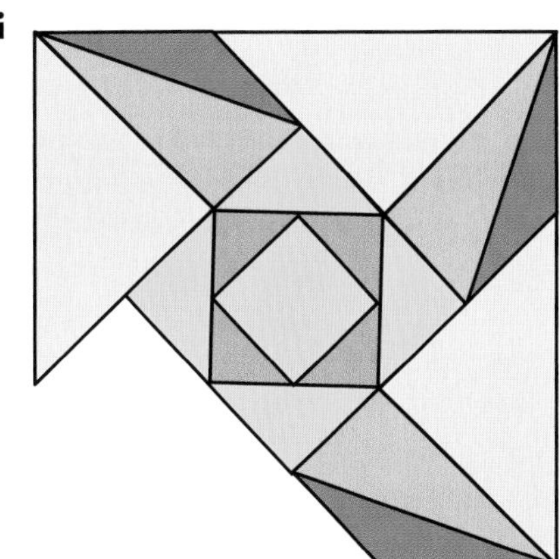

j

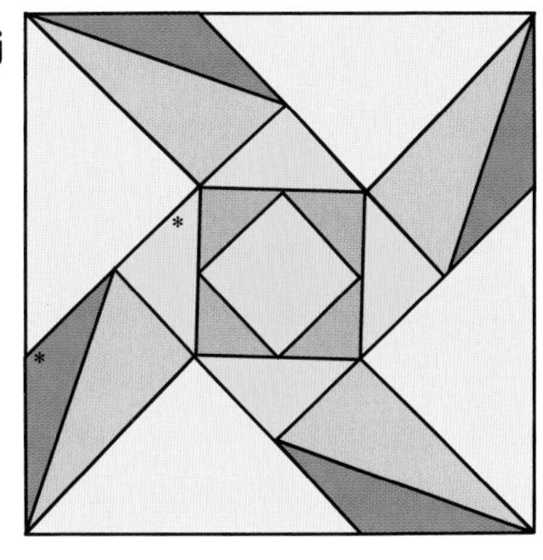

A block like Eccentric Star could be awkward to piece, especially when you're sewing by machine; however, if you use the partial seaming technique it becomes simple to piece and can be sewn with straight lines. Handle the long asymmetric triangular patches (the ones cut from template E) very carefully, as two of their edges are cut on the bias.

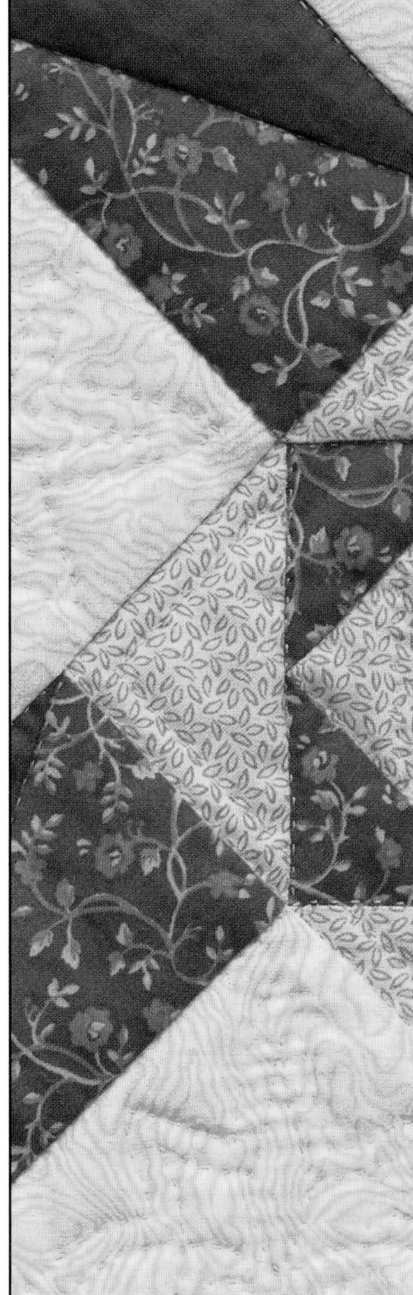

suggestions for alternative colourways

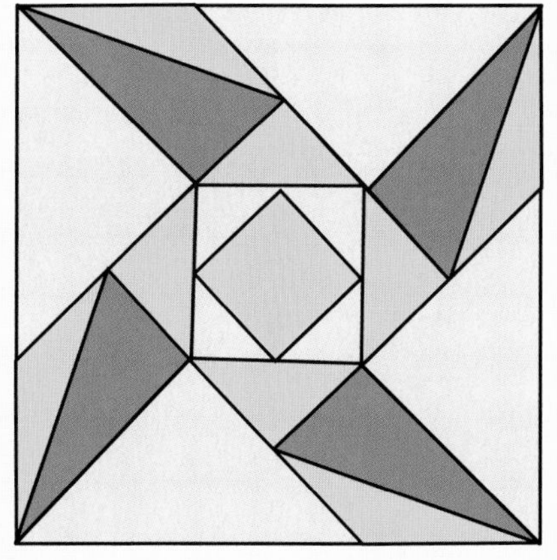

quilting idea

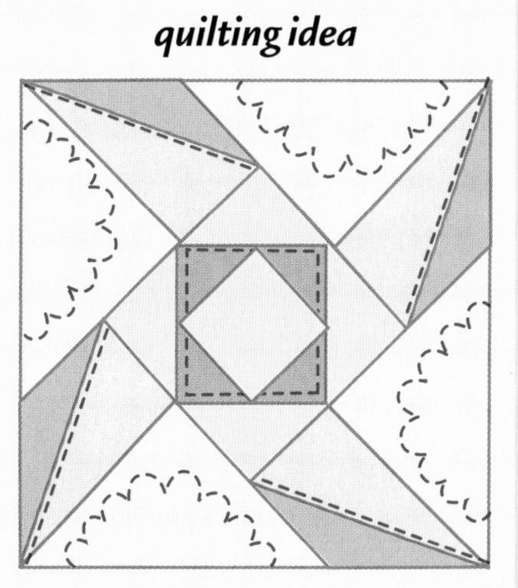

▪ BLOCK 14 ▪
Indian Wedding Ring

This variation on the well-known traditional Wedding Ring block offers more scope for using your scrap bag fabrics. It's a wonderful block to repeat across an entire quilt top, resulting in an interlinked pattern known as Double Wedding Ring.

■ **Grid**
this block is based on a 2 x 2 grid

■ **Techniques**
- piecing (see Piecing Your Patchwork on p12)
- curved seam patchwork (see p12)

■ **What you will need**
- basic supplies *(all-purpose sewing thread; needles or sewing machine; fabric scissors and thread-snipping scissors; pins; pencil)*

■ **Fabrics:** minimum 4

■ **Templates:** 7
you'll find the *Indian Wedding Ring* templates A-G on p86

■ Constructing the block

1 Join one D shape, alternate F and G shapes and one E shape as shown (**a**). Make eight arcs this way.

2 Join a small C square onto each end of one arc (**b**); make four units this way.

Join the other arcs onto the B shapes as shown (**c**). Join one of these units to a long arc (**d**); make four units this way.

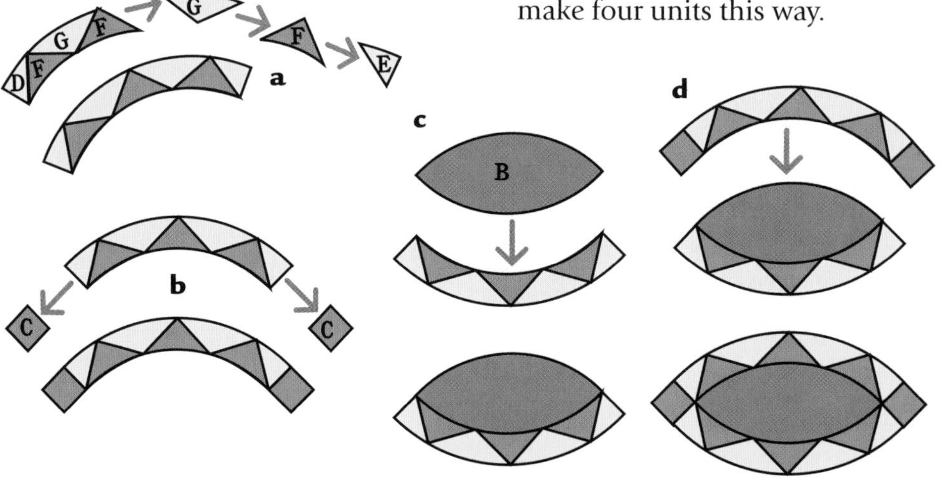

3 Add a large A shape to each side of each curved unit as shown (**e**).

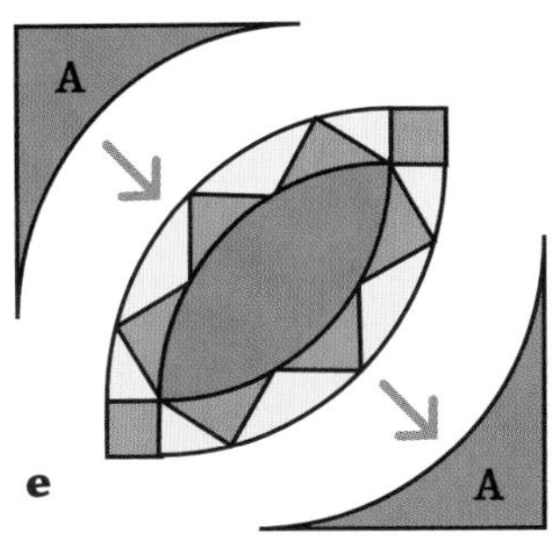

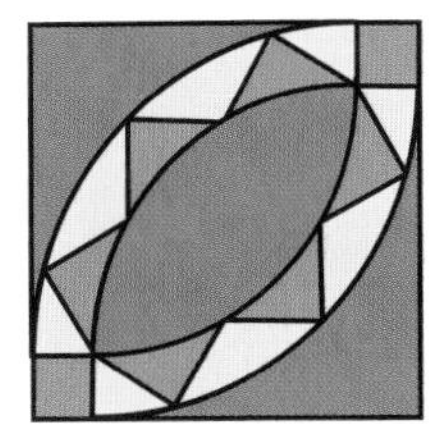

4 Join the square units in pairs in the arrangement shown (**f**), then join the pairs (**g**) to complete the block (**h**).

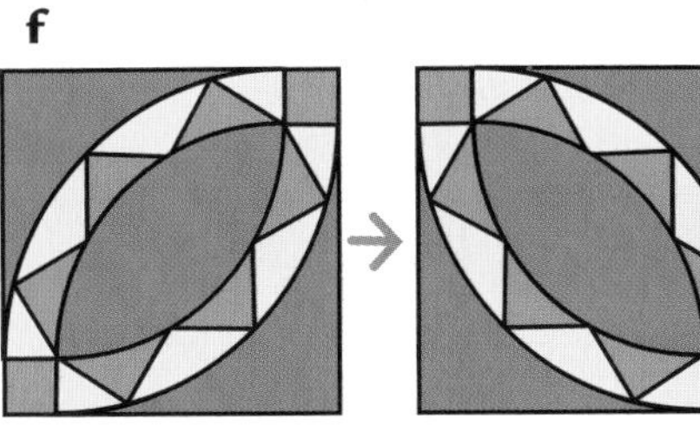

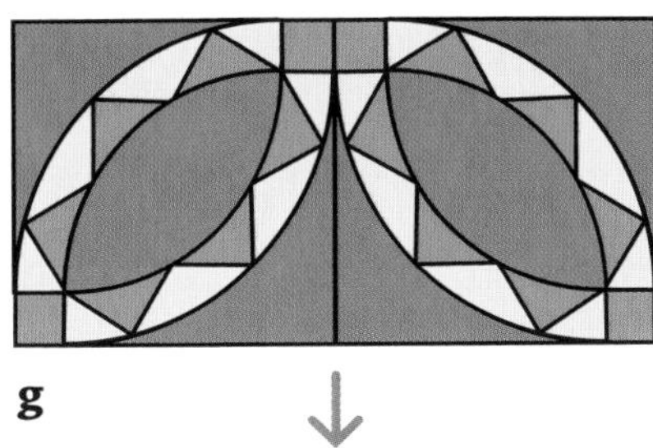

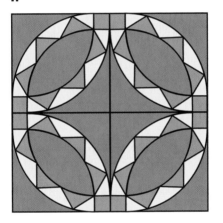

Diagram **i** shows the effect of using solid arcs rather than pieced ones.

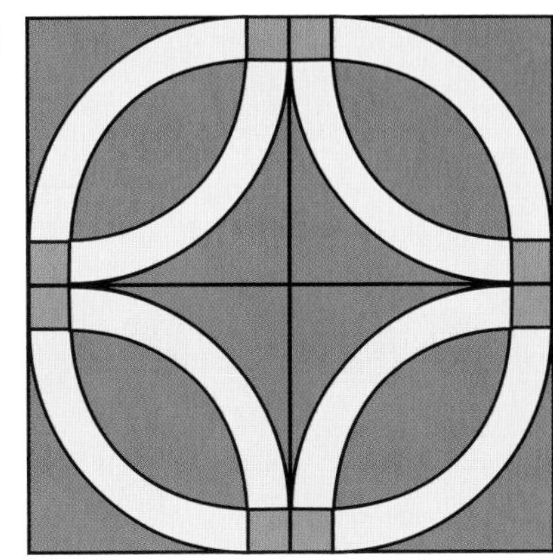

◆ TIPS ◆

If you're drafting your own pattern (see p103), you can make a further template for the central section and use one piece of fabric here, rather than having four seams in this space. Ensure that your seam allowance is tucked well to the back of the work when you sew together the two squares that sit on the outer edge of the block, so that the 'central' fabric doesn't get caught up and show through the seam at this stage.

suggestions for alternative colourways

quilting idea

▪ BLOCK 15 ▪

Rocky Road to Kansas

Rocky Road to Kansas gives you the opportunity to create your own fabric using pieces from your scrap bag to achieve a unique and individual end result; the randomly-patterned triangles add a rich texture to this simple-to-construct block.

■ **Grid**
this block is based on a 2 x 2 grid

■ **Techniques**
- triangles (see Piecing Your Patchwork on p12)
- crazy patchwork on a foundation
- mirror-image shapes (see p12)

■ **What you will need**
- basic supplies *(all-purpose sewing thread; needles or sewing machine; fabric scissors and thread-snipping scissors; pins; pencil)*

■ **Fabrics:** minimum 4
It's possible to use just one fabric for the crazy patchwork if it features a variety of colours and patterns across its surface. You'll also need a foundation fabric (eg calico) for the crazy patchwork shapes.

■ **Templates:** 4
you'll find the *Rocky Road to Kansas* templates A-D on p87

■ Sewing crazy patchwork

1 Cut a random-shaped piece of one of the fabric scraps and pin it in position, right side up, on one of the foundation triangles (**a**).

2 Lay another scrap on top, right side down, and stitch a seam (**b**). Fold the new patch to the front and press (**c**).

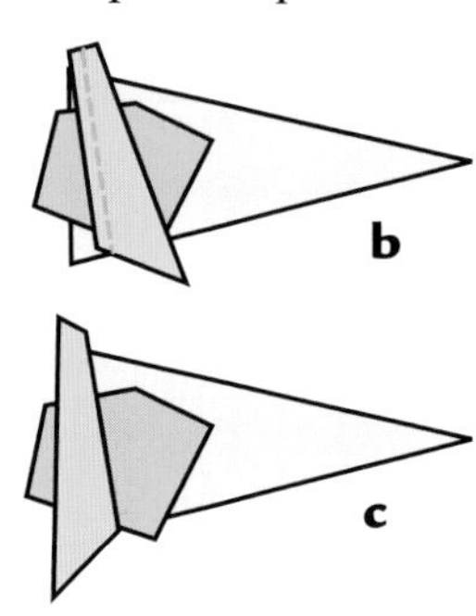

3 Continue adding scraps this way until the whole foundation triangle has been covered (**d**); trim the edges of the crazy-pieced patches to fit the foundation triangle (**e**). Make four shapes this way (**f**), varying the arrangements of fabric within them.

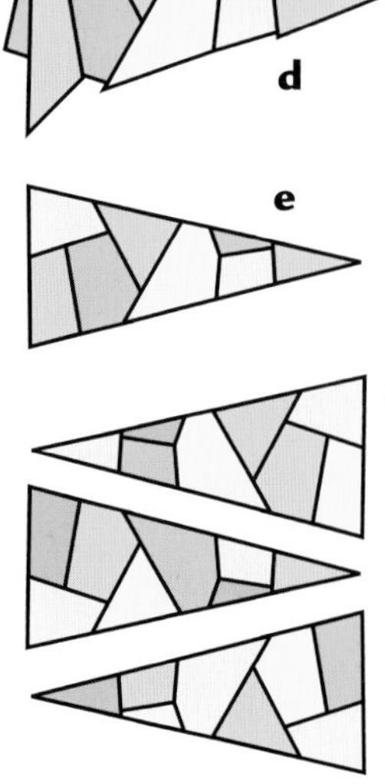

Constructing the block

4 Add an A triangle and a B triangle to the sides of one of the pieced triangles (**g**),

g

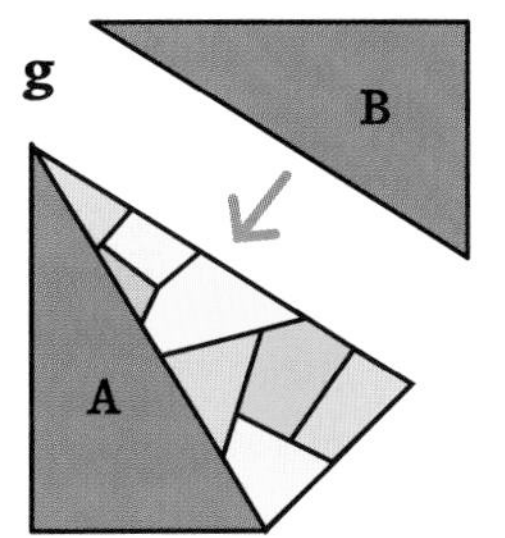

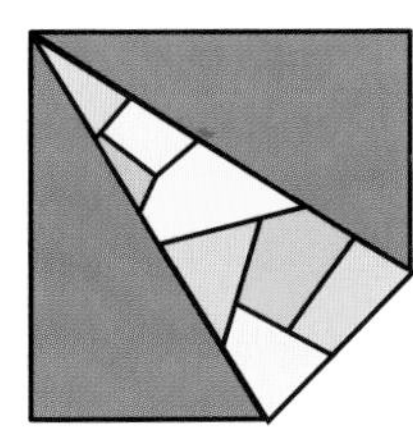

then add a small D triangle to the angled corner of the shape (**h**). Make four units this way.

h

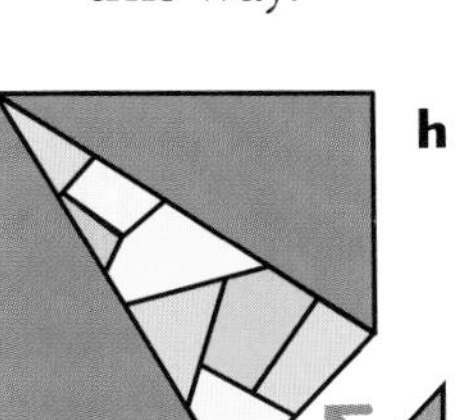

5 Join the units in pairs (**i**),

i

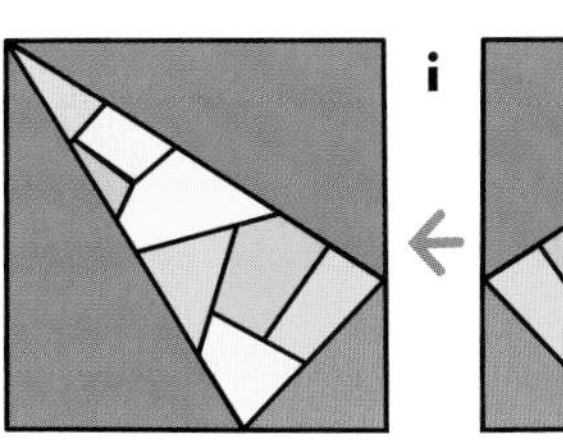

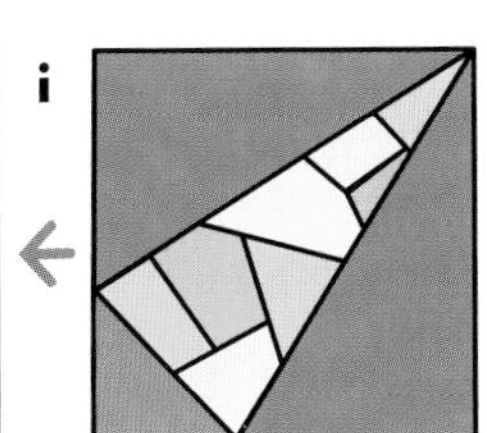

then join the pairs together (**j**) to complete the block (**k**).

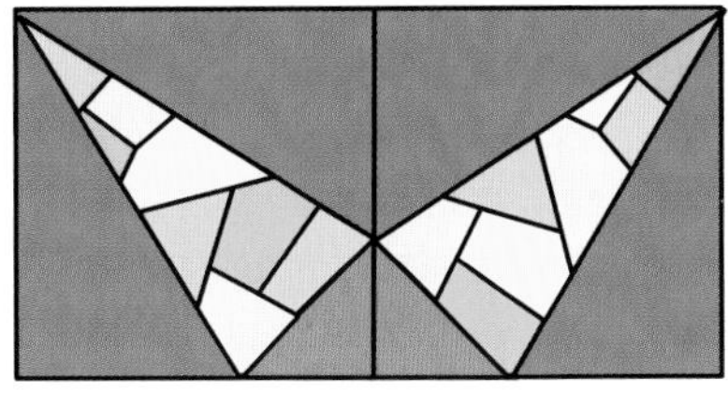

j

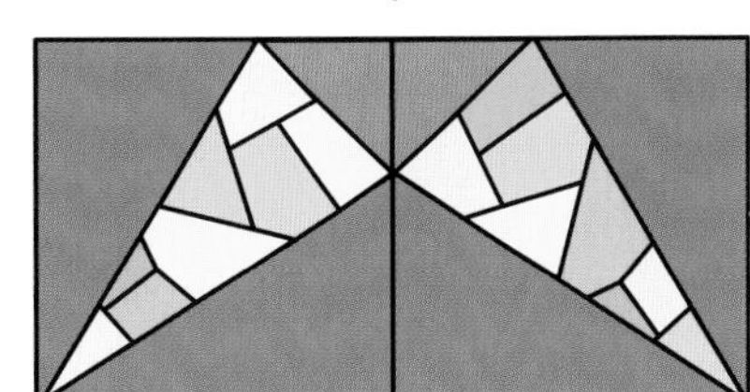

k

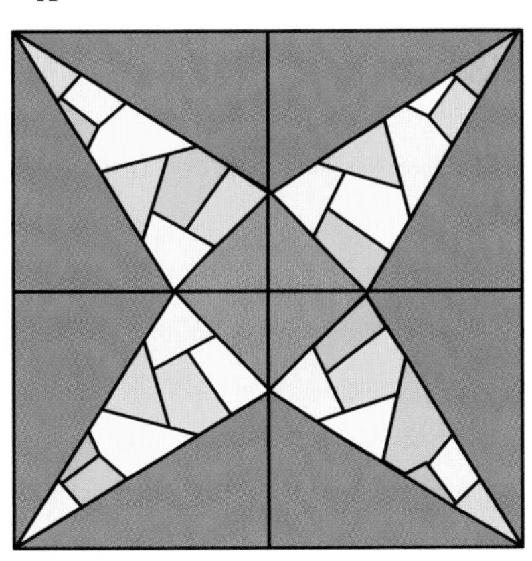

◆ TIPS ◆

Choose a light-coloured foundation material for the long triangles and make sure it's plain – a print might show through the surface fabrics. Use scraps of fabric for the crazy patchwork that are too small for anything else. Use lots of different prints if you prefer, but keeping to one colourway for the crazy patchwork will make it easier for you to choose a good, strong contrast colour for both the 'background' fabric and/or the central square. If you're hand-quilting, avoid quilting within the crazy patchwork sections as it will be very difficult to stitch through all the seams and the extra foundation material.

suggestions for alternative colourways

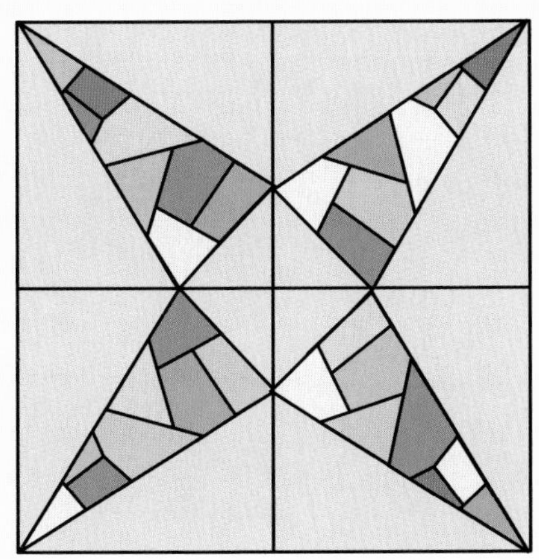

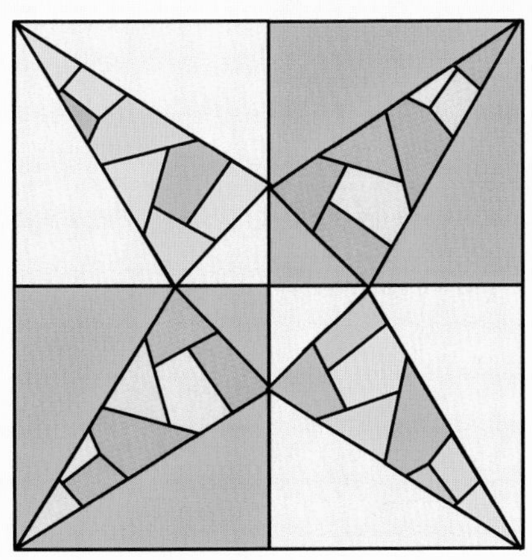

quilting idea

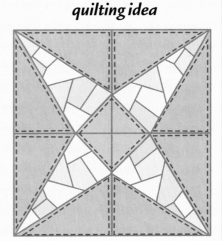

■ BLOCK 16 ■

Goose in the Pond

The traditional Flying Geese patchwork triangles are instantly recognisable within this beautifully symmetrical variation; in this version the 'geese' are shown flying inwards, towards the 'pond' in the centre.

■ **Grid**
this block is based on a 5 x 5 grid

■ **Techniques**
- squares and rectangles (see Piecing Your Patchwork on p12)

■ **What you will need**
- basic supplies *(all-purpose sewing thread; needles or sewing machine; fabric scissors and thread-snipping scissors; pins; pencil)*

■ **Fabrics:** minimum 3

■ **Templates:** 4
you'll find the *Goose in the Pond* templates A-D on p87

■ Constructing the block

1 Join the B triangles in pairs to create 12 small BB squares (**a**).

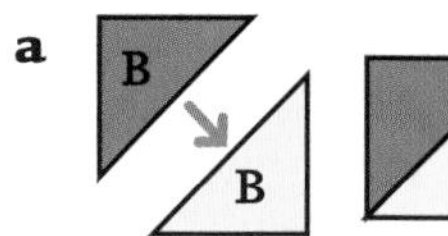

2 Join three D patches in alternating colours as shown to create a strip (**b**); make eight strips like this. Use the other D patches to create four strips as shown (**c**). Join three of these strips to create a square chequerboard design (**d**); make four squares in this way.

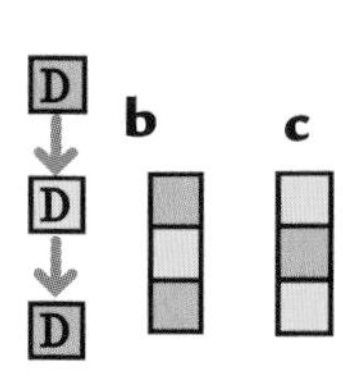

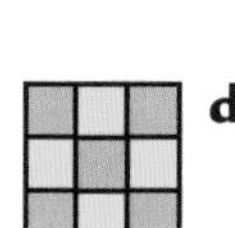

3 Join three C strips as shown to create a square (**e**); make four squares in this way.

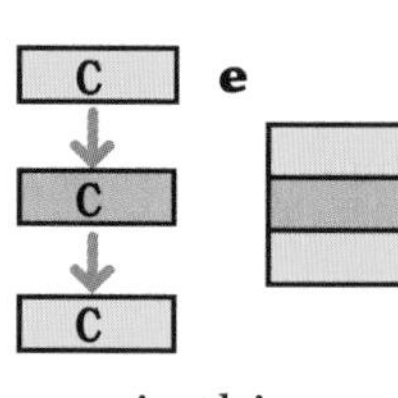

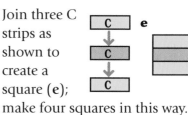

4 Make a strip from two BB squares, an A patch, and two more BB squares as shown in (**f**). Make two strips in this way.

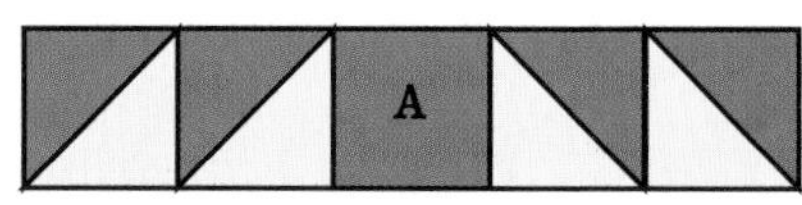

Make two shorter strips as shown (**g**).

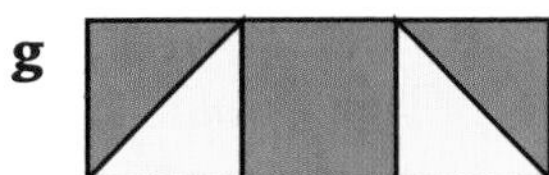

5 Create the three rows of the block centre as shown (**h**), then join these rows (**i**).

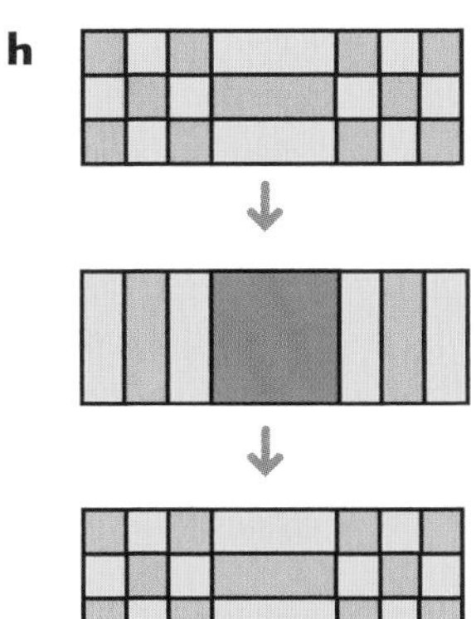

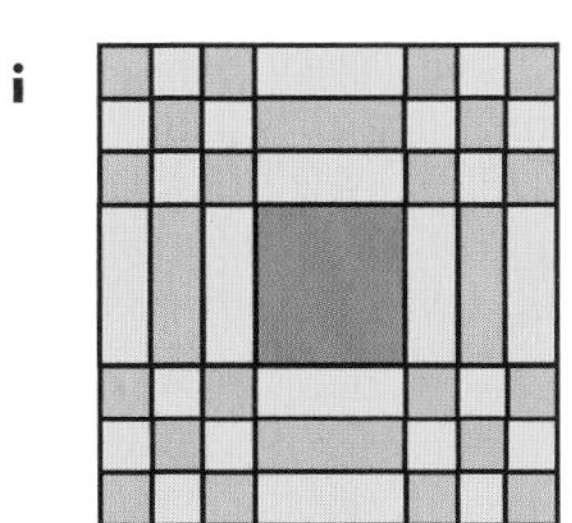

Join the two remaining short strips to the sides of the block centre (**j**), then add the longer strips to the top and bottom to complete the block (**k**).

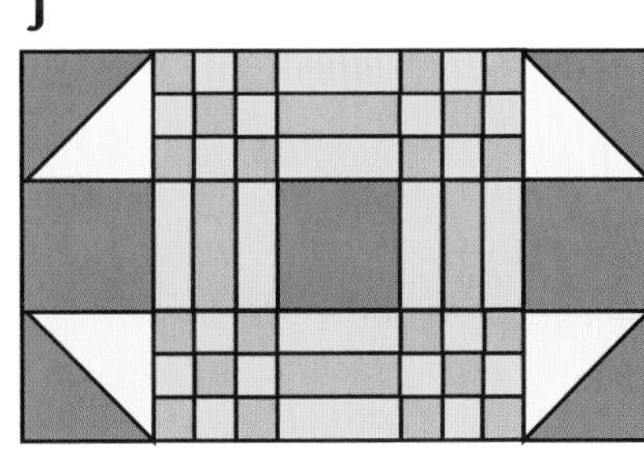

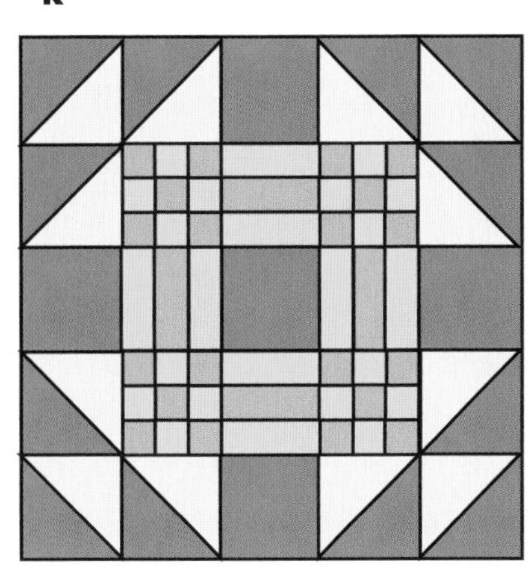

◆ **TIP** ◆

Use a boldly contrasting colour scheme to achieve a striking end result for this simple-to-sew patchwork block.

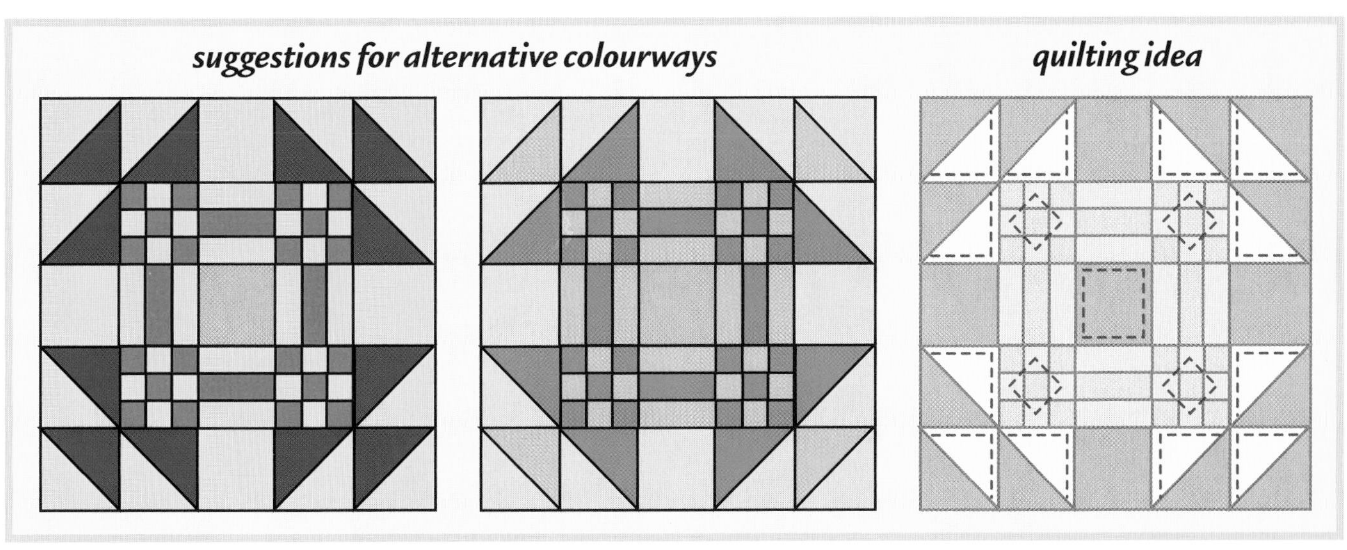

■ BLOCK 17 ■

Mariner's Compass

Mariner's Compass is one of the more complex blocks to be found in the patchwork world. You can alter and add to the traditional design in many ways; as you vary the numbers of 'spikes' and combine these with different centres, you'll find that the appearance of the compass changes dramatically.

■ **Grid**
this block is based on a 2 x 2 grid

■ **Techniques**
- piecing, triangles (see Piecing Your Patchwork on p12)
- hand-sewn appliqué (see p13)

■ **What you will need**
- basic supplies *(all-purpose sewing thread; needles or sewing machine; fabric scissors and thread-snipping scissors; pins; pencil)*
- freezer paper
- tacking thread and needle
- paper-cutting scissors

■ **Fabrics:** minimum 3

■ **Templates:** 6
you'll find the *Mariner's Compass* templates A-F on p88

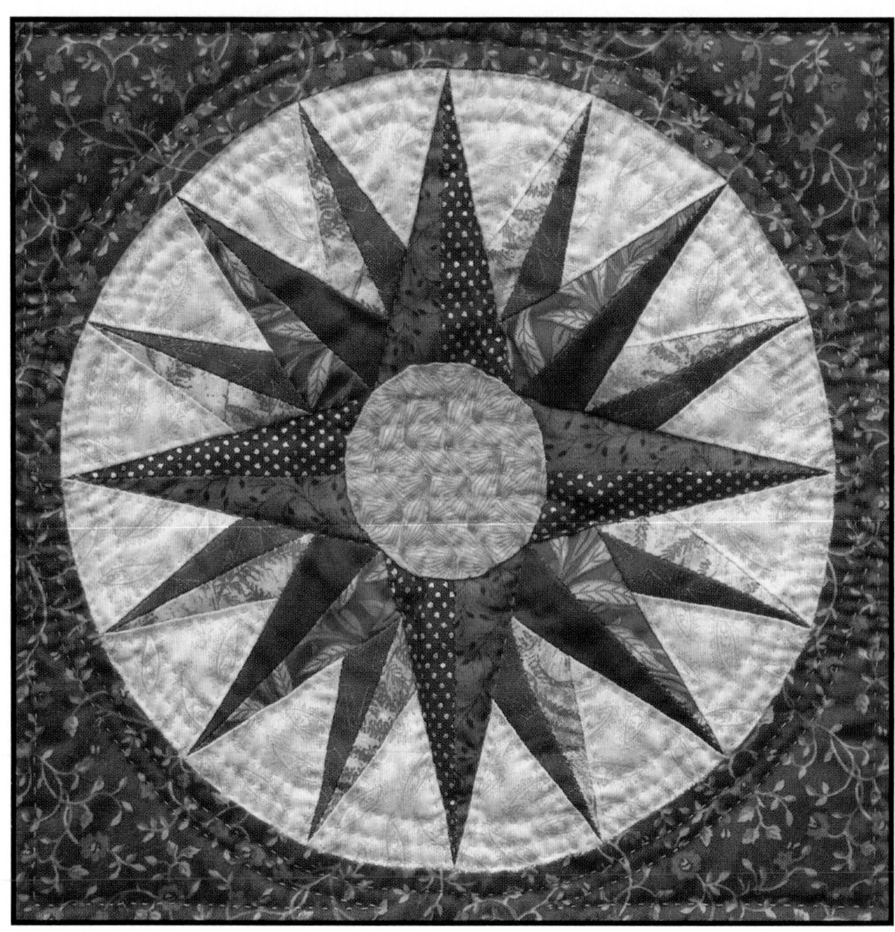

Making a split-colour spike

Join two fabrics by sewing-machine and press the seam open. Lay the fabric strip right side down, then position the relevant spike template so that it lies centrally over the opened seam; draw round the template (**a**), then cut the shape out plus a seam allowance all round (**b** and **c**).

a

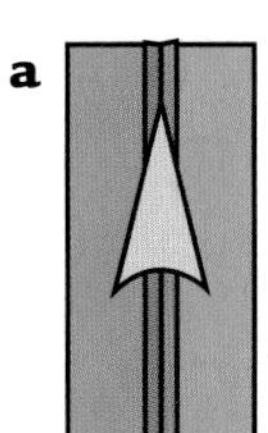

b

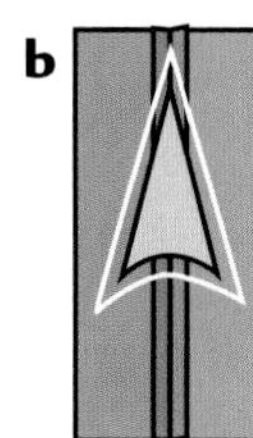

c

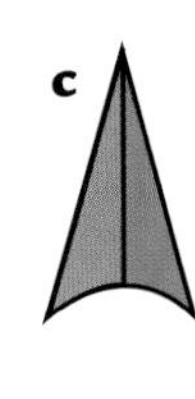

It's easier to make split-colour spikes this way than to make two separate templates and then have to join two long, thin patches of fabric.

Constructing the block

1 Add a wedge-shaped A piece to each side of a B shape (**a**); the B shape can either be a solid colour or pieced as above. Make eight units this way.

a

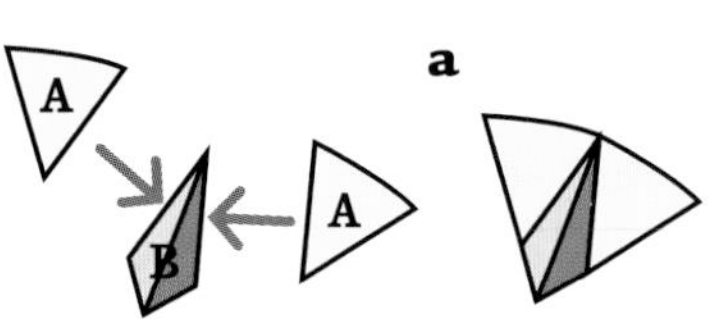

2 Add an ABA unit to each side of a C shape as shown (**b**). Add this shape to the side of a D patch (**c**), then join an F shape to the outside (**d**). Make four units this way.

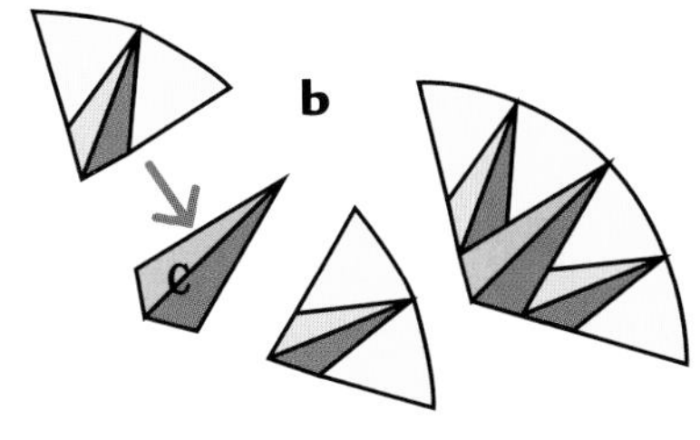

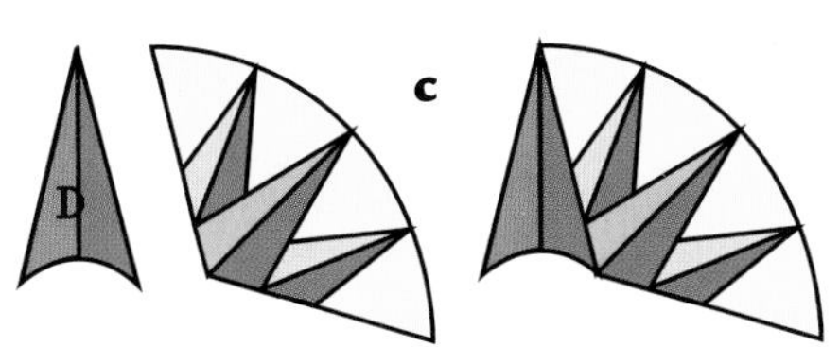

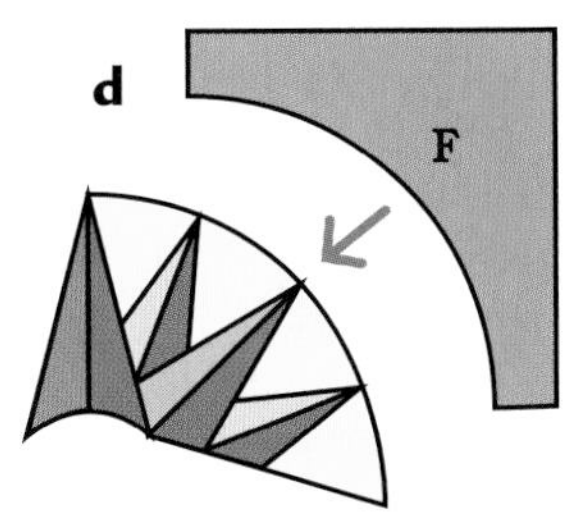

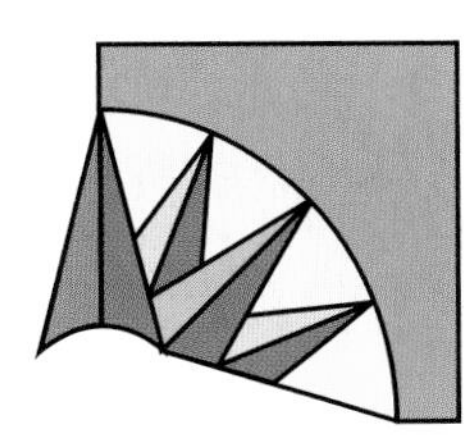

3 Join these units in a circle (**e** and **f**). You'll find that there's a slight angle in each seam where

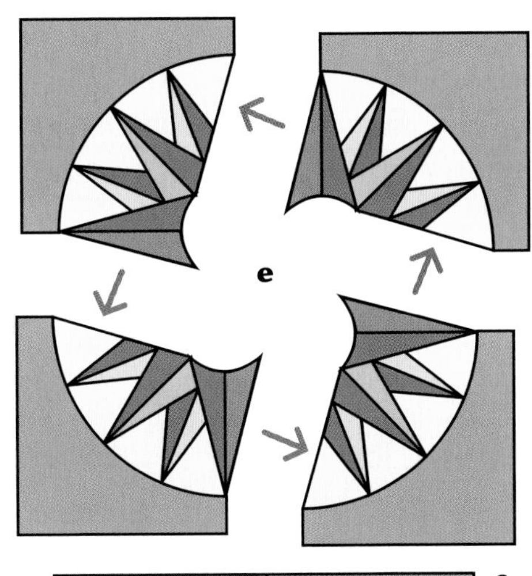

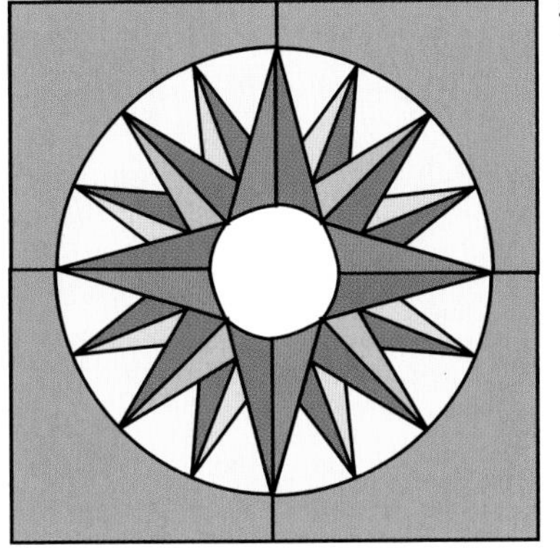

the compass design meets the background fabric; if you're sewing by hand this angle will be very easy to deal with. If you're stitching by machine, sew up to the angle, then lower the needle and pivot the fabrics slightly so that you can set off stitching in a straight line again.

4 Using appliqué over freezer paper (see p14), pin/tack and then use appliqué stitch to add the circle in the centre of the patch (**g**). Diagram (**h**) shows the effect of constructing the same block with solid spikes rather than pieced ones.

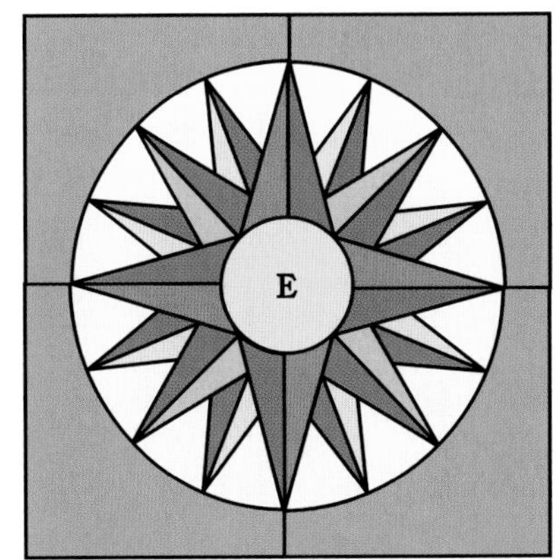

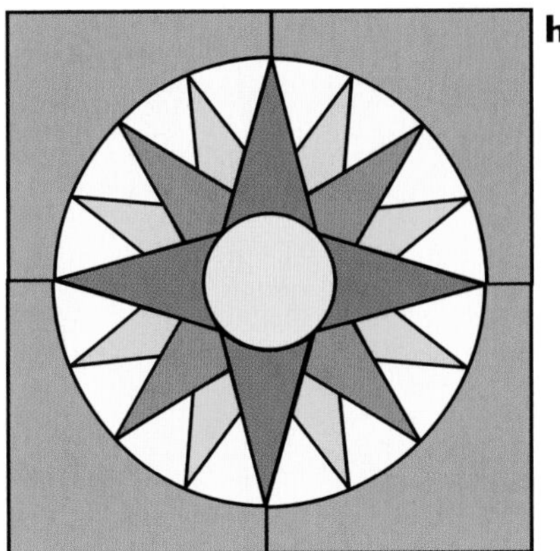

◆ **TIP** ◆

It's just as easy to stitch Mariner's Compass by hand or by machine. If you're hand-sewing, cut your 'spike' template in half to make two separate ones for the 'split colour' effect. Alternatively use spikes of solid colour.

suggestions for alternative colourways

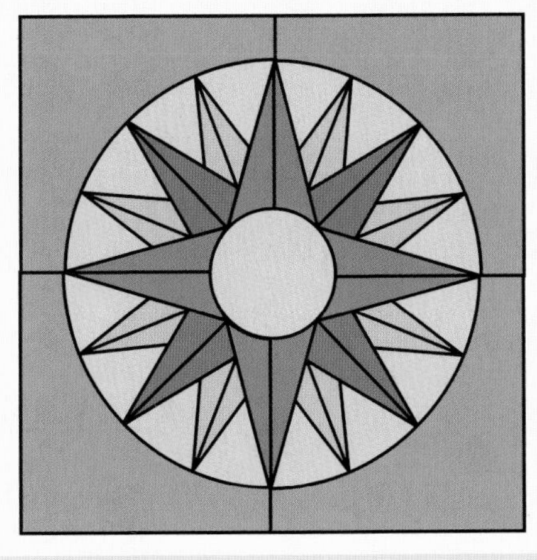

quilting idea

▪ BLOCK 18 ▪

Quartered Card Trick

The well-known Card Trick block offers a wonderful optical illusion – it looks like four fanned-out playing cards, with each one positioned in front of the other, with the added illusion of looking as though they're all sitting on a background fabric. It's an interesting challenge to take four smaller versions of the design and combine them in the same block. (This idea can also be used to show you how a block will look when it's repeated across an entire quilt top.)

- **Grid**
  this block is based on a 6 x 6 grid

- **Techniques**
  - triangles and squares (see Piecing Your Patchwork on p12)

- **What you will need**
  - basic supplies *(all-purpose sewing thread; needles or sewing machine; fabric scissors and thread-snipping scissors; pins; pencil)*

- **Fabrics:** minimum 5

- **Templates:** 5
  you'll find the *Quartered Card Trick* templates A-E on p89

▪ Constructing the block

1 All the time that you're constructing the block, pay very careful attention to which colour goes where. Join two D triangles as shown (**a**); create four small square patches this way (**b**), each time using one 'background' shape and one of each of the four 'playing card' fabrics.

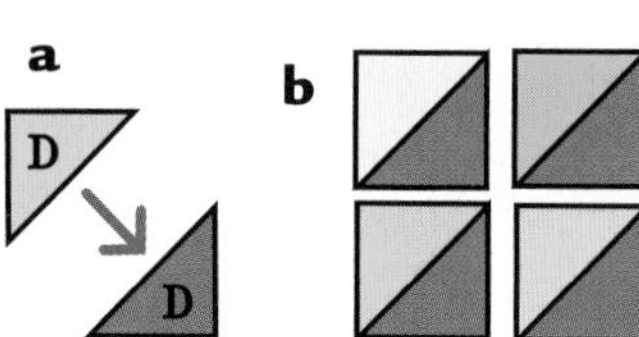

2 Join two small E triangles (**c**), then add a larger D triangle to the shape (**d**); make eight small square patches this way, making two patches in each of the colour arrangements shown (**e**).

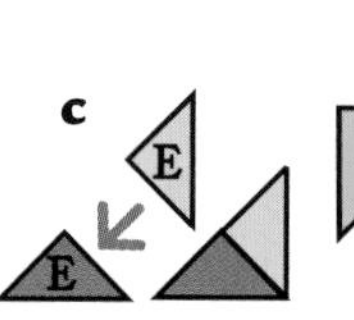

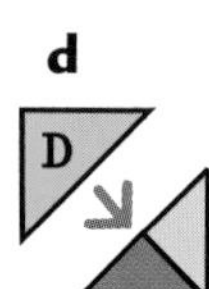

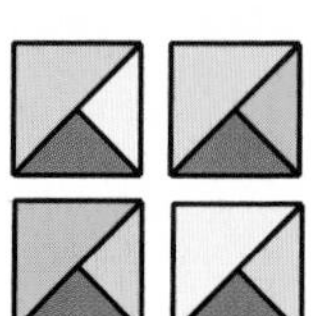

3 Join sets of four small E triangles first into pairs (**f**) and then into fours (**g**), arranging the colours as shown each time. Make four units this way.

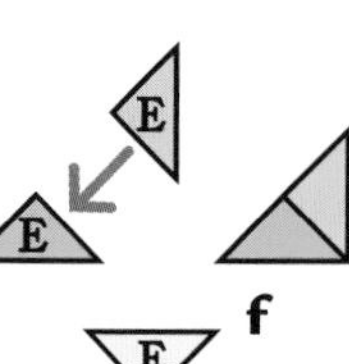

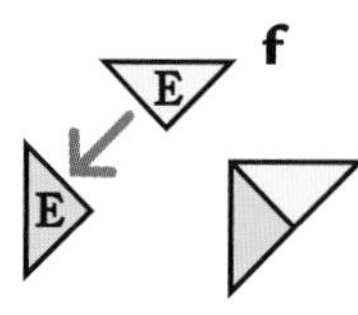

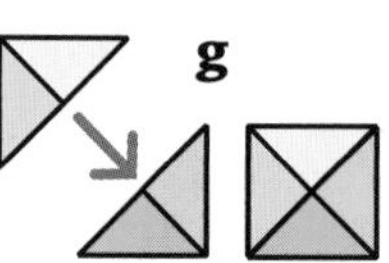

4 Add medium D triangles to opposite sides of the central A square, then add two more to the remaining sides, following the colour arrangement carefully (**h**).

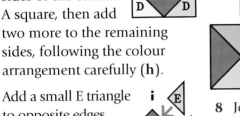

5 Add a small E triangle to opposite edges of a small B square as shown (**i**), then add a D triangle to this shape (**j**). Make two units in the arrangement shown in (**k**), and two as shown in (**l**).

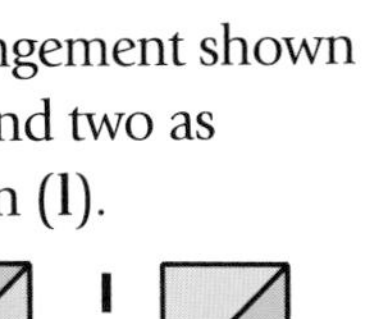

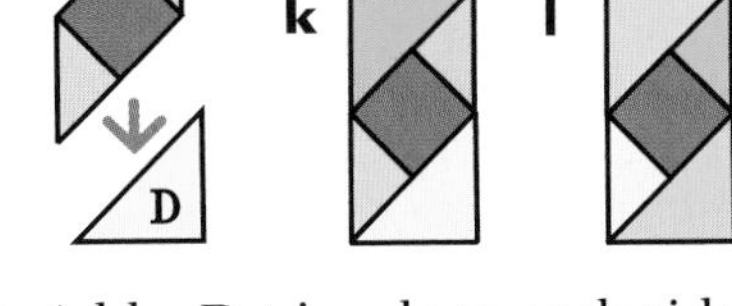

6 Add a D triangle to each side of a large C triangle; make four units this way, arranging the colours as shown (**m**).

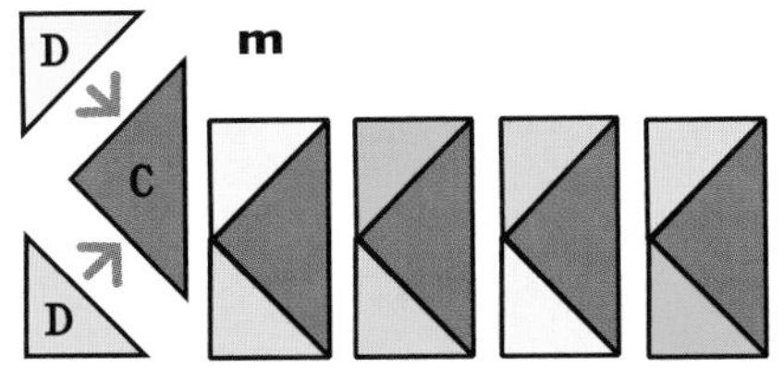

7 Join the units from step 5 to the units from step 6, watching the colours carefully so that you end up with the four arrangements shown (**n**).

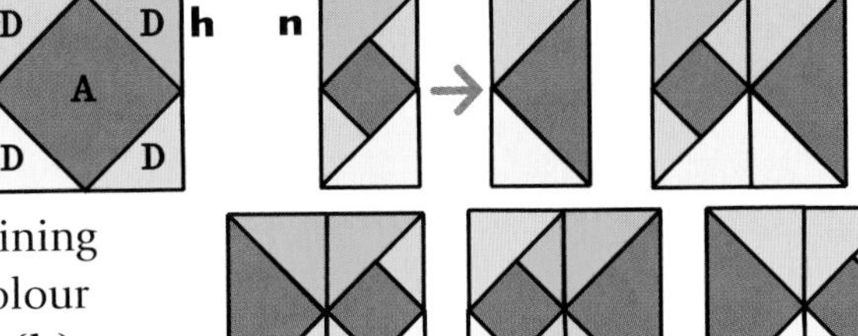

8 Join the units from steps 1, 2 and 3 first into pairs and then into fours (**o**), so that you end up with the four arrangements shown . You now have nine square patches in total.

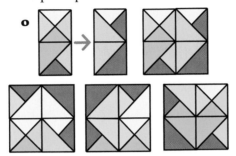

9 Join these patches first into rows as shown (**p**),

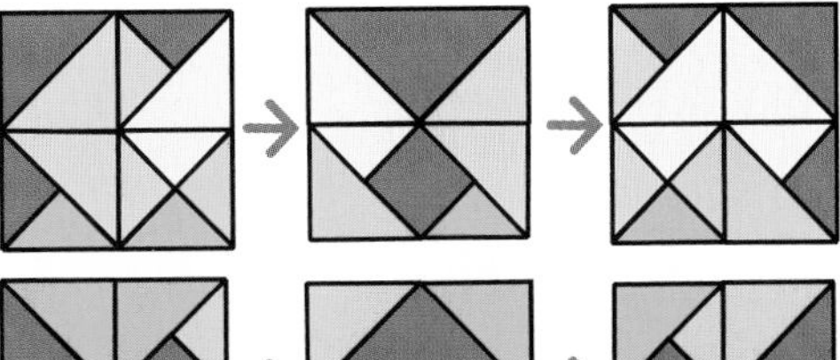

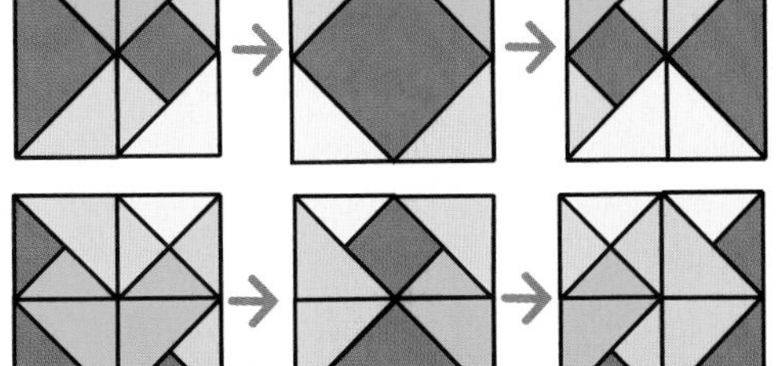

and then join the rows (**q**) to complete the block (**r**).

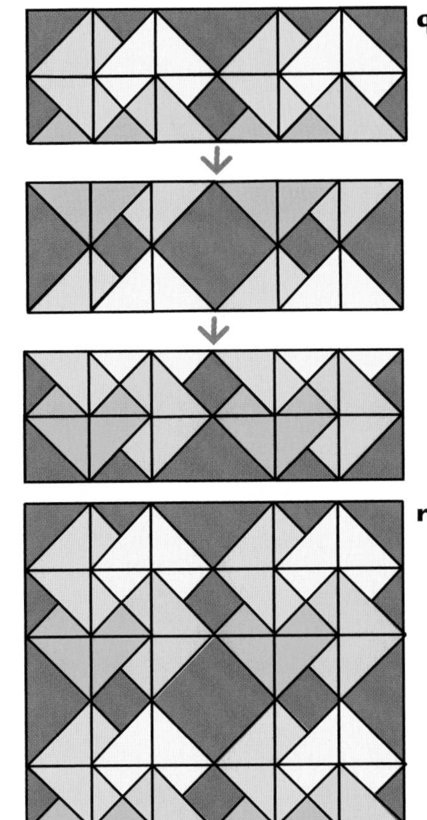

◆ TIPS ◆

Restricting yourself to a simpler colour scheme (one 'background' fabric and a different fabric for each 'playing card') will help simplify what could otherwise become an over-busy block. The four 'playing card' fabrics can all be from the same basic colour; just choose different prints and tonal values.

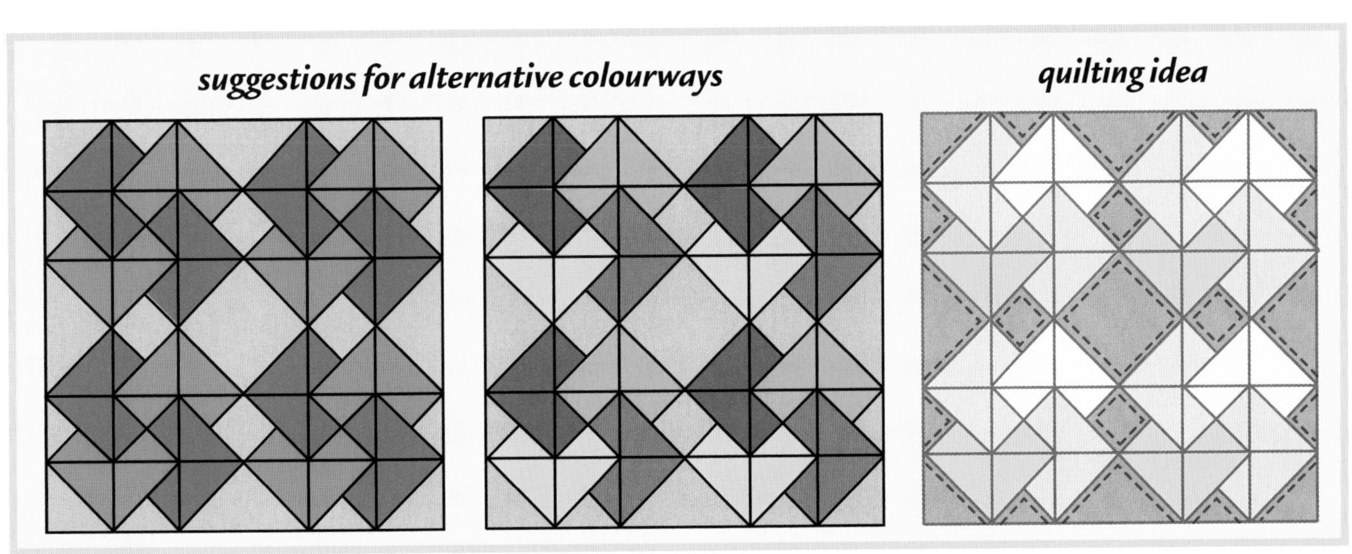

■ BLOCK 19 ■

Basket of Scraps

It's easy to see the four baskets that make up the *Basket of Scraps* block. Indeed, if you like the idea, the collections of 'scraps' in each basket can be literally that; cut them from assorted fabrics from your scrap-bag to create a posy of patterns and colours in each corner of the block.

■ **Grid**
this block is based on a 5 x 5 grid

■ **Techniques**
- triangles, rectangles, squares and rhomboids (see Piecing Your Patchwork on p12)
- asymmetric shapes (see p12)
- mirror-image shapes (see p12)

■ **What you will need**
- basic supplies *(all-purpose sewing thread; needles or sewing machine; fabric scissors and thread-snipping scissors; pins; pencil)*

■ **Fabrics:** minimum 3

■ **Templates:** 6
you'll find the *Basket of Scraps* templates A-F on p89

■ Constructing the block

1 Join one B triangle to the top of one E rhomboid as shown (**a**); make four units using the E shape of one colour (**b**), and four using the E shape cut from another (**c**).

2 Join one B triangle to the top of one F rhomboid in the same way, making four units using the F shape of one colour (**d**), and four using the F shape cut from another (**e**).

3 Join the EB and FB units in pairs to create four units as shown in **f**, and four as shown in **g**.

4 Add a D triangle to the right-hand side of one BEF unit as shown (**h**); make four units in this way. (Be careful that you're joining the triangles to the sides of the correct units!) Now make four units by adding D triangles to

the left-hand sides of the remaining BEF shapes (**i**).

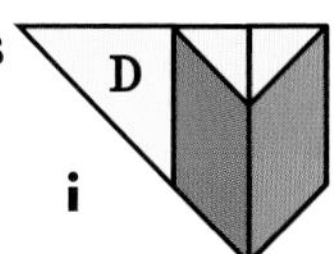

5 Join the DBEF shapes as shown to create four new units (**j**), then add a D triangle to the bottom of each unit (**k**).

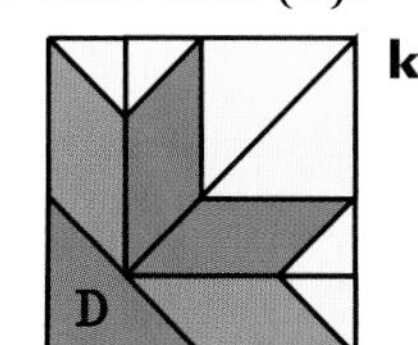

6 Add a small B triangle to each side of the A square (**l**).

7 Add one large unit to each side of a C rectangle as shown (**m**);

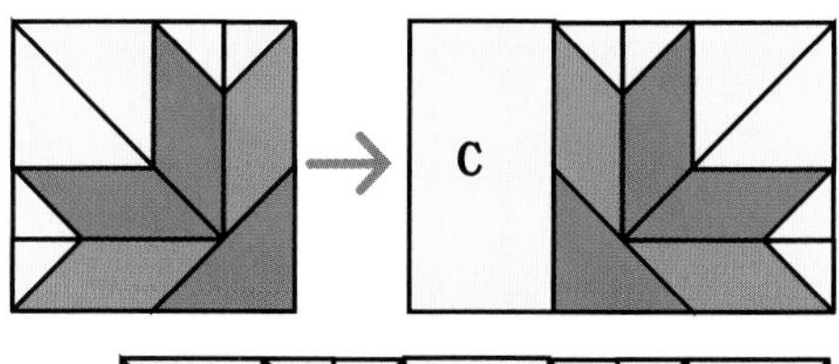

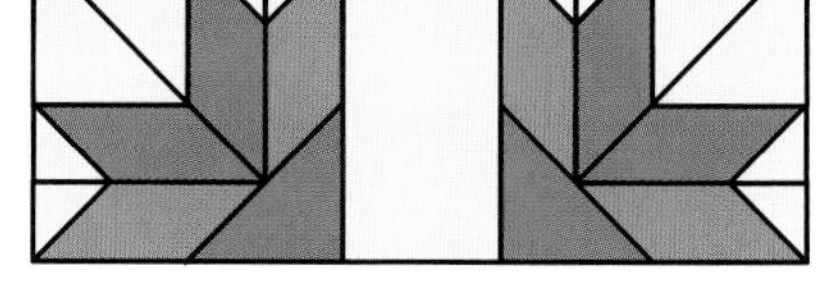

make two units this way. Add one C rectangle to each side of the AB square (**n**) to create the central row of the block.

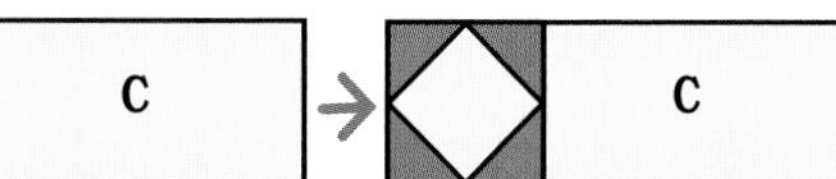

Join the three rows (**o**) to complete the block (**p**).

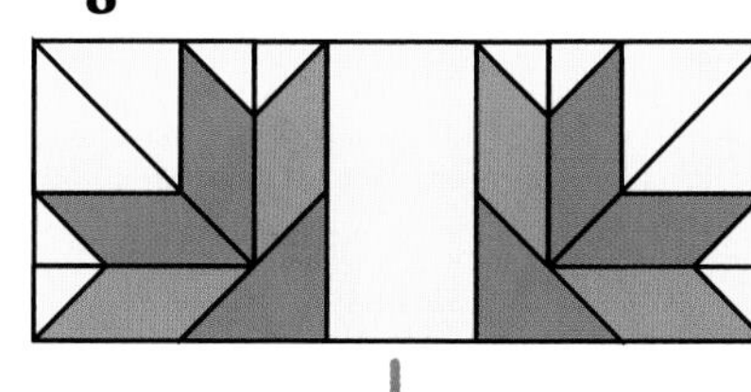

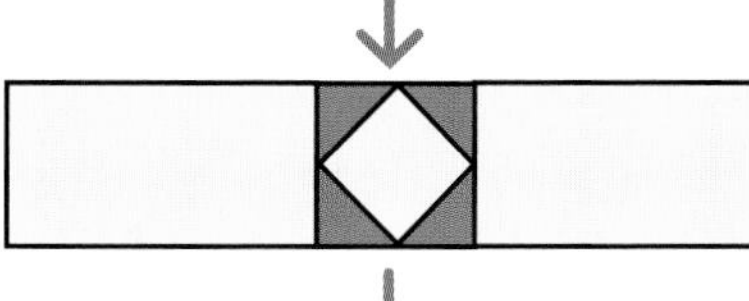

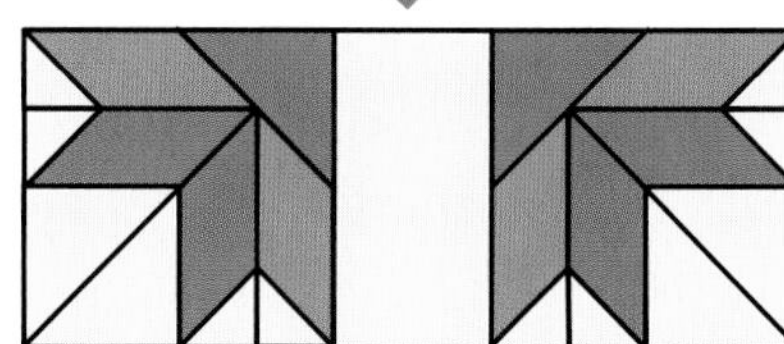

◆ **TIPS** ◆

When dealing with rhomboids, especially the ones for this block, do make sure that you use your SG (straight grain) arrows for stabilising the shapes where possible. Also, take care that you use the correct rhomboid template for cutting the correct fabric – it's easy to make a mistake here.

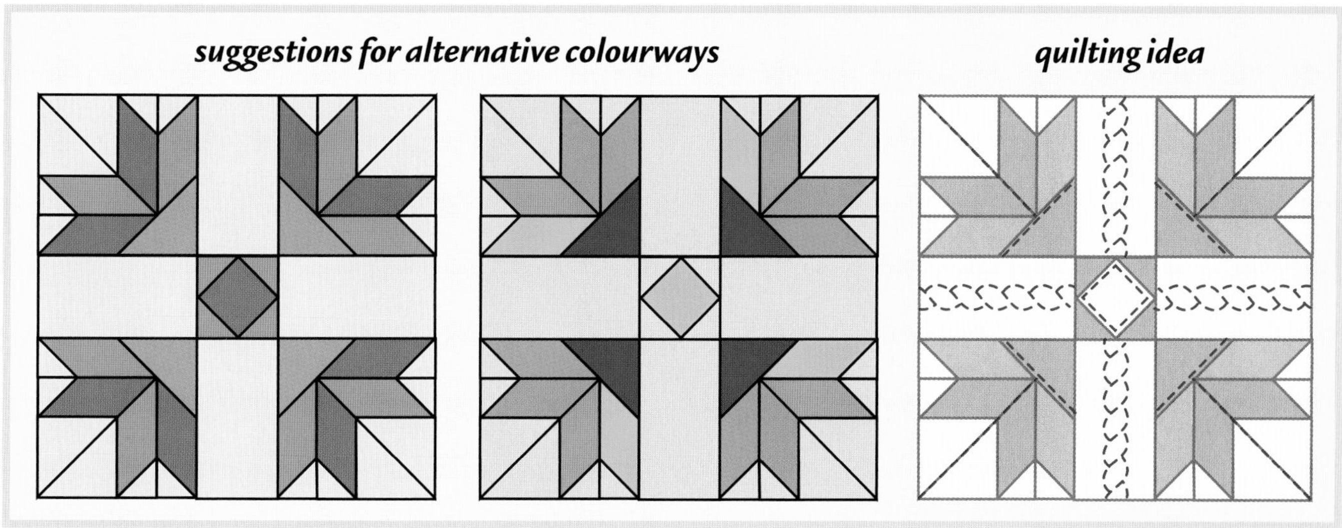

BLOCK 20

Californian Sunset

If you browse through books of patchwork blocks, you'll find countless star patterns in different arrangements; this interesting one is constructed within a traditional 9-patch (3 x 3) grid. The broken circles interconnecting with the arms of the stars highlight the shimmering heat radiating from the sun setting in the Californian sky.

Grid

this block is based on a 3 x 3 grid (9-patch)

Techniques

- triangles and squares (see Piecing Your Patchwork on p12)
- asymmetric shapes (see p12)
- mirror-image shapes (see p12)

What you will need

- basic supplies *(all-purpose sewing thread; needles or sewing machine; fabric scissors and thread-snipping scissors; pins; pencil)*

Fabrics: minimum 4

Templates: 10
you'll find the *Californian Sunset* templates A-J on p90

Constructing the block

1 Join one G triangle and one I triangle as shown (**a**); make four units this way. Join one H triangle and one J triangle as shown (**b**); make four units this way.

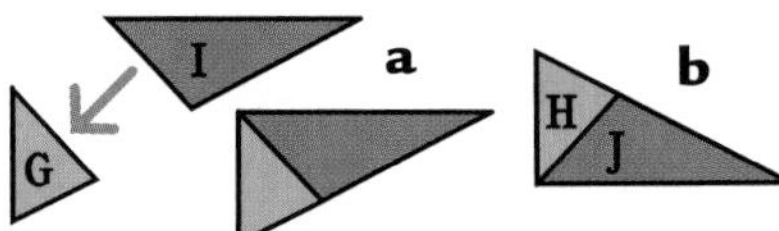

2 Join one GI unit to the side of one large F triangle, and one HJ unit to the other side as shown (**c** and **d**); make four units this way.

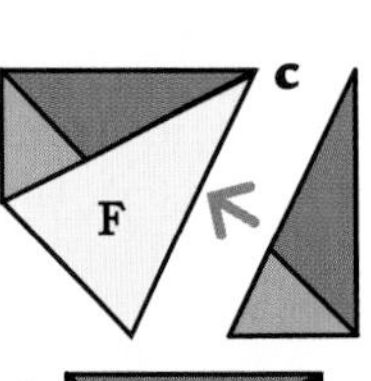

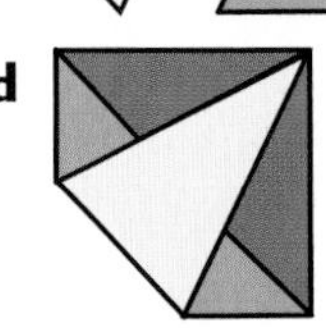

3 Add a B triangle to the angled edge of one FGHIJ unit as shown (**e**); make four units in this way. These will become the corner units of the block.

4 Join two E triangles in contrasting colours as shown, then add a third E triangle to create a strip (**f**). Add another E triangle to the bottom edge as shown to create a large pyramid (**g**),

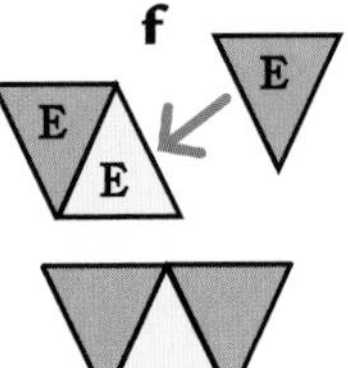

then join a D triangle to one side and a C triangle to the other, as shown (**h** and **i**). Create four units this way; these will become the side units of the block.

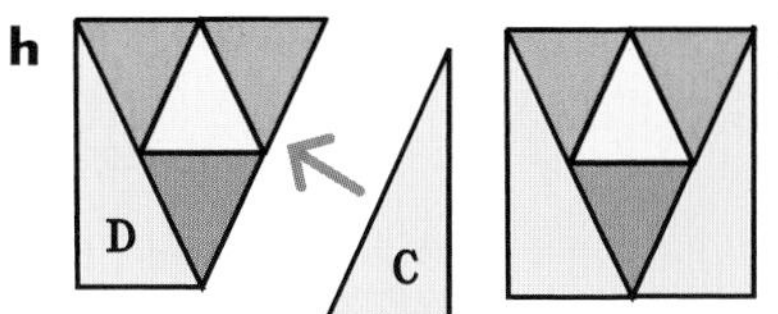

5 Add a B triangle to each edge of the A shape to create the central square of the block (**j**).

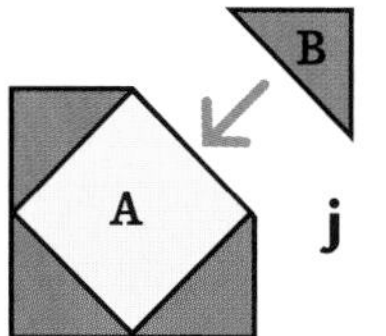

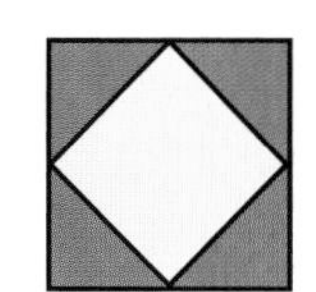

6 Join two corner units to a side unit as shown (**k**); create two strips in this way.

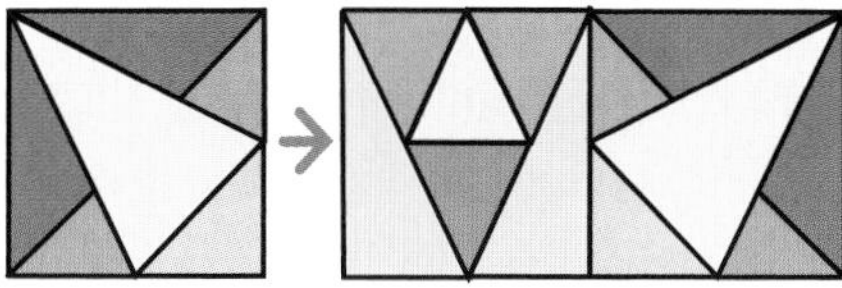

Join the remaining two side units to the central square (**l**).

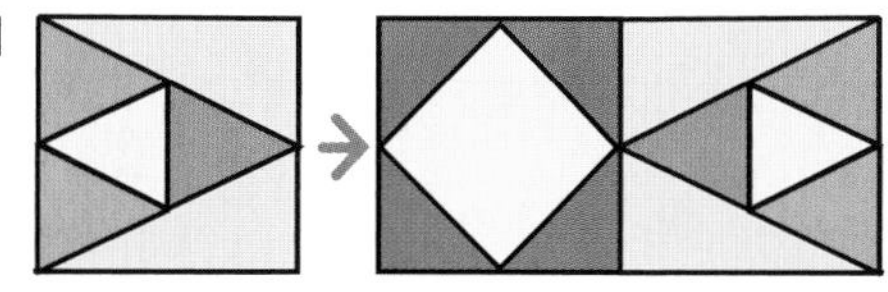

7 Join the rows as shown (**m**) to create the finished block (**n**).

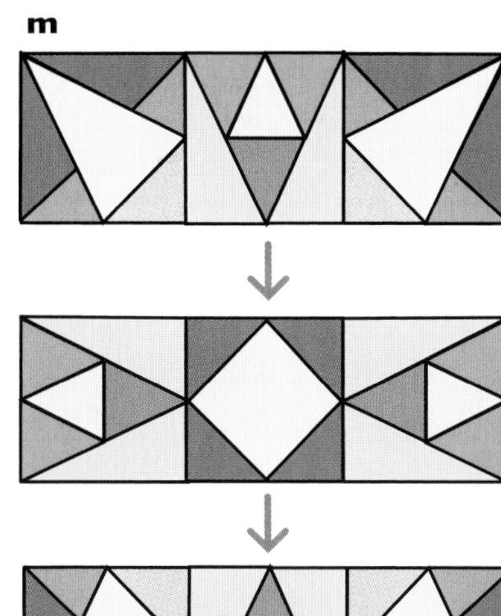

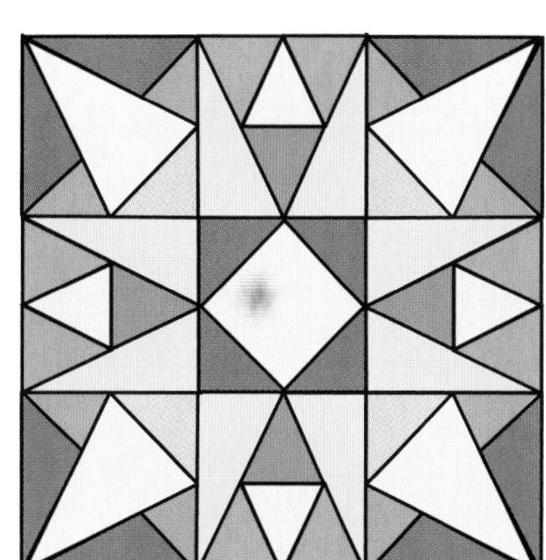

◆ TIPS ◆

Use two of your brightest coloured fabrics to highlight the spikes emanating from the two stars. Be careful when you're dealing with asymmetric shapes that look similar (ie, the small triangles sitting either side of the large spike in the outer corner squares); it's easy to make a mistake here.

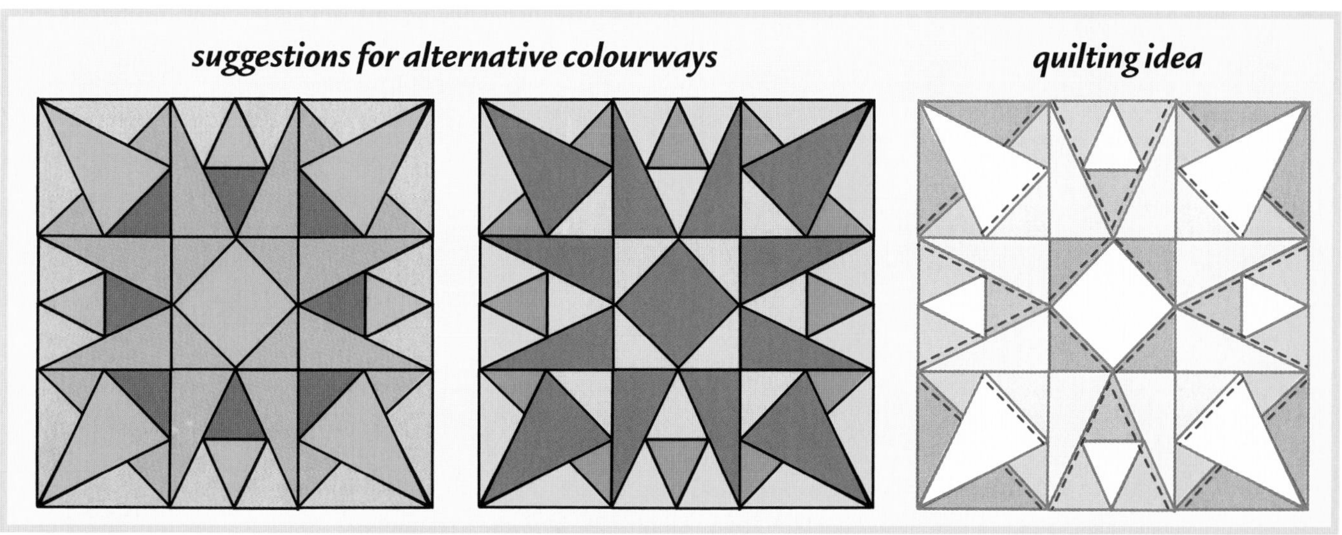

▪ BLOCK 21 ▪

Interlocking Squares

Here's a patchwork block that produces a wonderful optical illusion: the squares seem to weave in and out of each other. Don't be put off by the complex appearance of the block; it can actually be pieced very quickly and easily; you can vary the final effect depending on the fabrics that you choose. The large central octagon provides an ideal 'canvas' for an interesting quilting design or motif.

▪ Grid

this block is based on a 2 x 2 grid

▪ Techniques

- triangles, octagon, trapezium (see Piecing Your Patchwork on p12)
- rhomboids/asymmetric shapes (see p12)

▪ What you will need

- basic supplies *(all-purpose sewing thread; needles or sewing machine; fabric scissors and thread-snipping scissors; pins; pencil)*

▪ Fabrics: minimum 3

▪ Templates: 7

you'll find the *Interlocking Squares* templates A-G on p91

▪ Constructing the block

1 Join one B triangle to each corner of the A octagon to create the centre of the block (**a**).

2 Join a D rhomboid to the right-hand side of a C shape as shown (**b** and **c**), then add an E triangle to the top of the

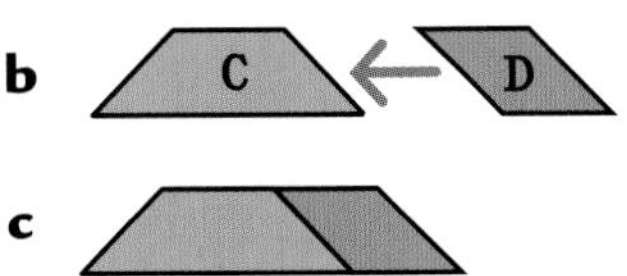

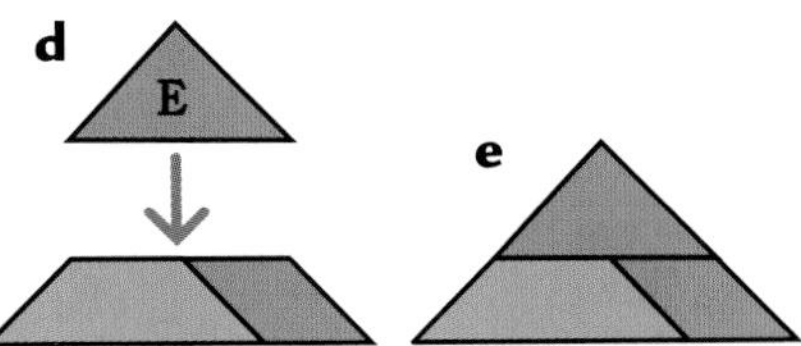

shape (**d** and **e**). Make four units this way.

3 Join one F triangle to the edge of one G shape as shown (**f** and **g**); make eight units in

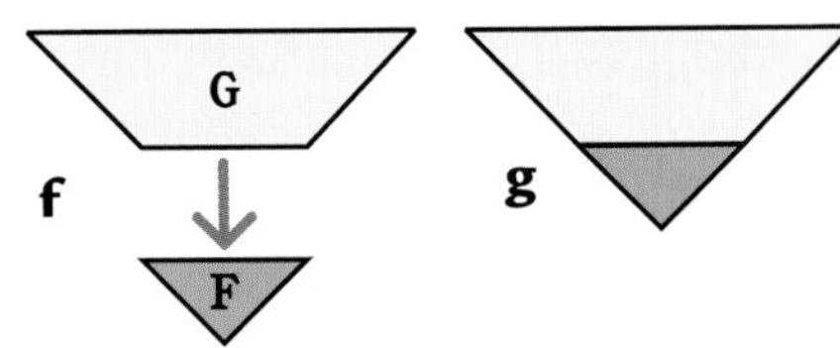

this way. Join the FG units in pairs as shown (**h**) to create four large triangles (**i**).

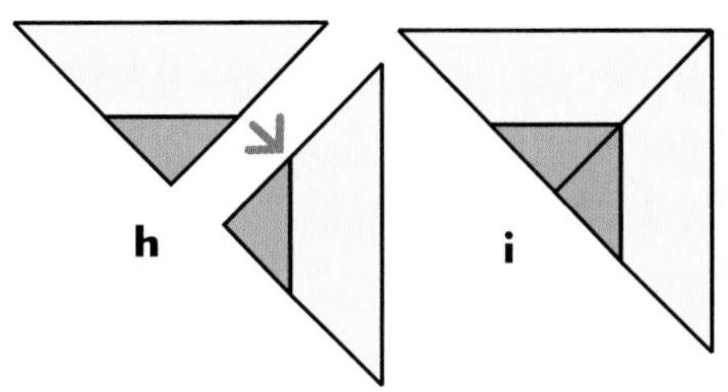

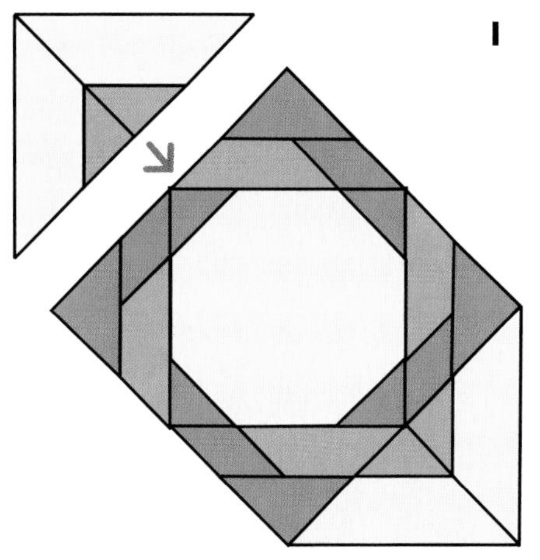

◆ TIP ◆

Three strongly contrasting fabrics are all you require for this block. Use slightly patterned fabrics that help to hide the seams; this will strengthen the optical illusion even further.

4 Join a DCE unit to each edge of the central square as shown (**j** and **k**), then add a GF unit to each edge of this new square (**l** and **m**) to complete the block (**n**).

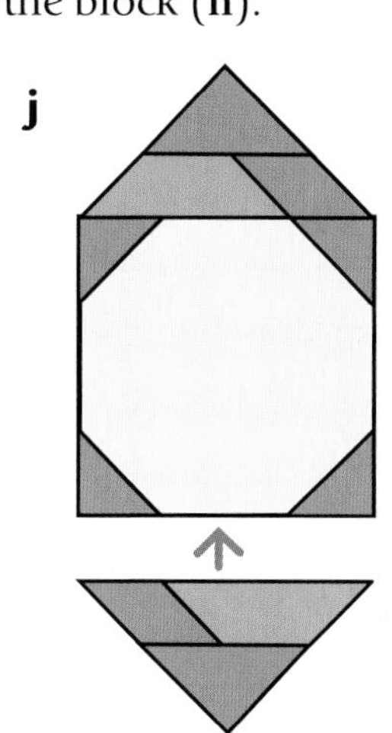

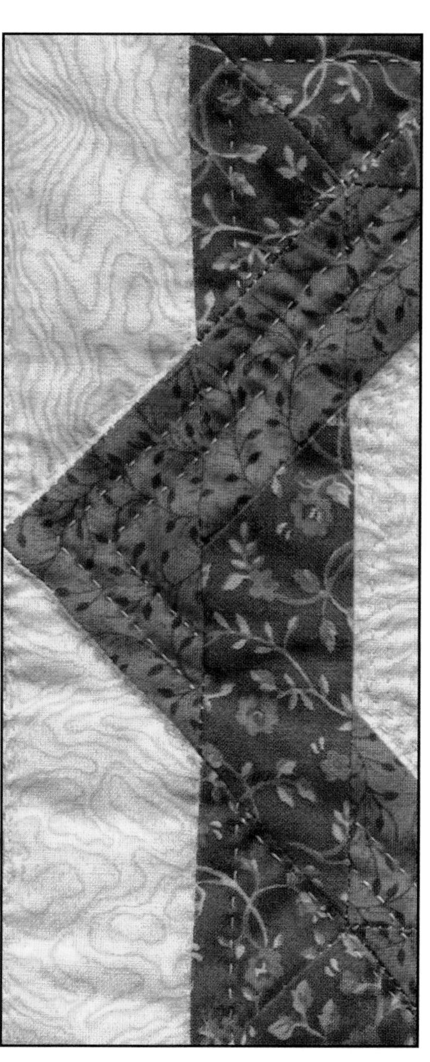

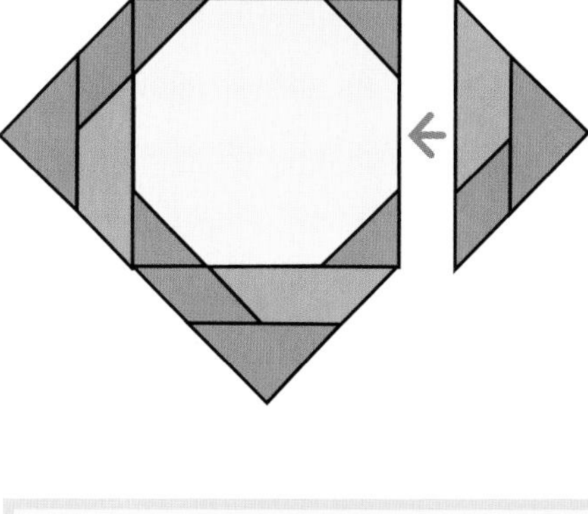

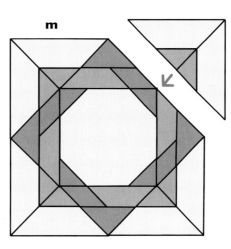

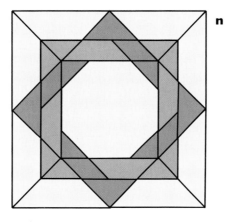

suggestions for alternative colourways

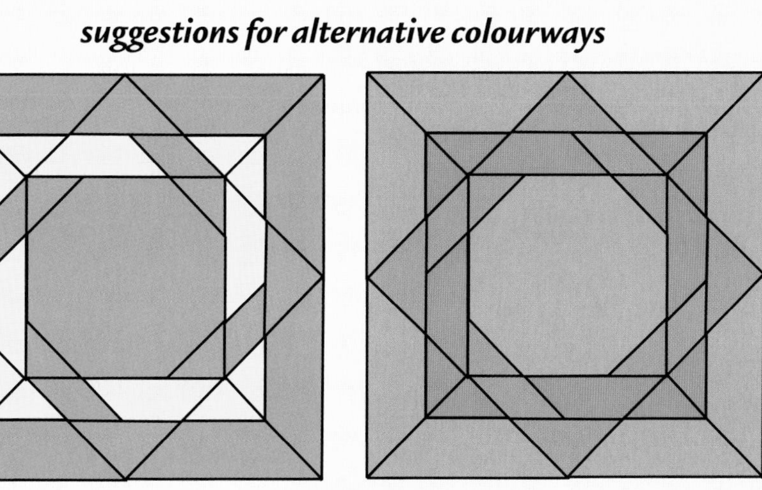

quilting idea

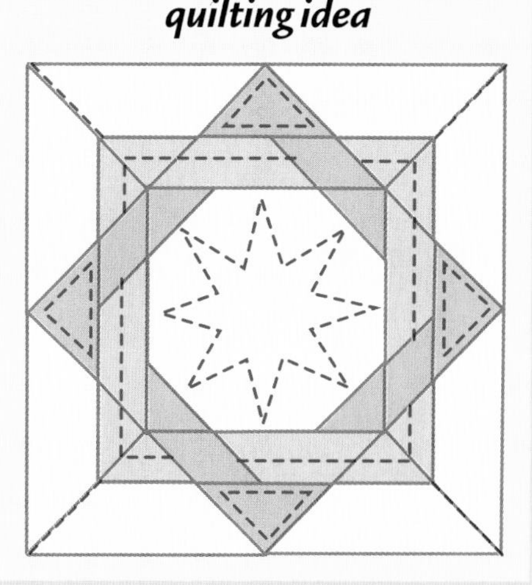

▪ BLOCK 22 ▪

Triple Star

This more complex star pattern will give you scope to use quite a few fabrics within the one block. The pattern really makes you look and look again – the grid is a real challenge to work out, but it's actually based on a traditional 9-patch layout.

■ **Grid**

this block is based on a 3 x 3 grid (9-patch)

■ **Techniques**

- triangles, squares (see Piecing Your Patchwork on p12)
- asymmetric shapes (see p12)
- mirror-image shapes (see p12)

■ **What you will need**

- basic supplies *(all-purpose sewing thread; needles or sewing machine; fabric scissors and thread-snipping scissors; pins; pencil)*

■ **Fabrics:** minimum 4/5

■ **Templates:** 11

you'll find the *Triple Star* templates A-K on p92

■ Constructing the block

1 Join a small B triangle onto each side of a C triangle (**a**); create four units this way. Join a small D square onto each end of a BCB unit (**b**); make two strips this way.

2 Join the remaining two BCB units to the sides of the large A square (**c**); make sure that you position the correct edges of the pieced units against the square. Join a pieced strip to the top and bottom of this unit as shown (**d** and **e**).

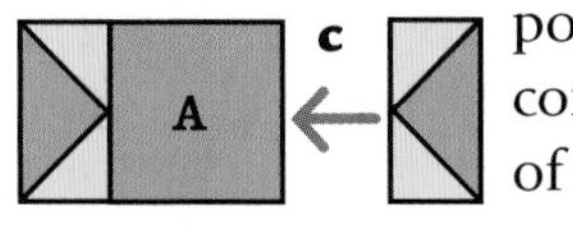

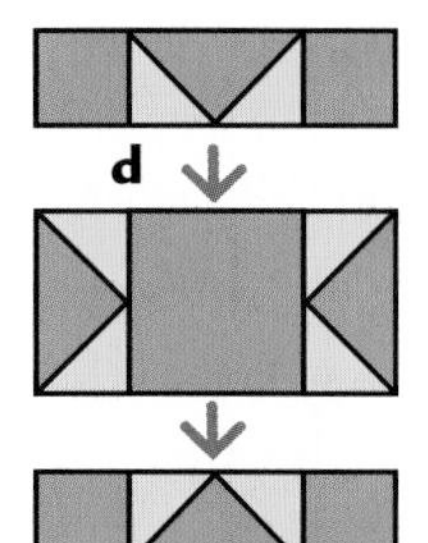

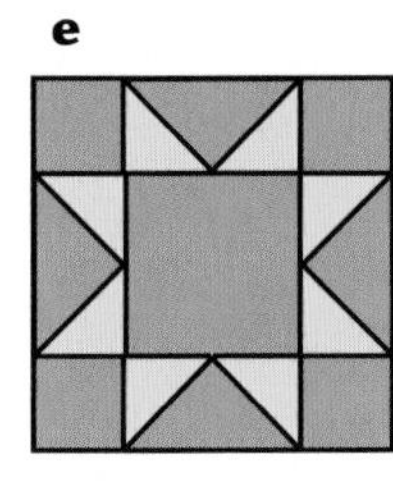

3 Add a small I triangle to the slanted end of an H shape as shown (**f**); create four units this

way (**g**), then make four more using the G shapes and I triangles (**h**).

4 Join one F shape to a GI unit (**i**); make four of these units (**j**), then make four mirror-image units by adding the E shapes to the HI units (**k**).

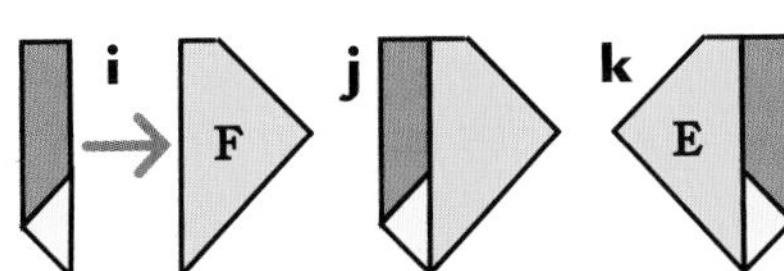

5 Add a large K square to the lower edge of the FGI shape as shown (**l**); add a C triangle to the upper edge of the EHI shape as shown (**m**), then join these two shapes (**n**). Make four complete units this way.

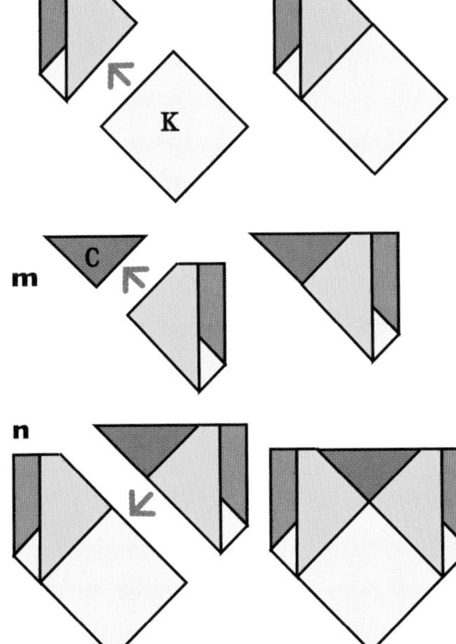

6 Add two of these units to opposite edges of the central square (**o**).

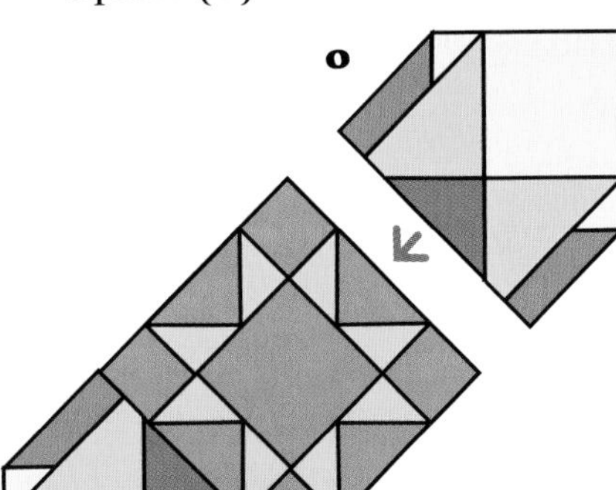

Join a J triangle to each side of the remaining pieced units (**p**) to create two large triangles (**q**), then add these triangles to the other two sides of the central square (**r**) to complete the block (**s**).

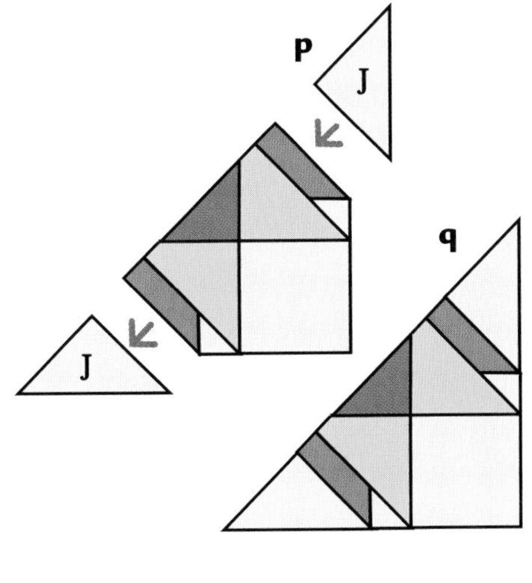

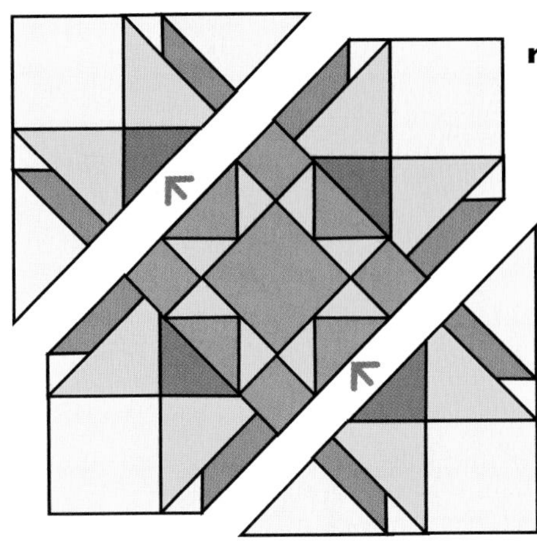

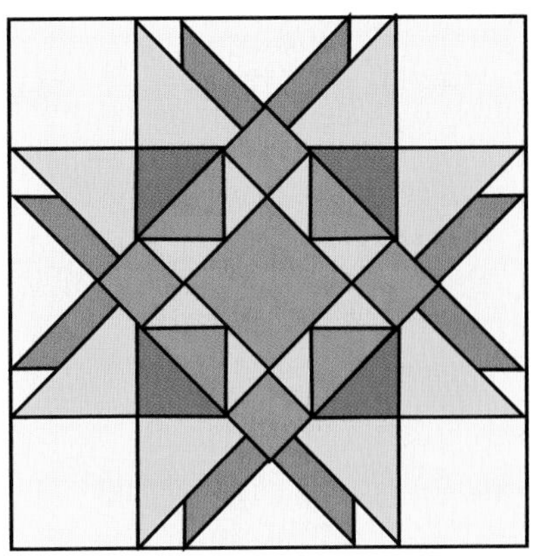

◆ **TIP** ◆

To achieve as much visual interest and contrast as possible, mix interesting prints with plains, and vary the tonal values used throughout the block.

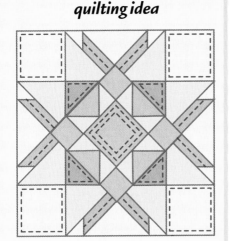

suggestions for alternative colourways

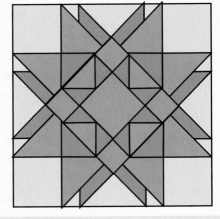

quilting idea

▪ BLOCK 23 ▪

Friendship Knot

This block provides an opportunity to use up your scraps of fabric for the little tufts at each knot; if you prefer a more formal arrangement of colours, you can achieve a three-dimensional look with the design. A large central square provides the opportunity for an interesting quilting design or motif.

■ **Grid**

this block is based on a 4 x 4 grid

■ **Techniques**

- triangles, squares (see Piecing Your Patchwork on p12)
- asymmetric shapes (see p12)
- mirror-image shapes (see p12)

■ **What you will need**

- basic supplies *(all-purpose sewing thread; needles or sewing machine; fabric scissors and thread-snipping scissors; pins; pencil)*

■ **Fabrics:** minimum 3

■ **Templates:** 6

you'll find the *Friendship Knot* templates A-F on p93

■ Constructing the block

1 Join a small C triangle to the edge of a D rhomboid as shown (**a**); make sure that you join the correct sides of each shape. Make four units as shown (**b**), and four units using the contrasting rhomboids (**c**).

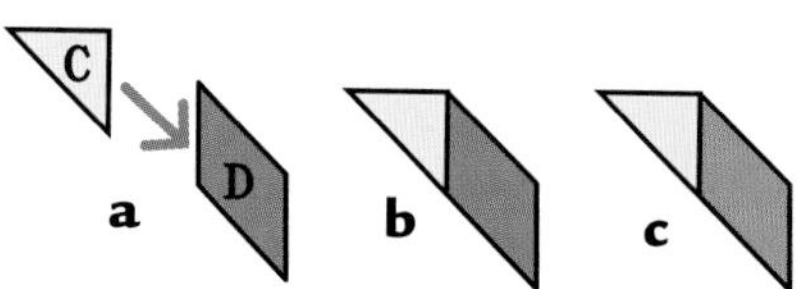

2 In the same way, make four units of E shapes plus C triangles (**d**), and four in the contrasting colour (**e**).

3 Join the CD and CE units in pairs as shown (**f**); make four pairs in one colourway (**g**), and four with the colours reversed (**h**).

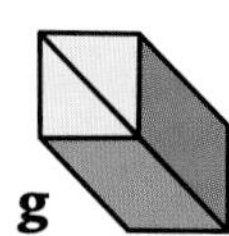

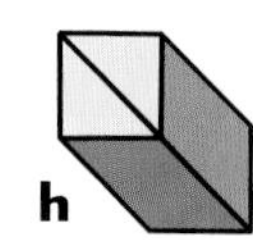

4 Add two C triangles to the outside edges of each of these shapes (**i**) to create four units in one colourway (**j**), and four in the other (**k**). These are the side units of the block.

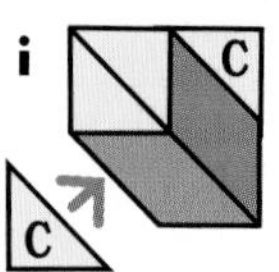

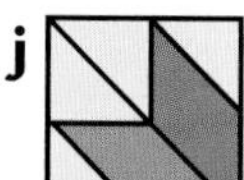

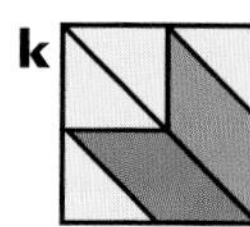

5 Add a C triangle to the edge of a B rhomboid, then add this unit to one edge of the large central A square (**l**). Add shapes to the opposite corner of the central square in the same way (**m**), and then to the

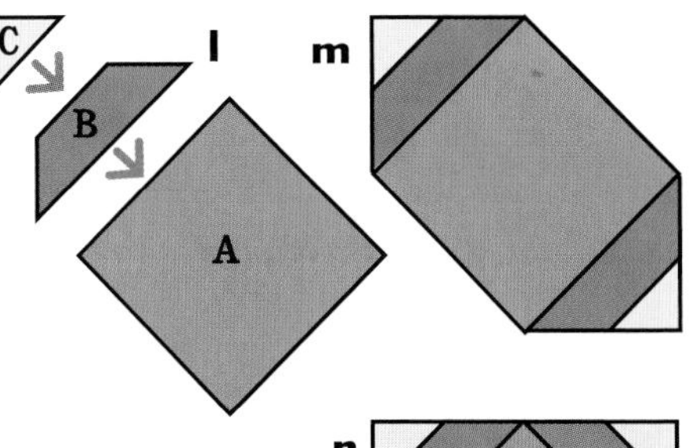

n

remaining edges to create the central unit of the block (**n**).

6 Join two square F patches and two of the pieced side units as shown (**o**); ensure that you're using the correct side units, in the correct orientation. Make two strips in the same way (**p**); these are the top and bottom rows of the block.

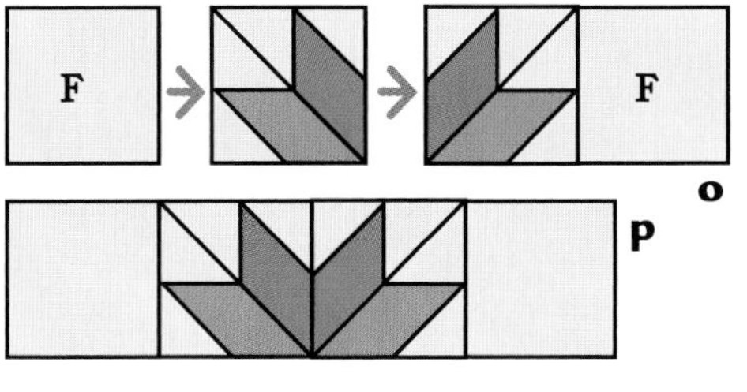

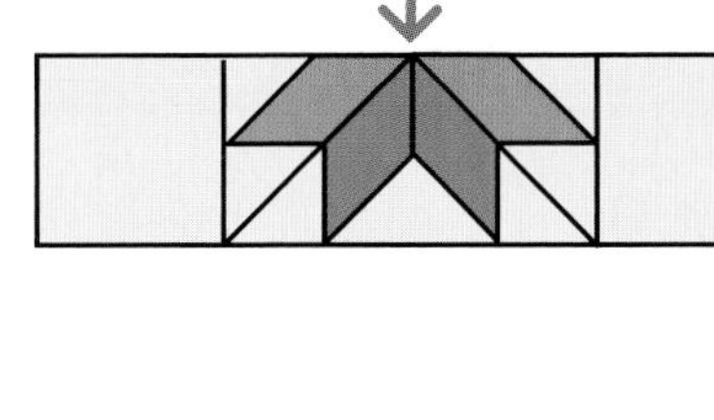

7 Join the remaining pieced side units in pairs (**q**), then add a pair to each side of the large central unit (**r**). Join the rows as shown (**s**) to complete the block (**t**).

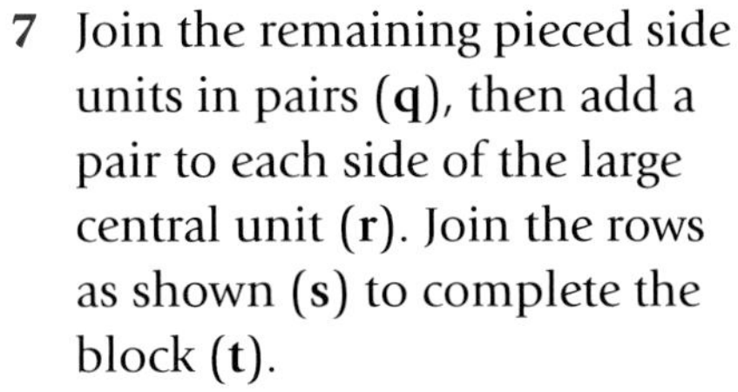

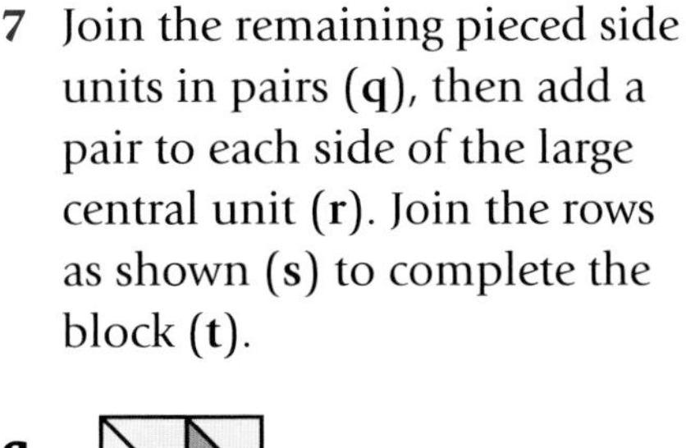

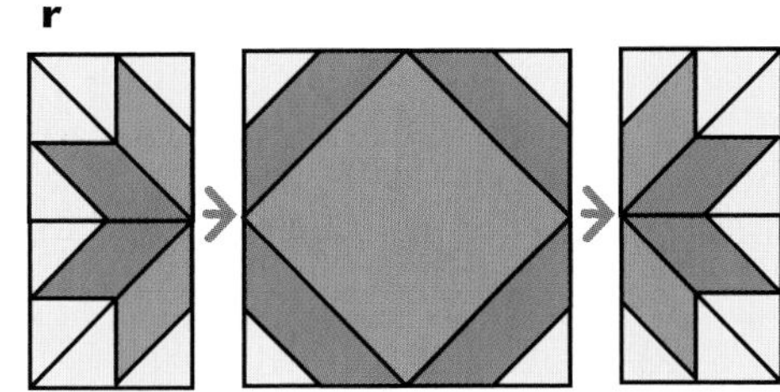

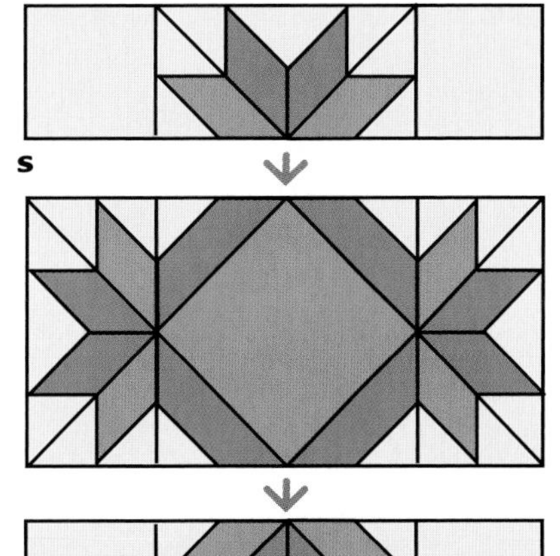

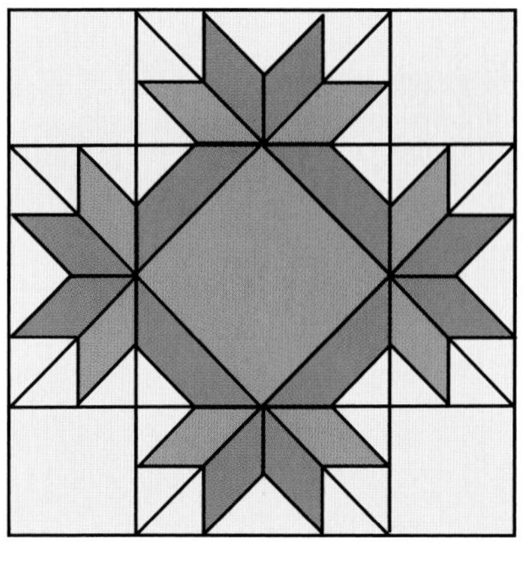

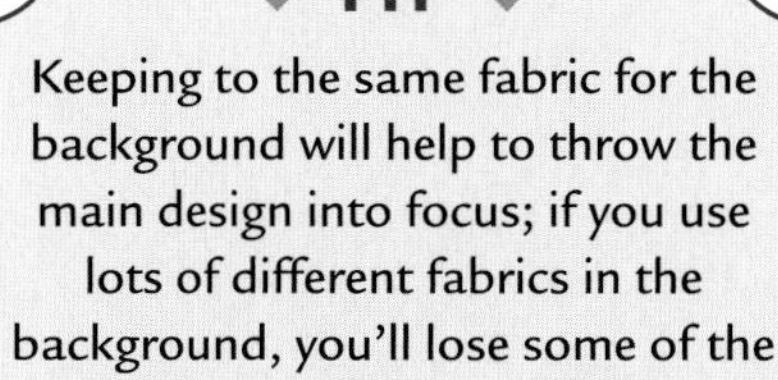

◆ **TIP** ◆

Keeping to the same fabric for the background will help to throw the main design into focus; if you use lots of different fabrics in the background, you'll lose some of the visual strength of the block.

suggestions for alternative colourways ***quilting idea***

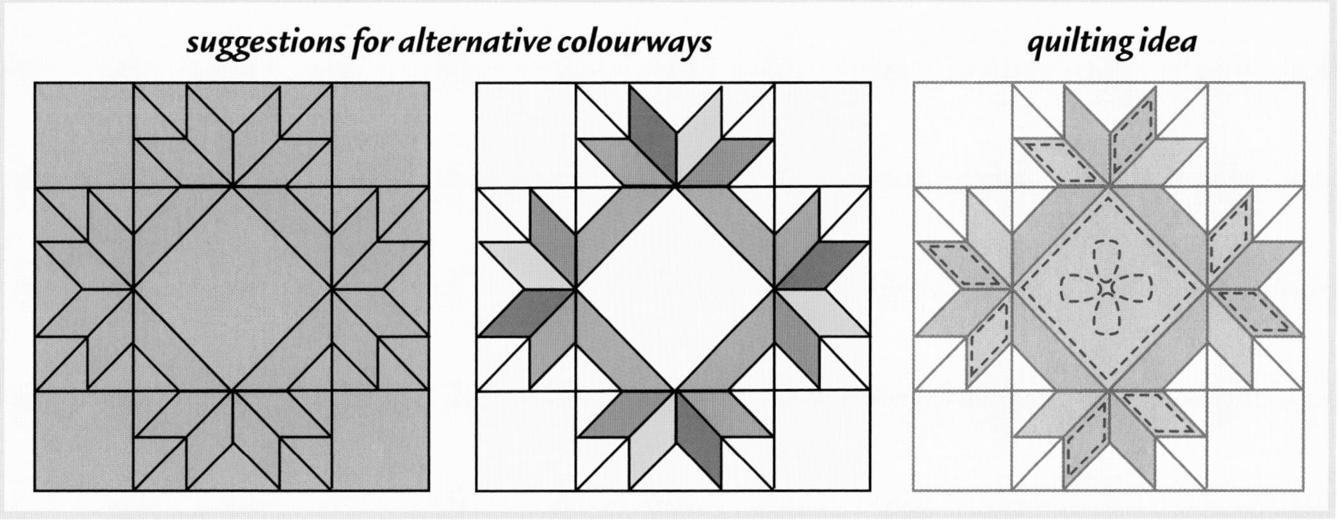

▪ BLOCK 24 ▪

St Benedict's Star

St Benedict's Star is a vibrant patchwork block based on a simple grid. If you choose quite a restricted colour-scheme, you'll find that this shows the design off to best effect. For a more dramatic effect, use two different colours or fabrics for the inner and outer star spikes.

Grid

this block is based on a 7 x 7 grid

Techniques

- squares, triangles, rhomboids (see Piecing Your Patchwork on p12)
- asymmetric shapes (see p12)
- mirror-image shapes (see p12)

What you will need

- basic supplies *(all-purpose sewing thread; needles or sewing machine; fabric scissors and thread-snipping scissors; pins; pencil)*

Fabrics: minimum 3

Templates: 5

you'll find the *St Benedict's Star* templates A-E on p94

Constructing the block

1 Join A patches in contrasting colours as shown (**a**); make 8 units this way. Join the units in pairs to create four chequerboard squares (**b**).

2 Join two C triangles in contrasting colours (**c**); make four units in this way. Join two B triangles in contrasting colours (**d**); make four of these units.

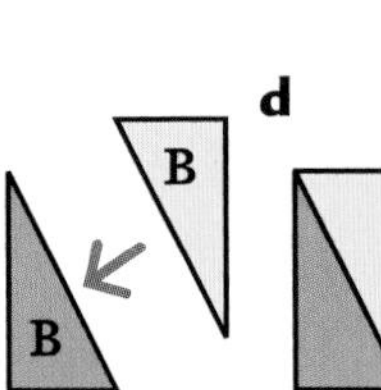

3 Join one CC shape to the side of a chequerboard square (**e**), then add a small A square to the end of a BB unit (**f**). Join these two shapes as shown (**g**); make sure that you're joining

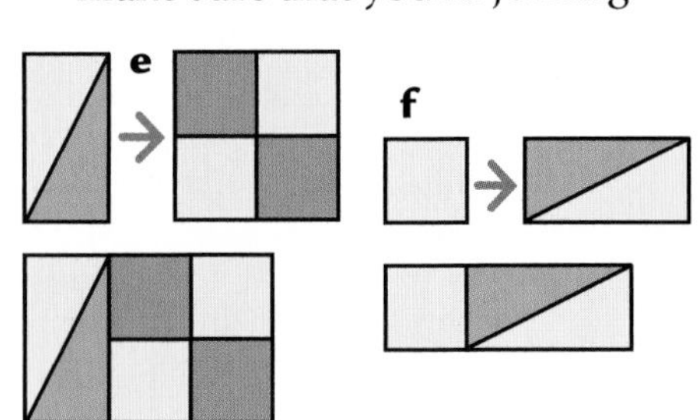

the correct sides of the patches each time. Make four units in this way; these become the corner patches of the block.

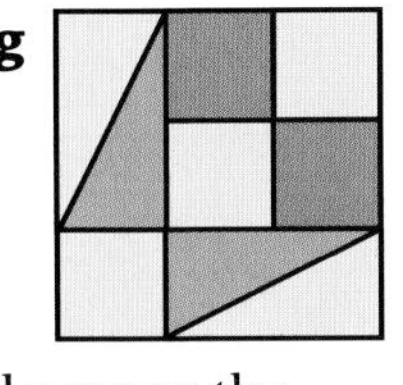

4 Add a D shape to each end of the E rhomboid (**h**). Join a D shape to one of the remaining B triangles (**i**); create two units this way.

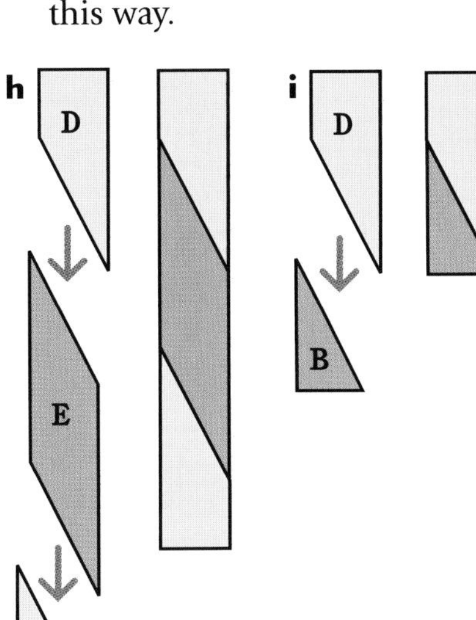

5 Join two corner patches with one of the DB shapes as shown (**j**); make two side units in this way.

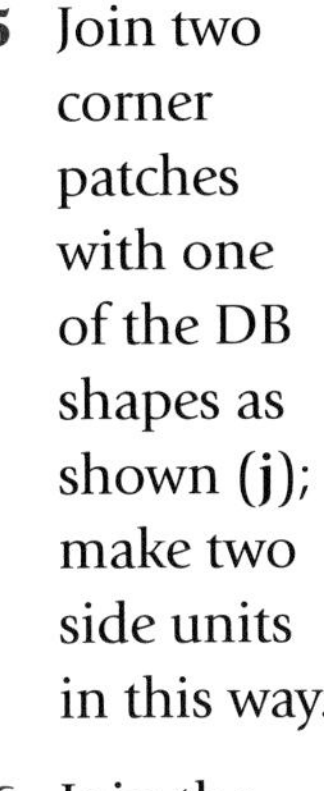

6 Join the side units round the long central strip as shown (**k**) to create the finished block (**l**).

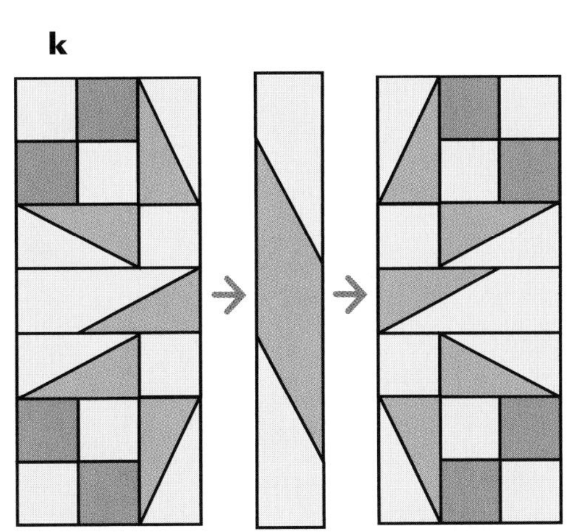

Ensure that you handle the central rhomboid shape very gently until you've stitched the complete block together. Although the two longer sides of the rhomboid are stabilised by placing the template on the straight grain of the fabric, this shape is particularly narrow and is easily distorted if you're not careful.

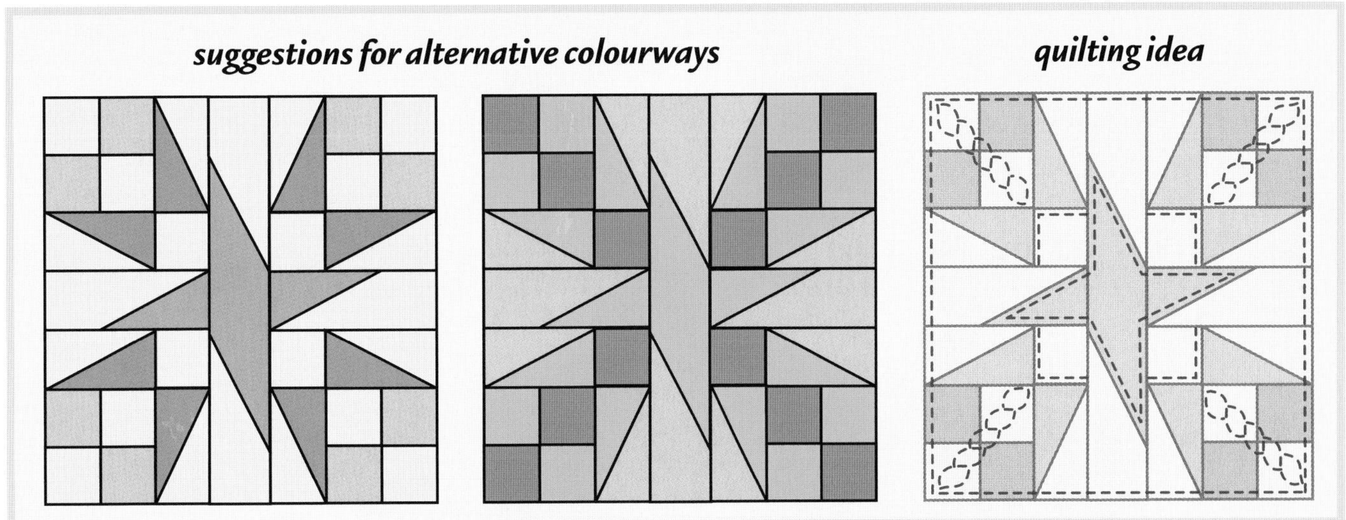

▪ BLOCK 25 ▪

Quilter's Dream

One of the more vibrant star patterns to be found in block patchwork, *Quilter's Dream* offers a lot of scope for using different colours and fabrics. Pick a strong and distinct 'background' colour to help make the star 'sing'. Once again, don't be put off by the complex appearance of this block; constructing the nifty 9-patch in the centre makes short work of putting it together.

■ **Grid**

this block is based on a 2 x 2 grid

■ **Techniques**

- squares, triangles, diamonds (see Piecing Your Patchwork on p12)
- mirror-image shapes (see p12)

■ **What you will need**

- basic supplies *(all-purpose sewing thread; needles or sewing machine; fabric scissors and thread-snipping scissors; pins; pencil)*

■ **Fabrics:** minimum 4

■ **Templates:** 8

you'll find the *Quilter's Dream* templates A-H on p95

■ Constructing the block

1 Join all the B squares in pairs of contrasting colours (**a**), then join the pairs as shown to create four chequerboard squares (**b**).

2 Add an F triangle to each top edge of an E rhomboid (**c**), then add a C and a D triangle to each edge of the pyramid (**d**). Make four units this way.

3 Join one chequerboard patch to each side of a CDEF unit as shown (**e**) – look carefully at which edges of the chequer-board patches are joined to which edges of the CDEF unit. Make two strips this way.

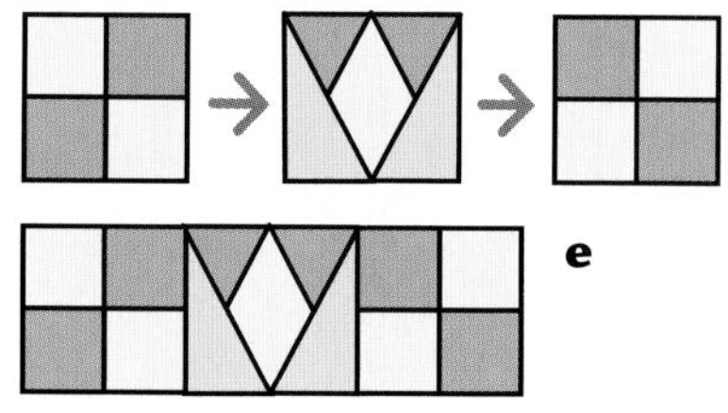

4 Create the central row of the 9-patch by adding the remaining CDEF units to the side of square A (**f**). Join the rows of

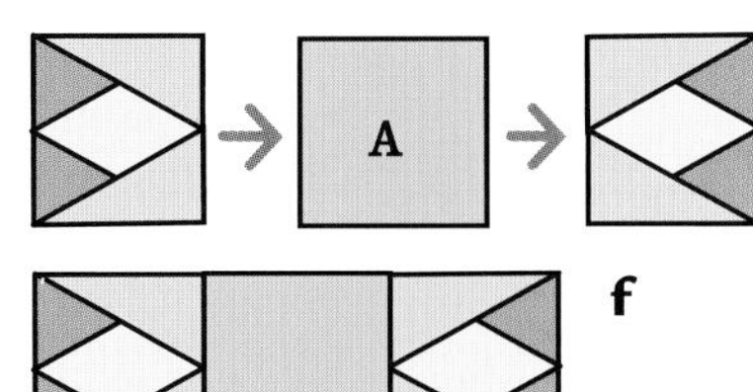

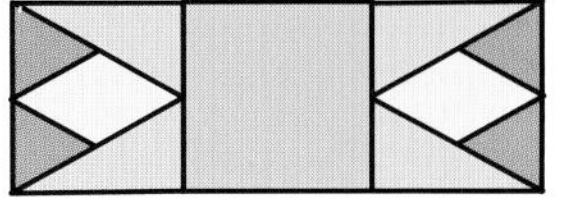

the 9-patch as shown (**g**) to create the centre of the block.

5 Add a C and a D triangle to the long sides of the H shape (**h**), then add a G triangle to each side (**i**) to create a large triangular unit (**j**). Make four units this way.

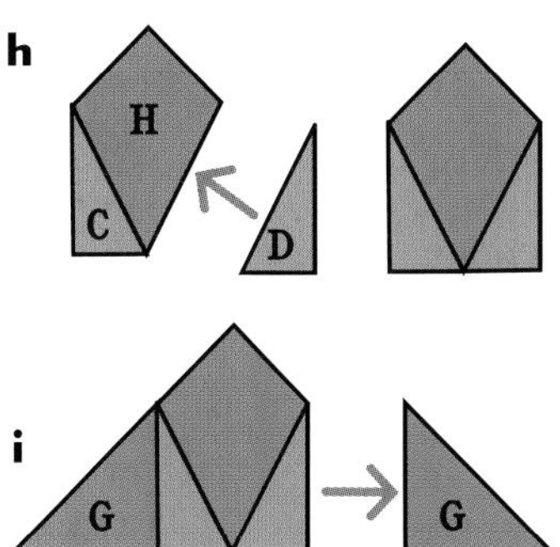

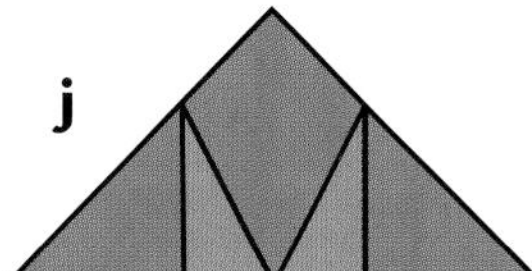

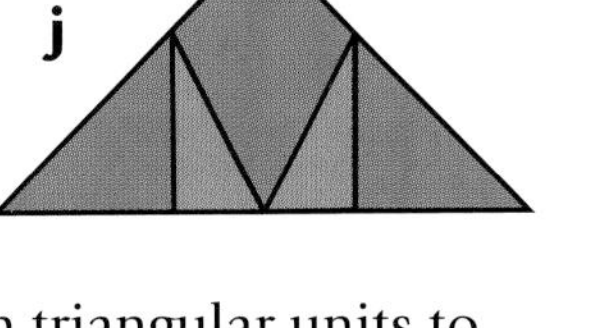

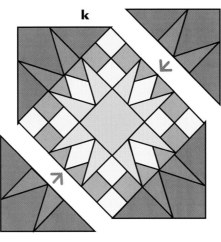

6 Join triangular units to opposite sides of the central 9-patch, then add the remaining two units (**k**) to complete the block (**l**).

k

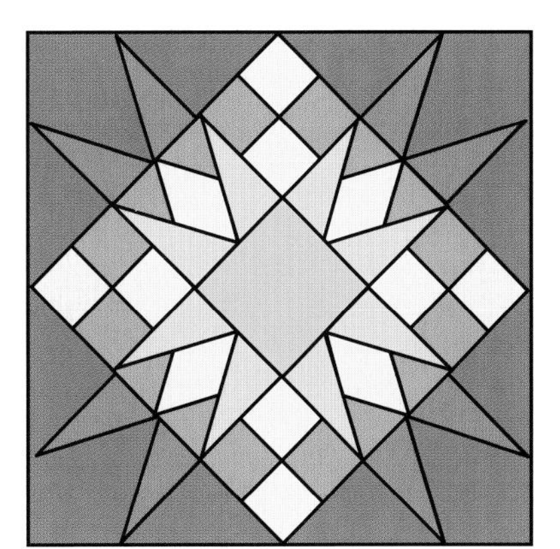

◆ TIP ◆

Placing two parallel sides of the diamond shape on the straight grain of the fabric helps to stabilise what could otherwise be an awkward fabric shape to handle.

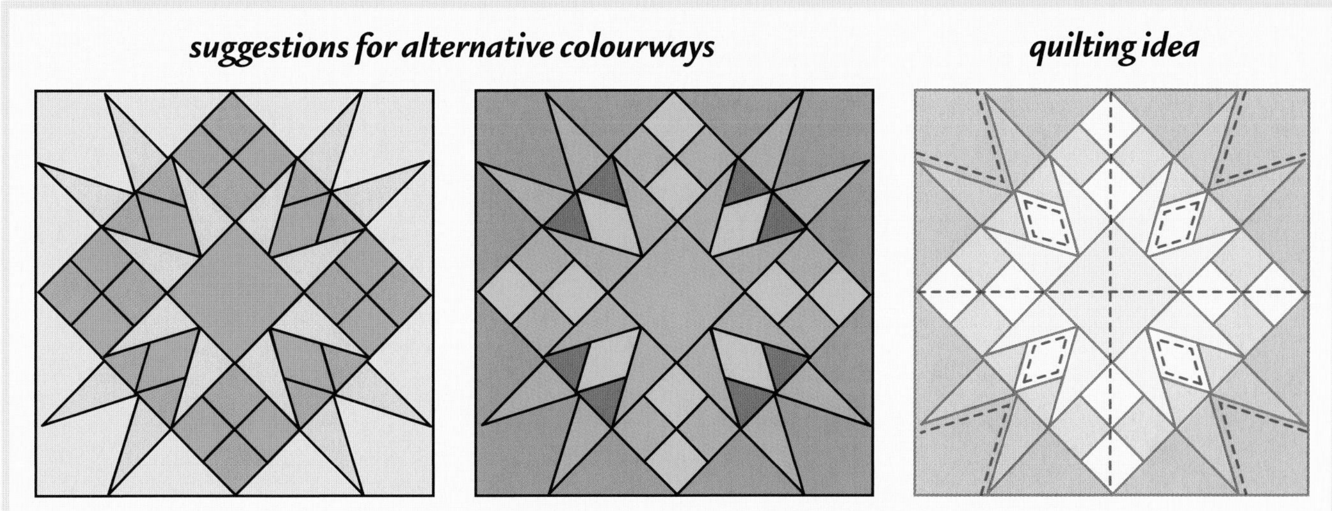

Assembling the quilt

Quilt as you go

Remember that this technique really does involve quilting 'as you go'. To benefit fully from this technique, you need to aim to:

- construct one block
- sew on the sashings
- layer and tack the block with its wadding and backing fabric
- quilt the block (not the sashings at this stage)
- then move on to the next block.

If you're tempted to make up all the blocks and then leave them in an ever-increasing pile to be quilted all at the same time, you'll miss out on the benefit of quilting 'as you go' (although it can be handy to stockpile several blocks at a time if you intend to quilt them on holiday or while travelling, for instance). Once you finish constructing a block, add the sashings (**a**), then layer the sashed block with its wadding and backing square (**b**).

a

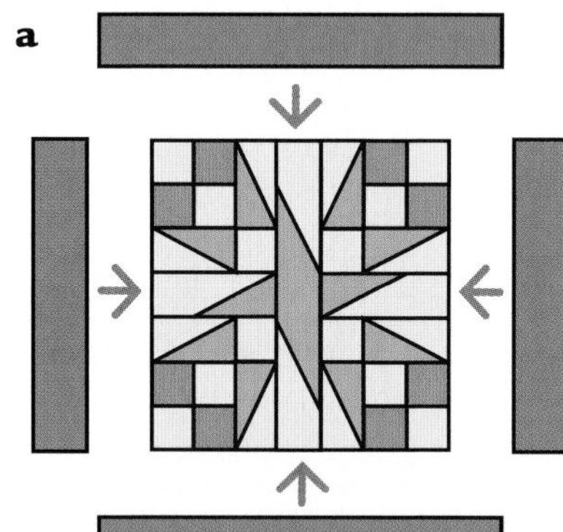

b

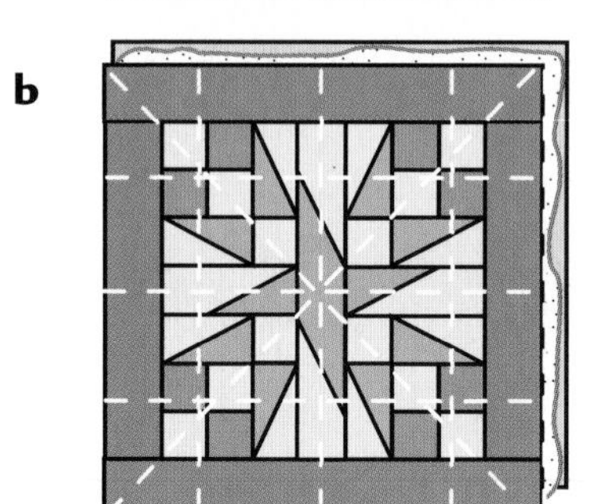

Quilting the blocks

My sampler quilt is totally quilted by hand. My instructions are given for 'lap quilting' – that is, hand-quilting without the use of a quilt frame or hoop. This is the method of quilting I prefer, but of course you're welcome to make your own choices for this stage.

If you have a quilting design that you'd like to trace, this needs to be marked on to the block before you layer your fabric 'sandwich' (**a**).

a

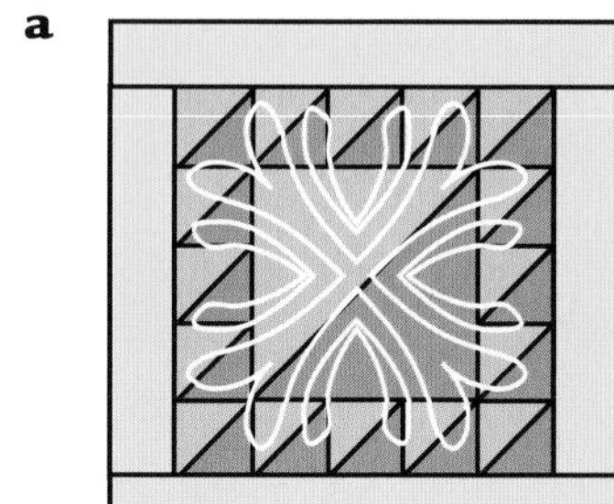

If you prefer to decide on the quilting design after the sandwich has been layered, tack each block in this way: top fabric uppermost, backing fabric face down and wadding in between (**b**).

Once you've layered and tacked each pieced block, there are many options open to you; you could choose to contour-quilt around each patch (**c**) or sew 'in the ditch' (that is, in the valley of each seam itself). Alternatively, you could use a ready-made or home-made quilting stencil and position the pattern either within the patches (if the design is small), as shown in (**d**), or so that the design covers the entire block (**e**). Whichever way you choose to quilt the block, ensure that you work from the centre of the design outwards.

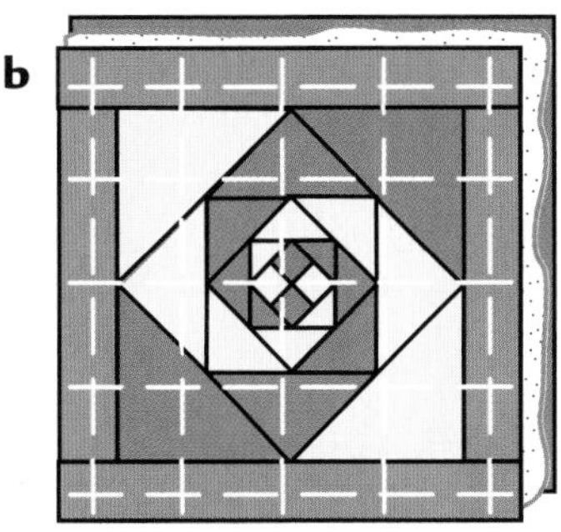

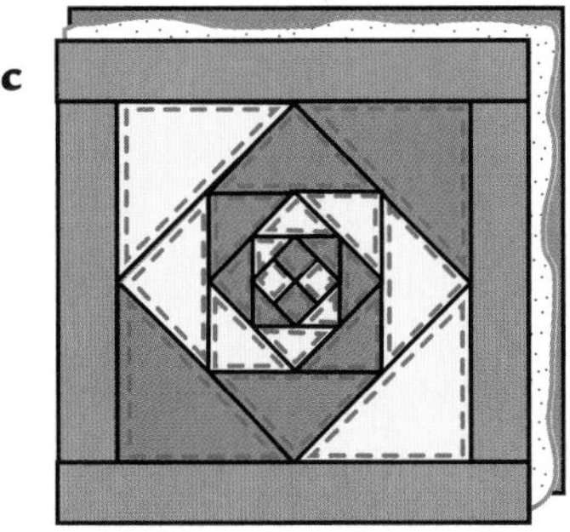

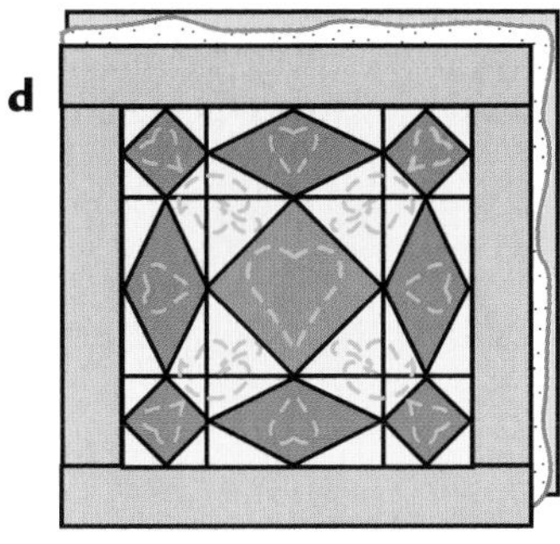

Hand-quilting

Choose a quilting needle (a 'Between' needle) that you're comfortable using, and a specialised quilting thread in a colour which complements your work. Ideally, keep the length of thread to 18in (45cm) maximum. Make a neat knot in one end; insert the needle into the quilt top about a needle's length away from the starting point for your stitching.

Pass the needle through the top fabric and the wadding only until it surfaces at your starting point, then gently pull the thread to 'pop' the knot into the wadding where it should be held securely.

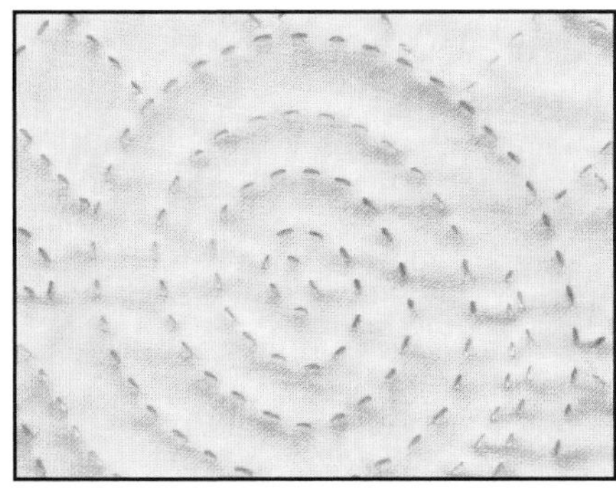

Working from the surface of the quilt, take the first stitch while holding your needle almost perpendicular (at right angles) to your work. Take several stitches onto the needle at once, catching up all three layers of your work, before pulling the needle and thread through – not too tightly, but just enough to allow the stitches to lie flat on the fabric surface. Continue to quilt round the lines of your design in this way.

To finish off a thread, make a neat knot in it about a stitch length away from your fabric. If you have room, take one more stitch; if not, take a backstitch: run the needle through the top fabric and wadding only, once more popping the knot into the wadding to secure the stitching, then snip off the remaining tail of thread.

Machine-quilting

The simplest method of quilting a block by machine is to contour-quilt your block design by stitching around the outlines of the patches. This stitching can be done 'in the ditch' (where the stitching sits in the valley of the seam itself), or just to one side of the seam where it will be more visible. You'll find that you get best results if you work with an even-feed foot (also known as a walking or dual-feed foot) fixed to your machine. If you don't have one of these, pin the seam to be sewn, placing the pins at right angles to the seam and at regular intervals – remove each pin before you reach it.

With just a little more concentration you can quilt decorative designs; try to choose a continuous-line design to avoid having to stop and start too often. You may need to practise this method of machine-quilting before working on your quilt.

Free-form (or random) machine-quilting requires you to lower the feed dogs on your sewing machine; if your machine doesn't have this facility, you may be able to cover the feed dogs with a piece of card or plastic. (You may also find that you need to adjust the tension on your machine and use a different-sized needle from usual.) Reduce the stitch length and width to nil. You'll find it easier to work free-form machine-quilting if the work is set into a machine-quilting or embroidery hoop and a machine-

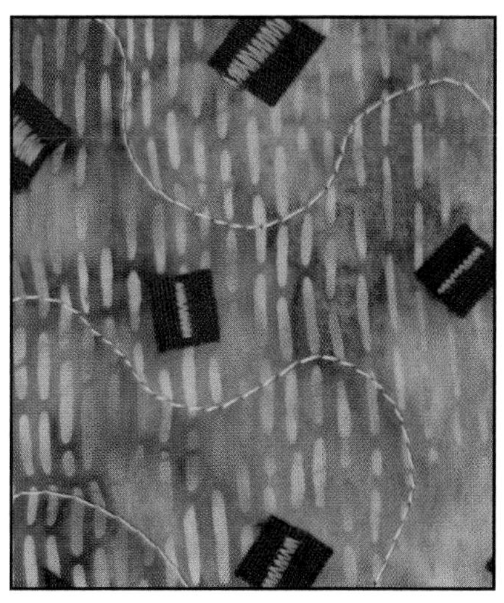

embroidery foot is fitted. Once again, practice makes perfect with this method – spend some time on a spare fabric 'sandwich' before working on your quilt.

Whichever method of machine-quilting you choose, take time to choose a suitable colour of thread for not only the top thread, but also for the bobbin thread. Make sure that you begin your work with both the top thread and the bobbin thread on the top surface of the fabric (so that the bobbin thread doesn't get caught up in the stitching on the back), and try to work your design from the centre outwards.

If your machine has the facility, use a locking stitch to begin and end each quilting line; if not, work two or three tiny stitches – back, forwards, back etc – on the same spot: this should be enough to secure the thread and you can just snip the stray threads away. If the threads don't lock, it's best to tie them off and thread them into the layers of your quilt with a needle.

Constructing the quilt centre

Once all your blocks have been constructed and quilted (and after awarding yourself a pat on the back for all your hard work), remove all the tacking and lay the blocks out on a large, flat surface. Choose a surface large enough for you to stand back, evaluate your work and find a pleasing arrangement by juggling the blocks around. Taking a photograph at this stage can help, if time allows (the benefits of digital cameras); if not, try a reducing glass (you can achieve the same effect by looking through your camera's viewing lens, by looking in the wrong direction through a pair of binoculars, or by using a security spyglass made for front doors).

Arrange your blocks so that you have a good balance of colours, tones and shapes across the quilt top; your arrangement may or may not be the same as mine. Once you've decided on the position of each block, pin a number and letter sequence to the blocks so that you can't make any mistakes when you're sewing them together: ie. 1a, 1b, 1c etc across the top row, 2a, 2b, 2c etc across the second row, and so on.

Begin by joining one pair of blocks in their sequence, making sure that the sides with the short sashings go together at this stage. Stitch the seam to join the two sashings first, pinning the wadding and backing fabric out of the way; finger-press this seam open (**a**). At this stage you'll find it handy to cut a piece of sturdy card and lay it over the back of the seam (**b**); this will prevent you from accidentally cutting the front of the work during the next stages.

Unpin the two pieces of wadding only and bring them down over the card so that they overlap; with scissors, cut right up the centre of the overlap and discard the surplus. You now have two pieces of wadding butting up perfectly to each other; whipstitch the edges together with generous stitches (**c**). Leaving the card in place, unpin the backing fabric; bring one piece

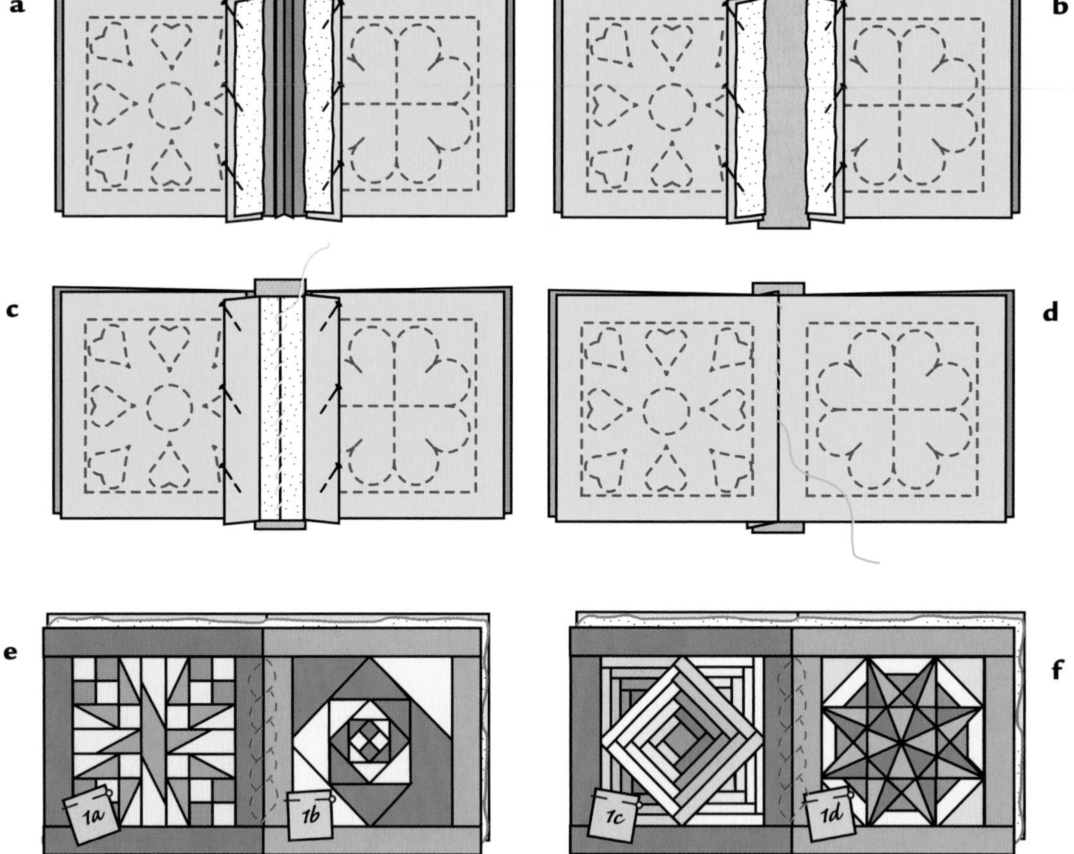

g

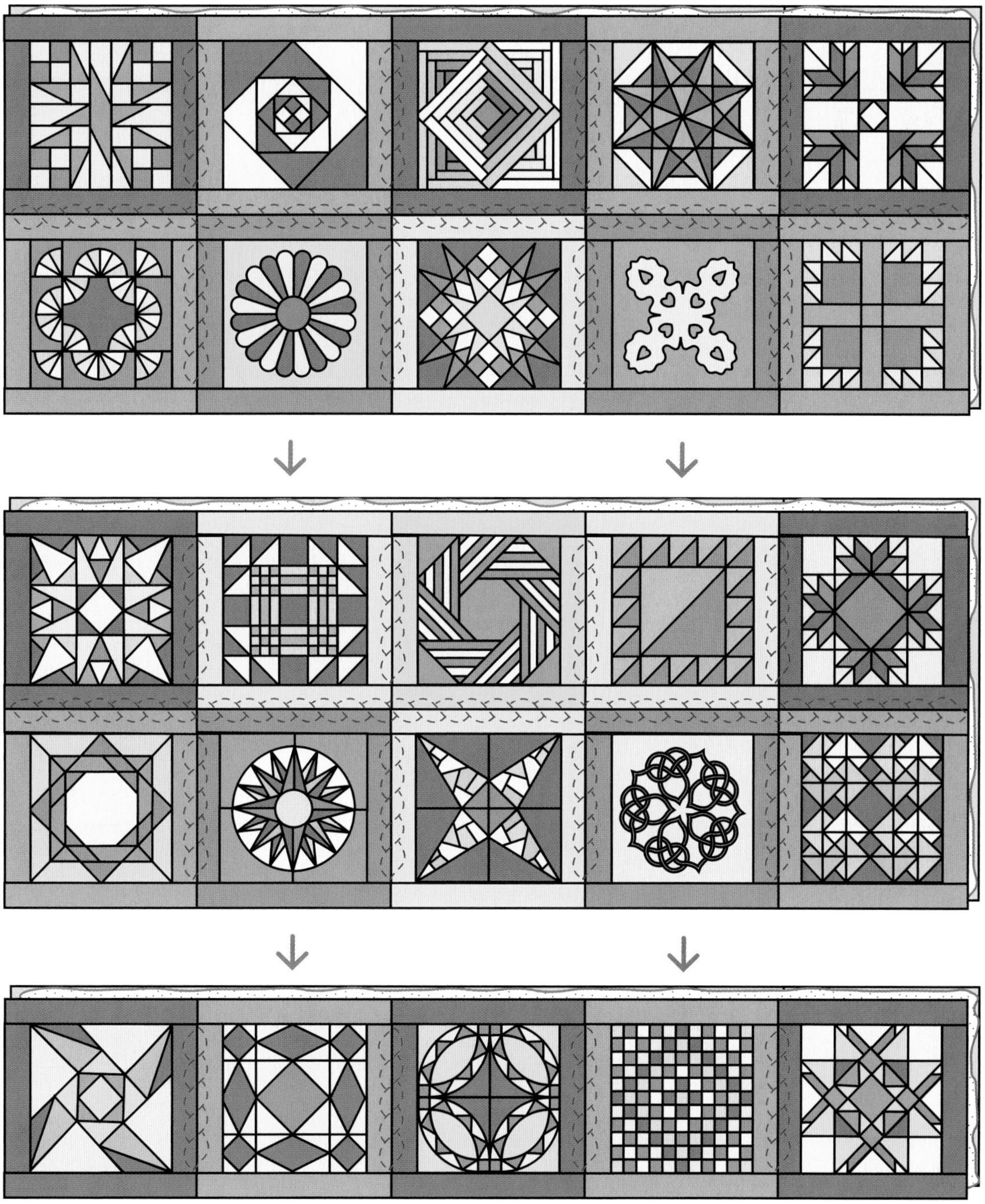

down so that it lies flat, then bring the other section down on top, folding the raw edge underneath; slipstitch this into place (**d**) and remove the card.

Once the first pair has been joined, re-tack the area of the short sashings and quilt within this area only (**e**); remember to leave the longer sashings free of quilting at this stage, ready for further construction.

Join a second pair of blocks (**f**) and quilt them in the same way. By joining pairs at a time, then joining the pairs to make one long strip, you'll avoid one end of the quilt becoming top-heavy and difficult to handle.

Once all the horizontal rows of blocks have been joined and quilted within the short sashing areas, it's time to join the long strips in pairs (**g**), then join the pairs to construct the entire quilt centre (as shown in **h** overleaf). Remember to quilt each long run of sashing as it's joined (still quilting 'as you go') – your quilt will be growing larger at this stage and working in pairs again will avoid one end of the quilt from becoming heavier than the other and tricky to handle.

Well done! Your quilt centre is finished. Now is the time to approach the borders.

Adding the borders

As I mentioned earlier, if the quilt is intended for a specific-sized bed your border measurements may already be dictated. If, on the other hand, you're happy to make a quilt regardless of specific measurements, ensure that the border measurement you opt for is in proportion to the quilt centre itself. (A good rule of thumb here is to take a border measurement of larger than the width of the block sashings, but no larger than your block size. Obviously, this is open to interpretation and you may prefer to add a larger border to bring your quilt up to the size that you'd like it to be.)

Sampler quilts destined for exhibition ought to be aesthetically pleasing and will generally require a border on all four sides to balance the design. If your quilt is destined for a bed with a headboard, footboard or other determining features, though, take this into consideration when you're designing the borders – for instance, you may prefer the pieced quilt centre to cover the pillows on your bed, in which case you could leave the top edge of the quilt without a border. Again, the choice is yours – it's your quilt.

If you want to make decorative borders – for instance pieced or appliquéd ones – think of them as long rectangular blocks. Do any patchwork or appliqué first, then follow the instructions below to layer and quilt the borders before adding them to the quilt centre.

Constructing the borders

If you're making the borders for your quilt the same way I've made mine, begin by constructing the border units from step (**a**) onwards; if you're using plain border strips, move straight on to step (**e**).

Join one 70in (175cm) gold strip and one red strip the same length as shown (**a**) to create a side unit; make two units this way. Join the remaining border pieces as shown (**b**, **c** and **d**) to create two units for the top and bottom of the quilt. Add any appliqué motifs that you choose using scraps of fabric from the rest of your quilt (**e**).

Layer each border unit with its wadding and backing fabric (**f**), tack the layers together and quilt

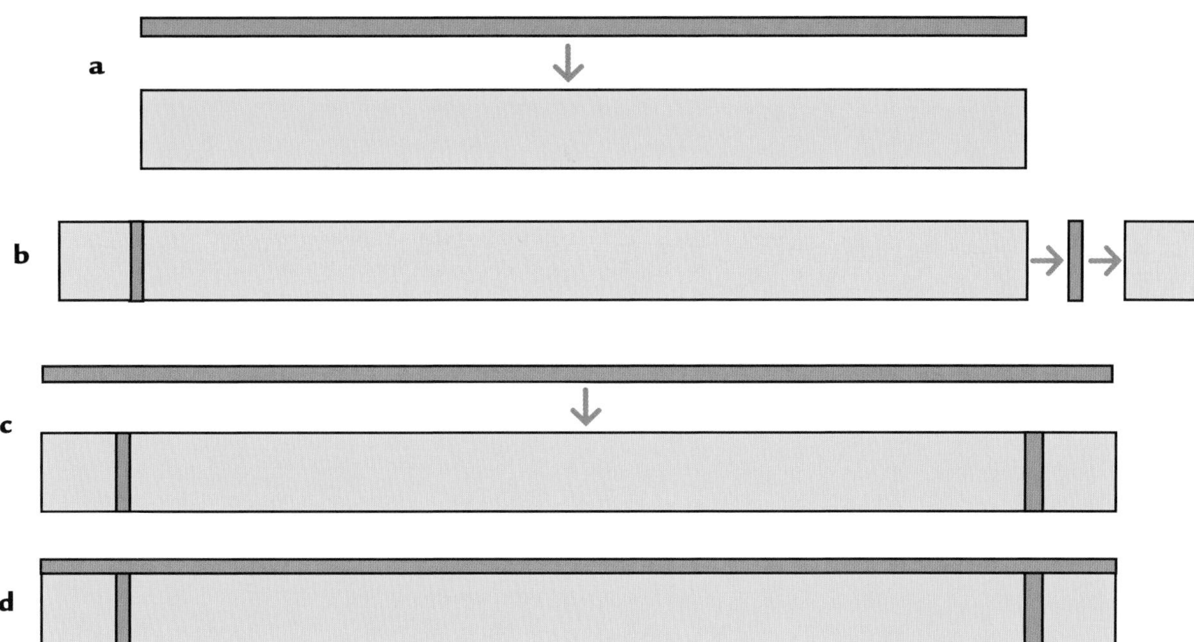

the majority of the border (**g**), leaving at least 2in (7.5cm) unquilted on the edges that are to be joined to the quilt centre.

Join the borders to the quilt centre, beginning with the borders on opposite sides (**h**), then adding the remaining borders at the top and bottom (**i**).

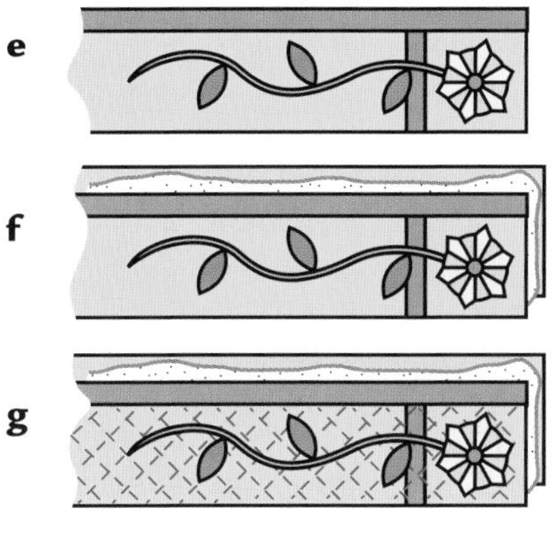

h

Once all the borders are in place (**j**), add any extra quilting to the areas which have been sewn together last.

i

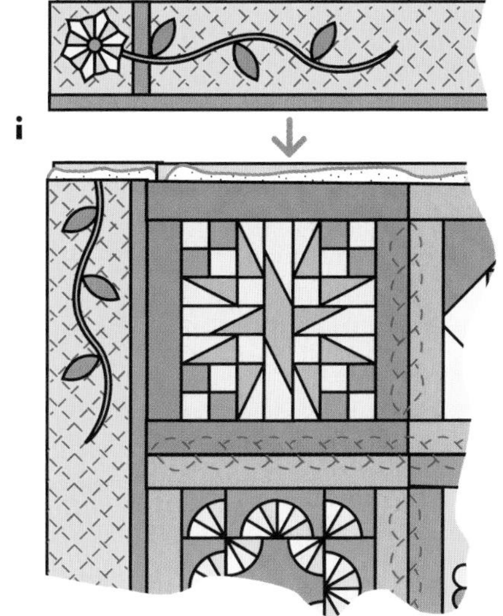

j

Binding

Fold the prepared binding strips in half down their length and press. Position one length of binding on the front of the quilt, aligning the raw edges, and pin in place (**a**); sew

a

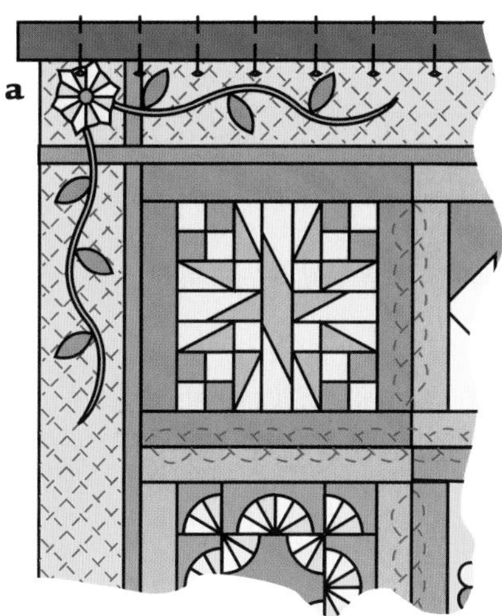

approximately ½in (1cm) in from the raw edges. At this stage, trim back any surplus wadding and backing fabric so that it's very slightly larger than your quilt top; this helps to pad the binding out a little. Push the folded edge of the binding to the back of the quilt and slipstitch it in place (as shown in **b** overleaf), covering the previous line of stitching.

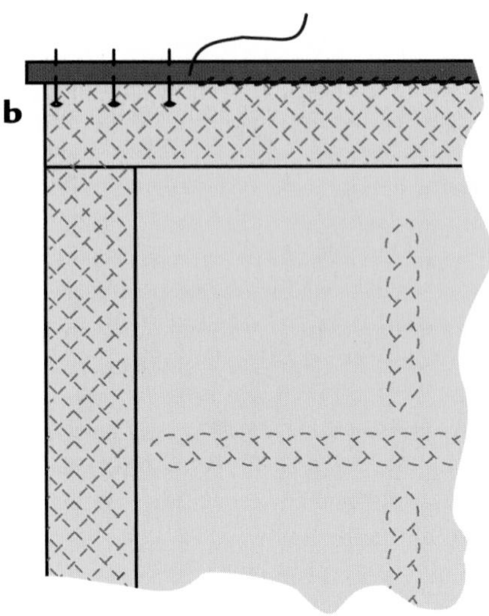

Repeat on the opposite side of the quilt and cut all the ends of the binding flush with the ends of the quilt top. Pin binding strips to the remaining edges of the quilt, leaving at least 1-2in (3-5cm) of excess binding fabric overhanging each end. Sew the strips in place (**c**),

then tuck the excess flaps of fabric inwards as you slipstitch the binding to the back of the quilt.

Remove any remaining tacking, then sit back and admire and enjoy the fruits of your labour.

Labelling your work

Don't forget to label your quilt somewhere – patchwork is an art form, and all artists that I know of sign their work for posterity.

Your 'label' or 'signature' can be as simple as adding your initials (although a full name might be better) and the year in which the quilt is finished. I usually stitch these basic details into the quilt somewhere – either on the back, or within one of the blocks or a discreet area of the border on the quilt front (**a**), just in case a 'stitched-on' label ever comes adrift. Use simple lettering to ensure that these details are legible.

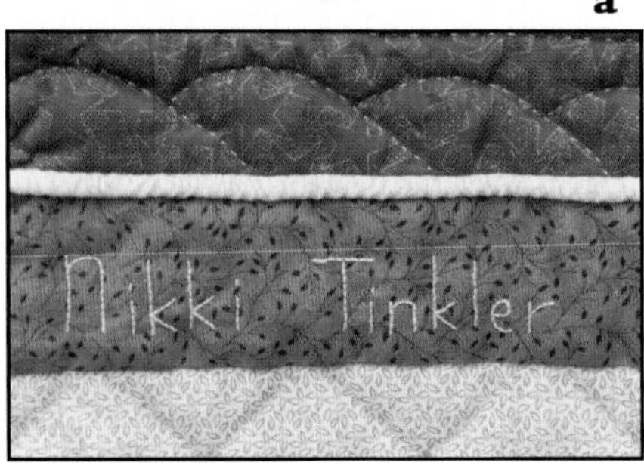

If you want to add a message which is too complicated to stitch, make a label which can be sewn to the back of your work (**b**). The simplest

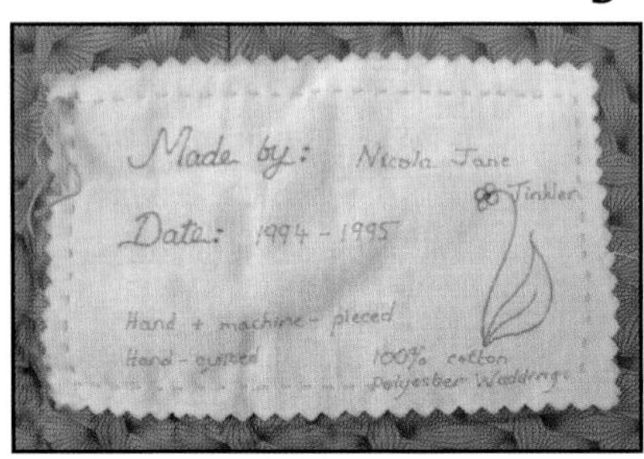

type of label I make uses calico (or other plain fabric) backed with medium- or heavy-weight iron-on interfacing to strengthen it. Use permanent fabric-marking pens to write any details on the calico, and

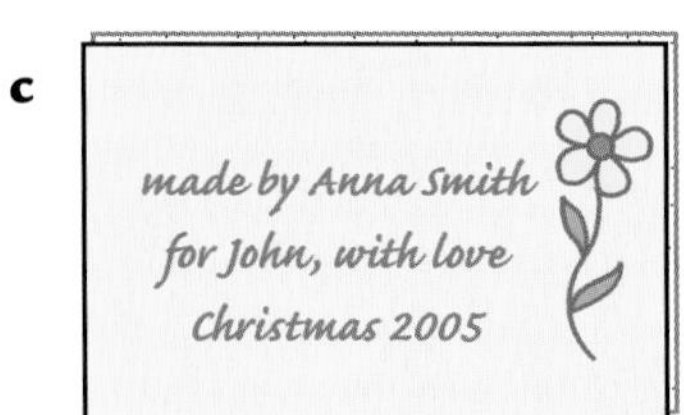

draw in any motifs (**c**). (If you need guide lines, rule these in with blue, water-soluble pen which can be removed afterwards). Or, if you prefer, stitch the details on the label, or print them. Iron the label onto the Vilene, and trim the edges to the required shape and size with pinking shears (**d**). Stitch the label to the backing fabric of the quilt, stitching just inside the pinked edge (**e**).

You could also write or stitch details in one patch of a small pieced block (**f**), or on a shaped appliqué patch (**g**) stitched to the back of the quilt.

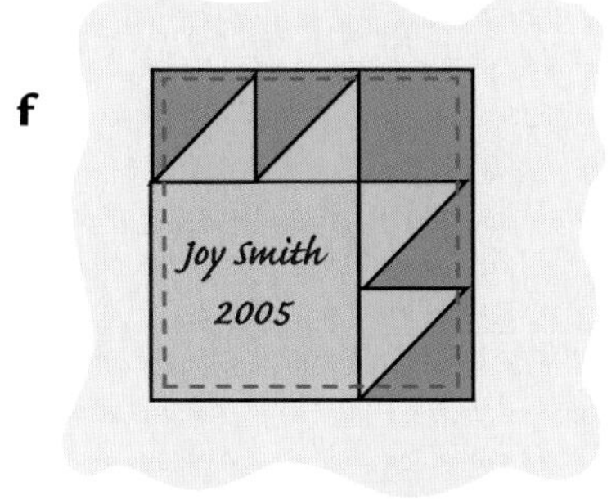

Displaying your quilt

If your work is to be hung/displayed as a wall-hanging (or exhibited in a quilt exhibition), you'll need to add a hanging sleeve or display loops. A hanging sleeve can simply be a surplus length of fabric, approximately 5in (10-12cm) x the width of your quilt; turn under and stitch a hem on all four edges, and slip-stitch the sleeve to the backing fabric at the top of the quilt (**a**).

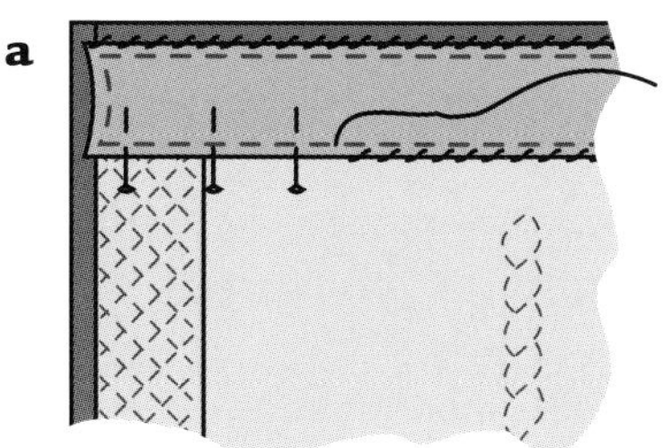

If you have enough fabric to make a tubular sleeve (**b**), this is even better. By adding a tube of fabric,

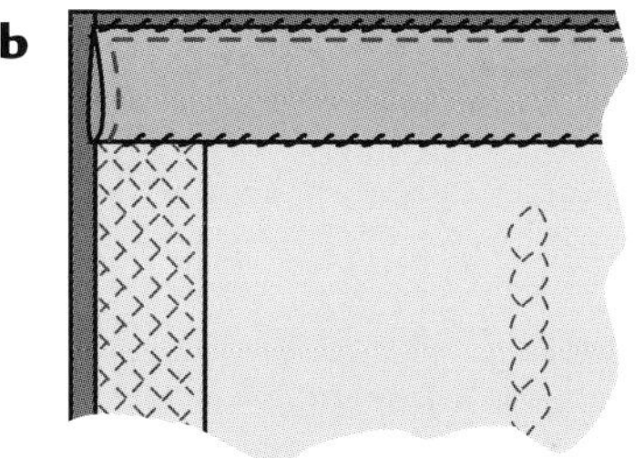

rather than a one-sided sleeve, you'll protect any quilting stitches (and the quilt itself) from any damage that might occur when a hanging pole is pushed through.

An alternative is to add display loops of fabric or tape to the top edge of the quilt (**c**); ideally these should be added as you stitch on the final binding, so that the raw ends can be concealed under the binding.

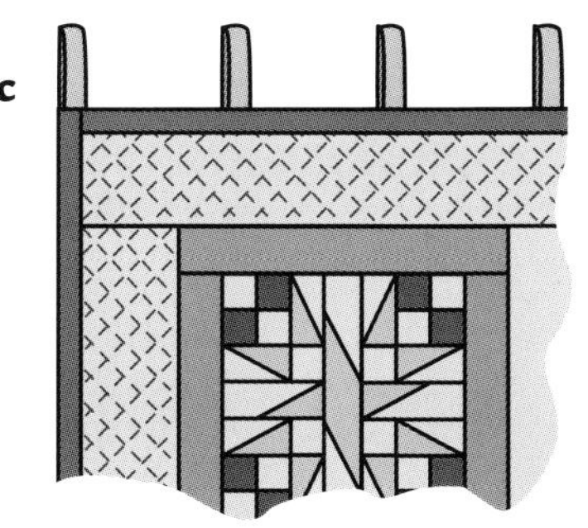

Looking after your quilt

You've put an enormous amount of time and care into creating your quilt; it would be a shame to waste it by not giving enough care and attention to cleaning, storage and general care of the quilt.

Cleaning

Before you began stitching your quilt, you should already have taken into consideration if it's going to be washed; if so, is it going to be laundered on a regular basis, or will the occasional wash be enough? If you're making a quilt for a baby, a child, or perhaps an elderly person in a residential home, make sure that the fabrics are pre-washed, and ensure that the complete quilt (including the chosen wadding and means of quilting) will all stand up to the rigours of regular machine laundering.

If your quilt is destined to be more decorative, though – perhaps placed on your bed only during daytime hours – and so won't require regular laundering, you can afford to give a little more time and care to the cleaning stage. A lot of people are tempted to give their precious quilts to a dry-cleaners: beware, though – not all waddings are suitable for dry-cleaning!

You could try machine-washing your quilt on a very gentle machine cycle intended for silks and woollens. Alternatively, choose a sunny summer day: fill the bath with hand-warm water and a delicate woollens detergent. Gently lower the quilt into the water, kneading the quilt to assist the cleaning process. Pull the plug to disperse the soapy water and refill the bath with clean rinsing water ; do this two or three times. Give the quilt a final rinse and let the last rinse water out; gently knead the quilt as much as possible to disperse any excess water, then roll the quilt carefully into a large sheet and carry the bundle onto a large area of clean lawn or patio where it can be laid out flat to dry gently. Don't lift a wet quilt and peg it to a washing line; the weight of all that wet fabric will put stress on the fabrics and the stitching.

Storing

If the quilt is going to be stored for any length of time, avoid plastic bags, which might cause a build-up of condensation and mould. Hunt out a shop selling acid-free tissue paper; wrap the quilt with layers of this tissue – try to pad out areas of folding which might cause permanent crease marks – and store the quilt away from direct sunlight. Shake it out regularly and refold it in different places to avoid permanent creasing.

General care

Old, faded quilts have their own charm, but unfortunately even bright new fabrics soon fade without any help, and it's nice to keep your fabric colours true for as long as possible. So, if your quilt is displayed on a bed and there's a danger of it frequently lying in direct sunlight, try to avoid the problem: during the part of the day when the sun shines in, pull the curtains, cover the quilt with a spare sheet or turn the quilt reverse side up.

The same goes for quilts that are hung on a wall – try to find a wall that isn't targeted by bright sunshine if at all possible. If the quilt is quite large and heavy, do give it a 'rest' from time to time; hanging up for a long time can cause stress on the fabrics and the stitching. Take the quilt down, shake out any dust, and let it recuperate for a week or so before re-hanging it.

The Templates

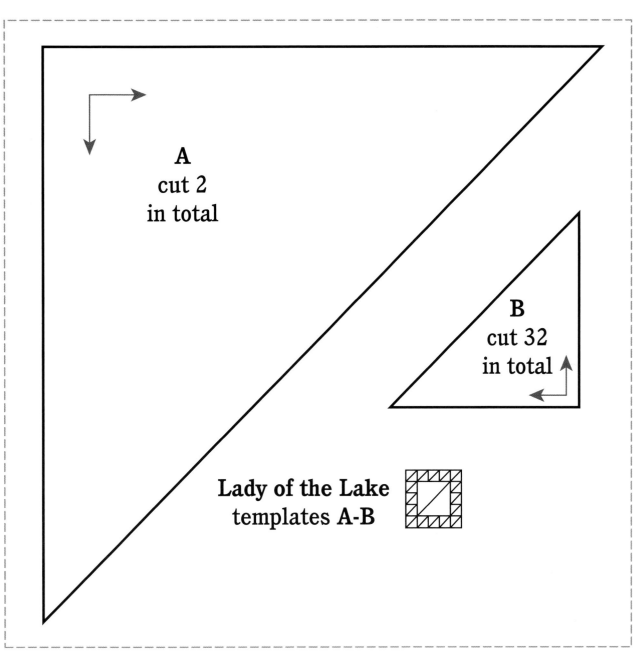

A
cut 2
in total

B
cut 32
in total

Lady of the Lake
templates **A-B**

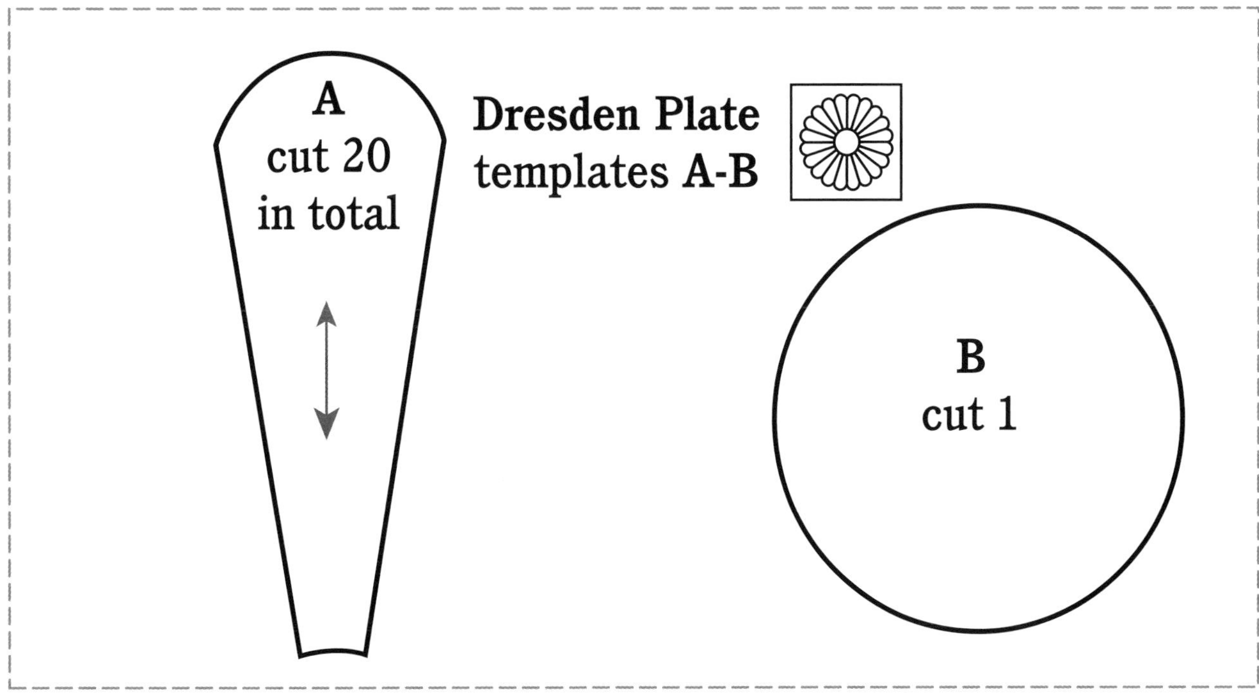

A
cut 1

B
cut 4

G cut 16

F
cut 4

E
cut 8
! FLIP !

C
cut 4

D
cut 8
! FLIP !

Storm at Sea
templates A-G

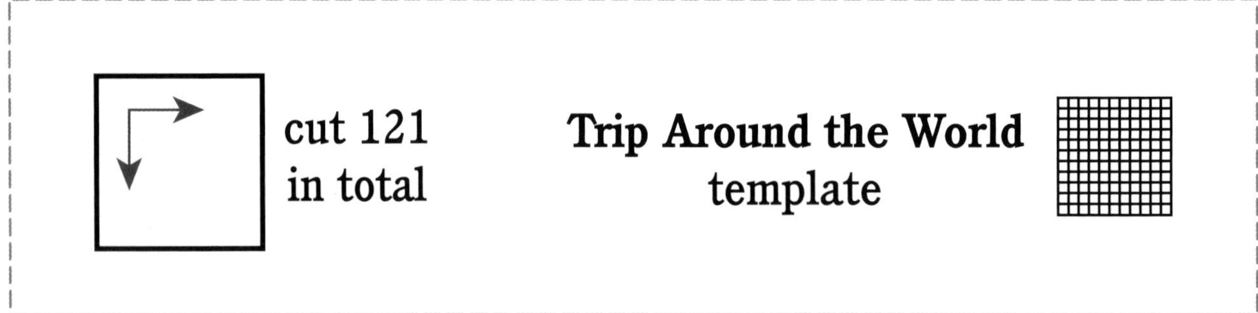

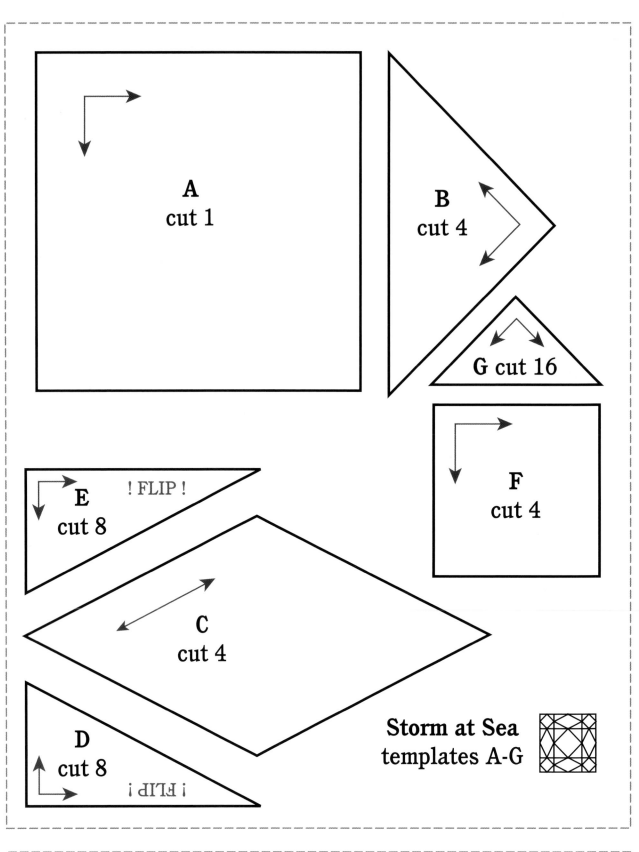

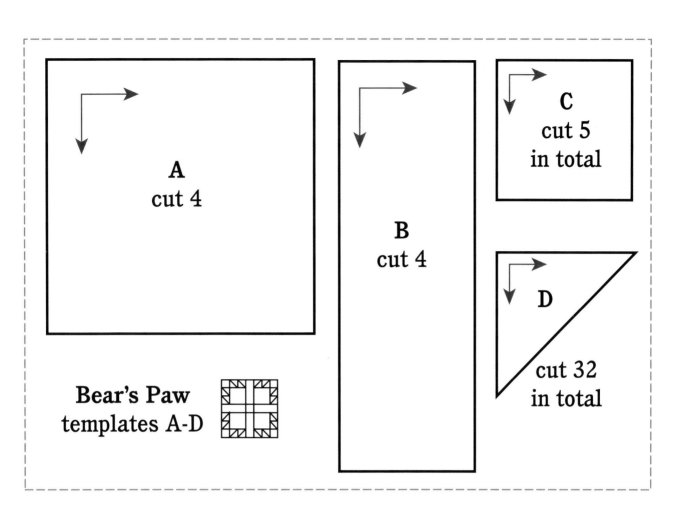

A
cut 4

B
cut 4

C
cut 5
in total

D
cut 32
in total

Bear's Paw
templates A-D

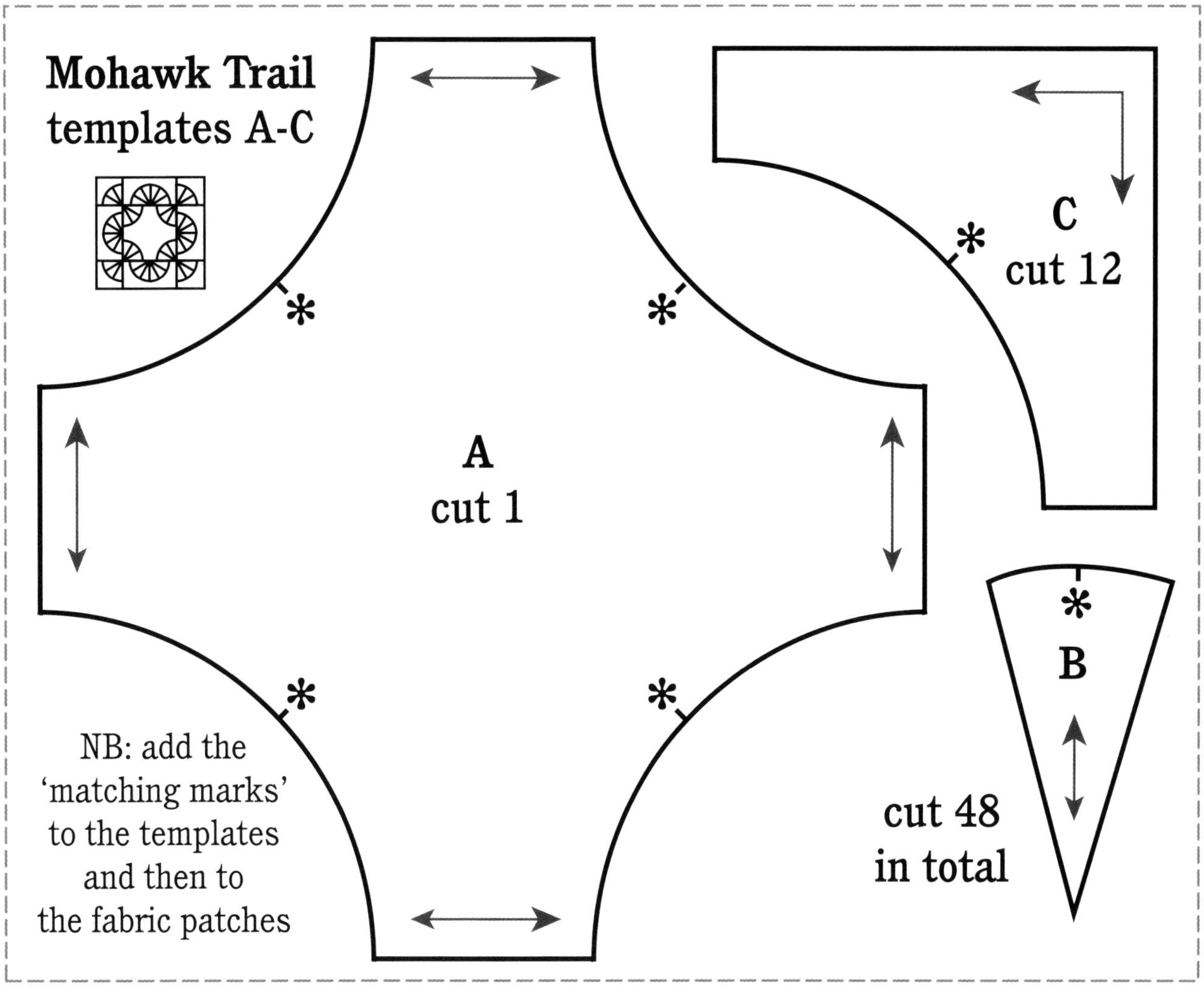

Mohawk Trail
templates A-C

A
cut 1

C
cut 12

B
cut 48
in total

NB: add the 'matching marks' to the templates and then to the fabric patches

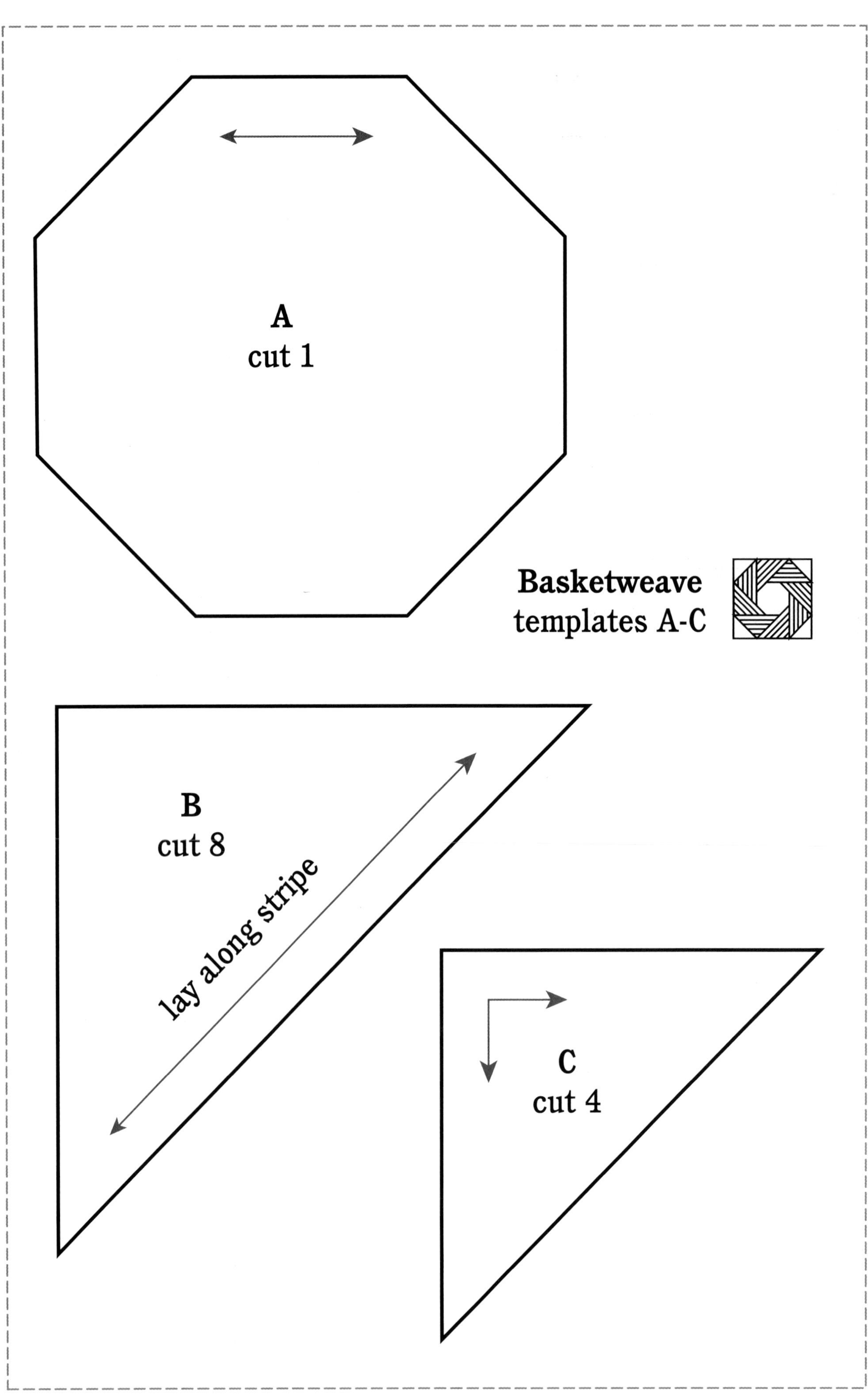
A
cut 1
Basketweave
templates A-C
B
cut 8
lay along stripe
C
cut 4

Snail Trail
templates A-F

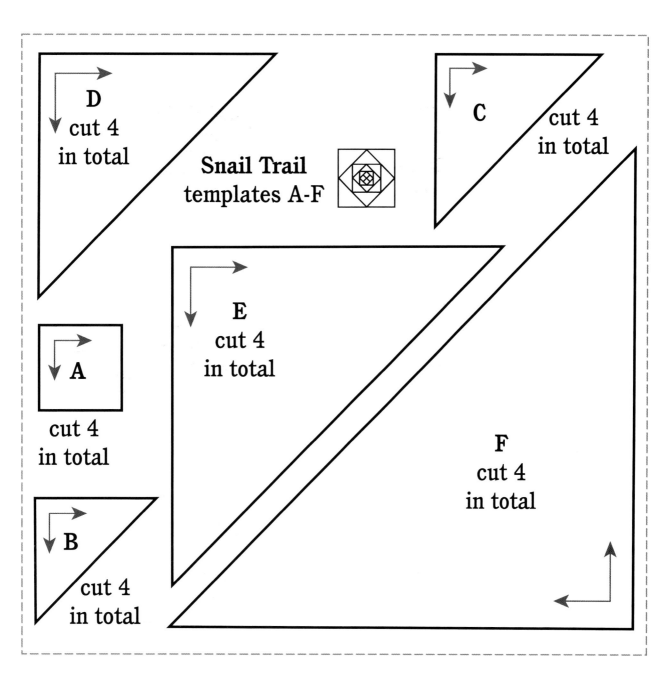

D
cut 4
in total

C
cut 4
in total

E
cut 4
in total

A
cut 4
in total

F
cut 4
in total

B
cut 4
in total

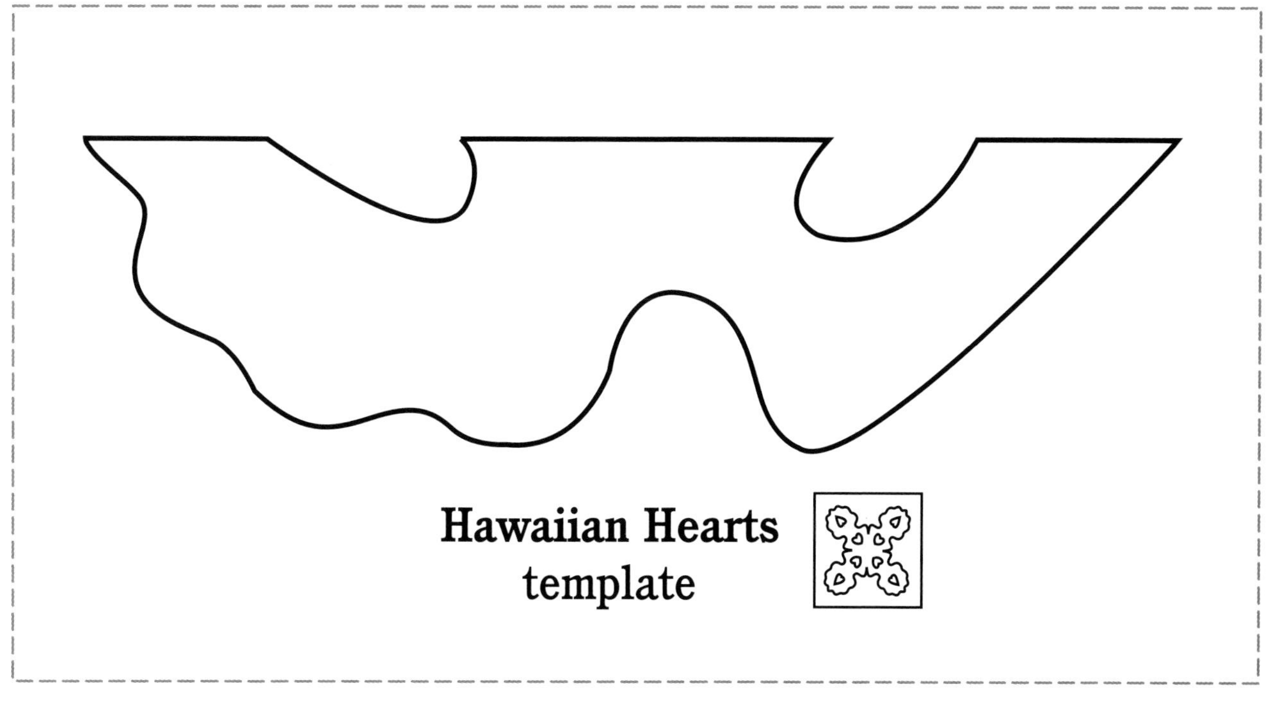

Celtic Knot
template

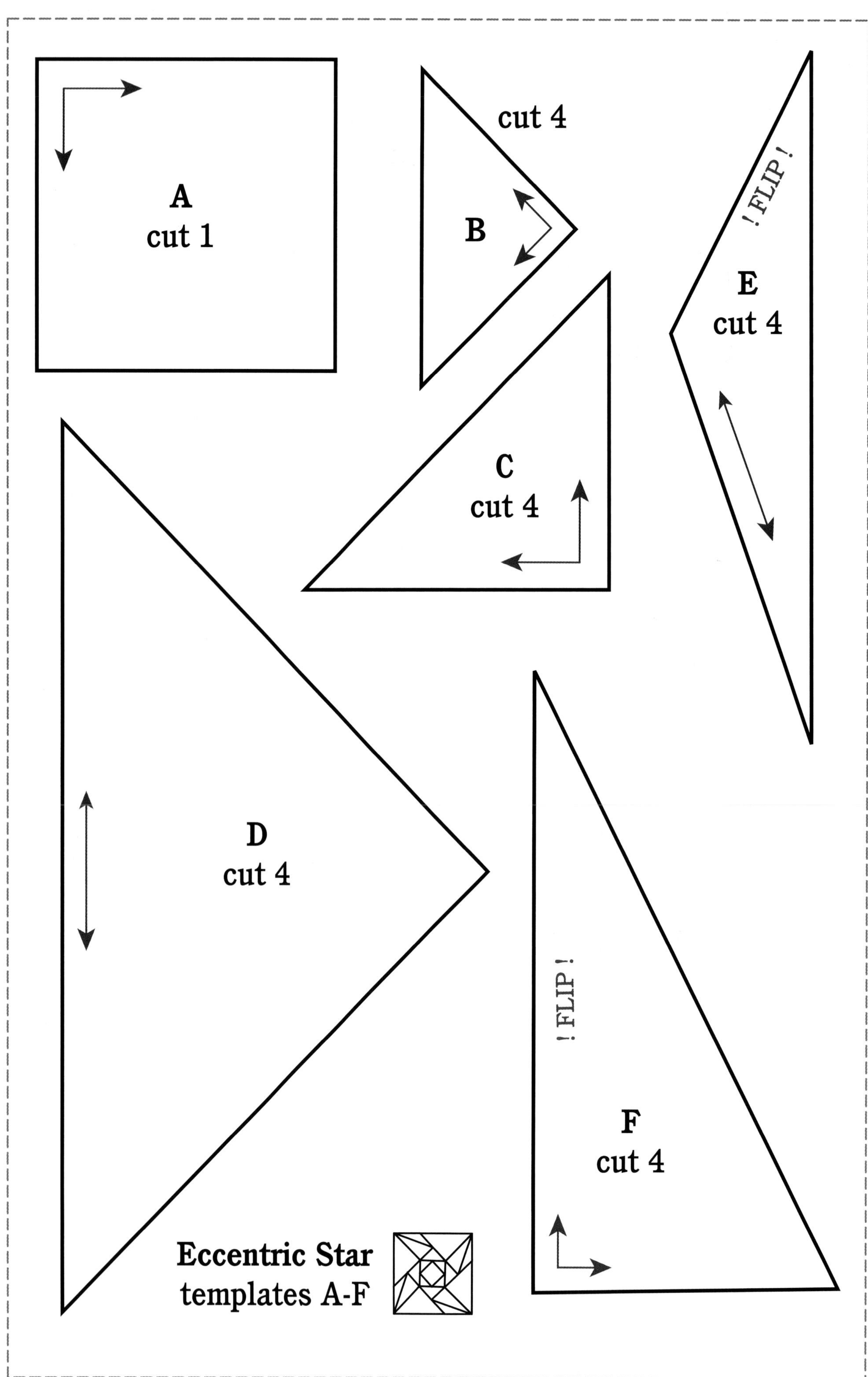
A
cut 1
cut 4
B
! FLIP !
E
cut 4
C
cut 4
D
cut 4
! FLIP !
F
cut 4
Eccentric Star
templates A-F

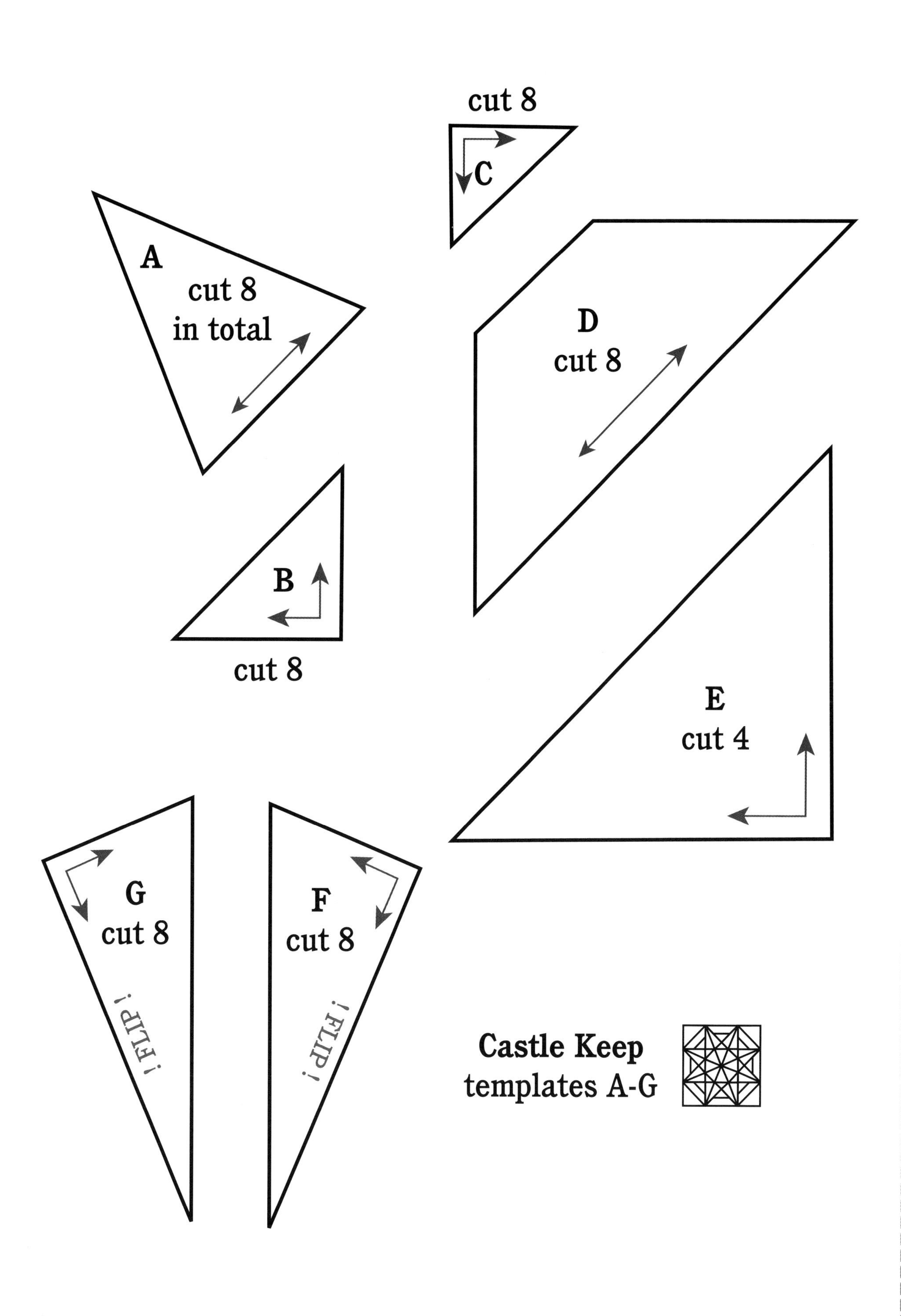
cut 8
C
A
cut 8
in total
D
cut 8
B
cut 8
E
cut 4
G
cut 8
¡FLIP¡
F
cut 8
¡FLIP¡
Castle Keep
templates A-G

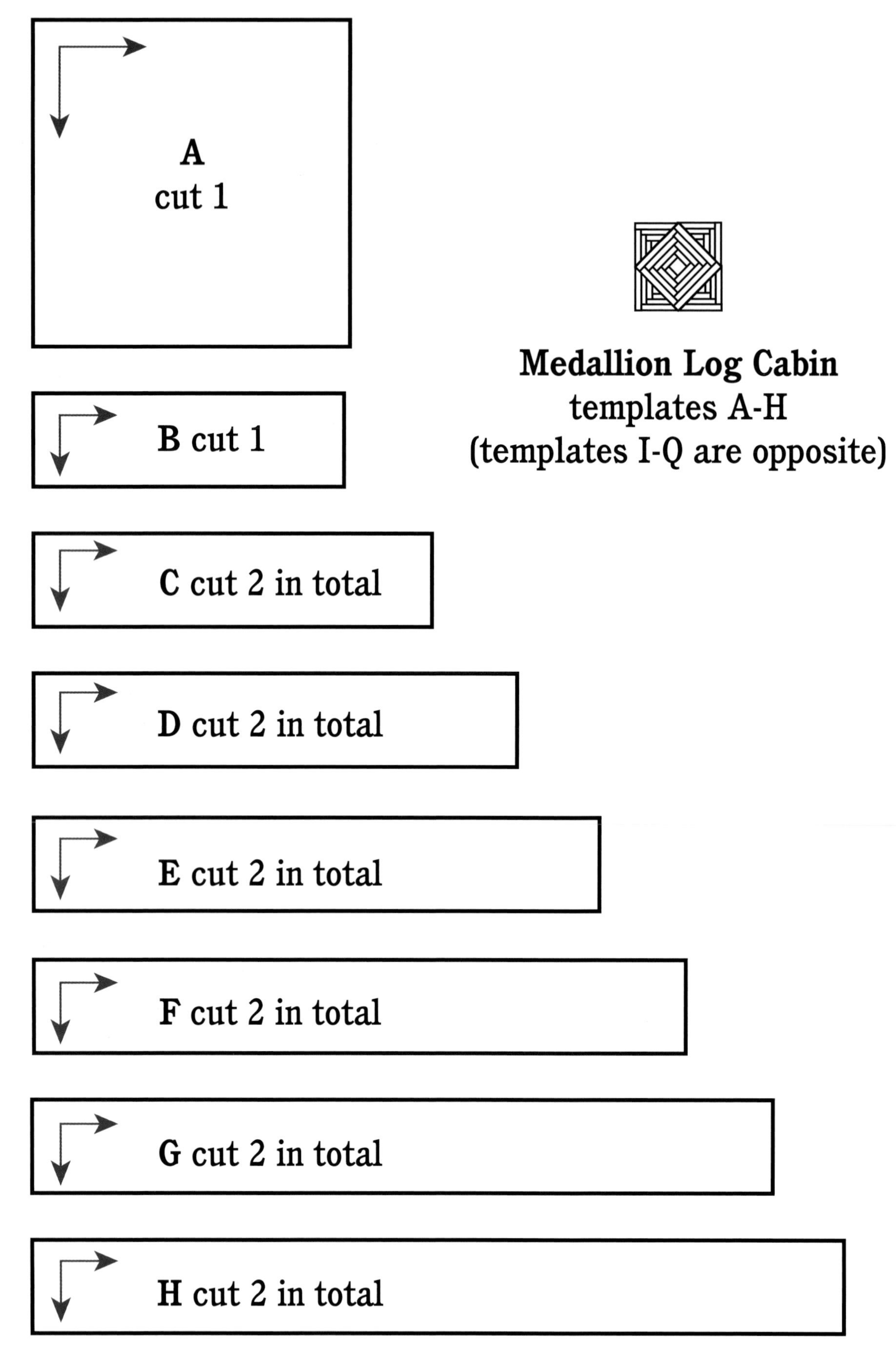

Medallion Log Cabin
templates A-H
(templates I-Q are opposite)

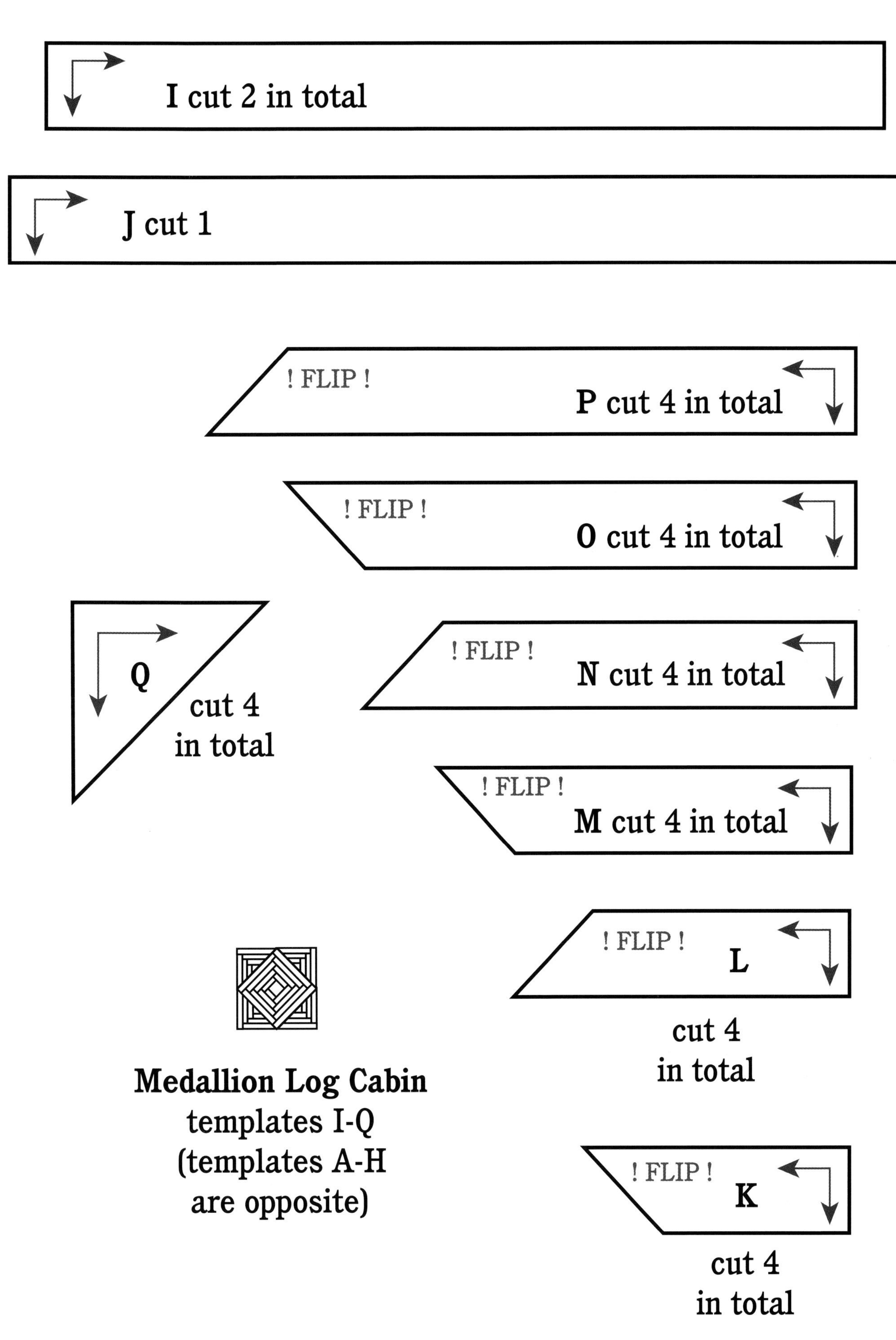

Medallion Log Cabin
templates I-Q
(templates A-H
are opposite)

B
cut 4

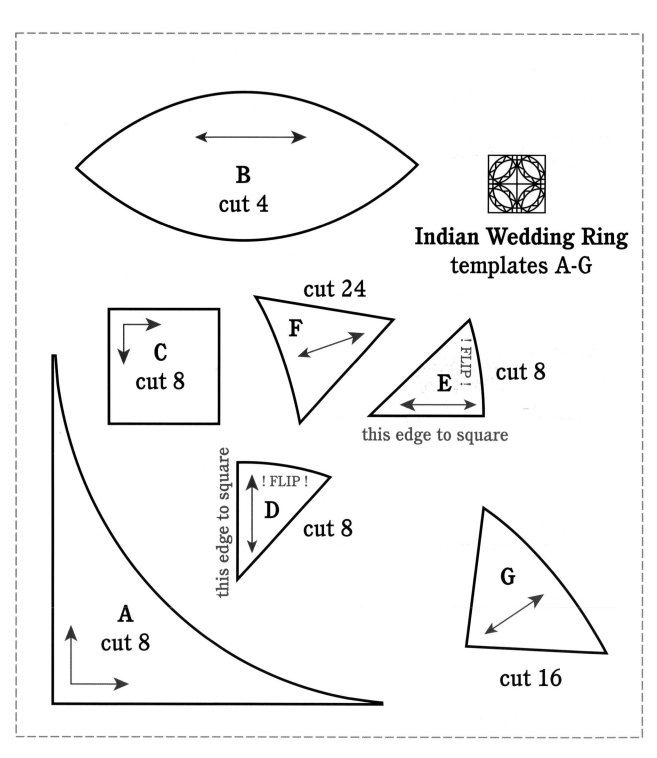

Indian Wedding Ring
templates A-G

cut 24

F

C
cut 8

! FLIP !
E
cut 8

this edge to square

this edge to square

! FLIP !
D
cut 8

G

A
cut 8

cut 16

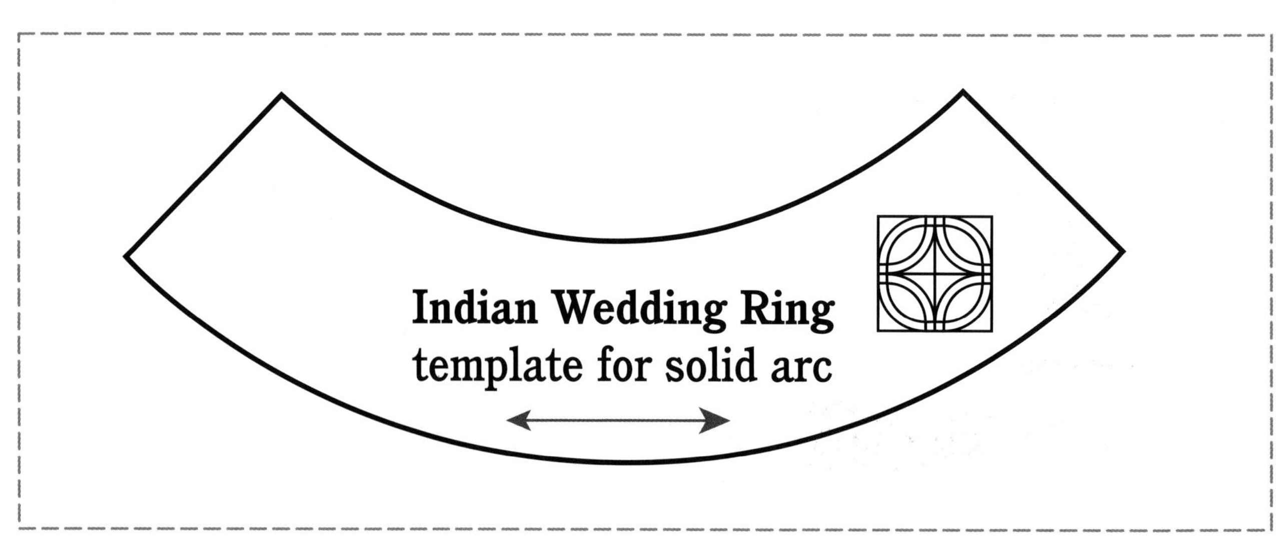

D
cut 4

B
cut 4

! FLIP !

A
cut 4

! FLIP !

C
cut 4 in
foundation
fabric

Rocky Road to Kansas
templates A-D

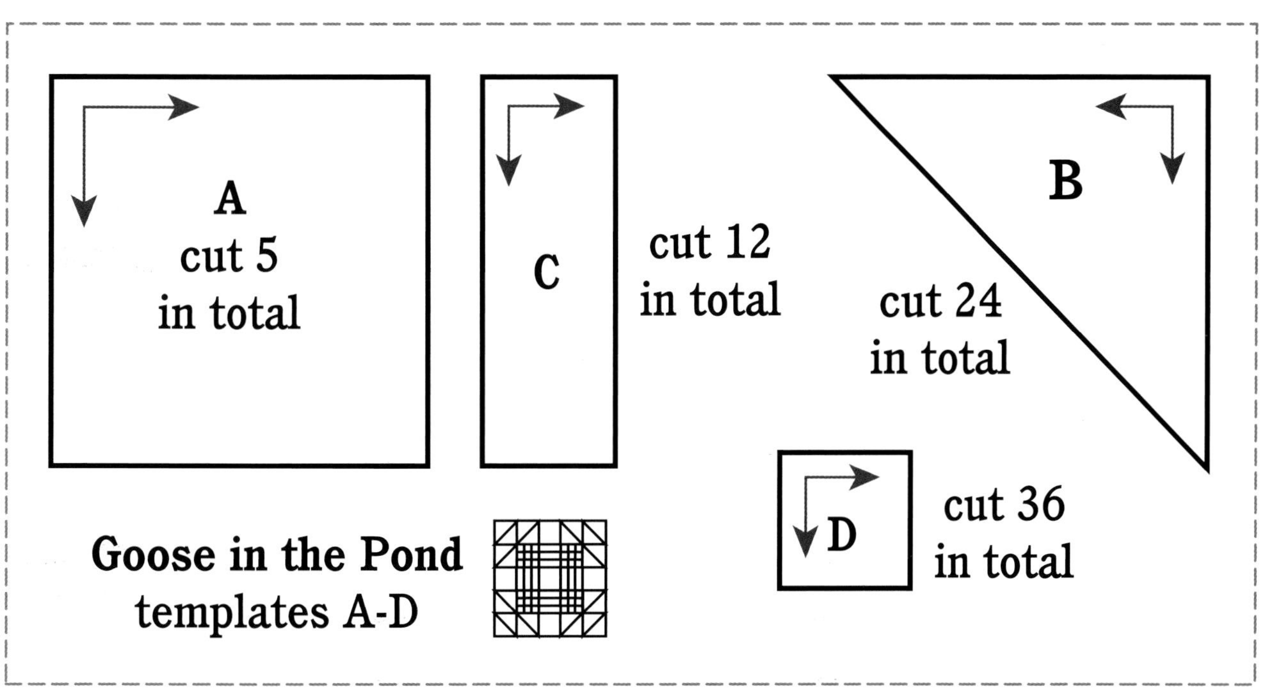

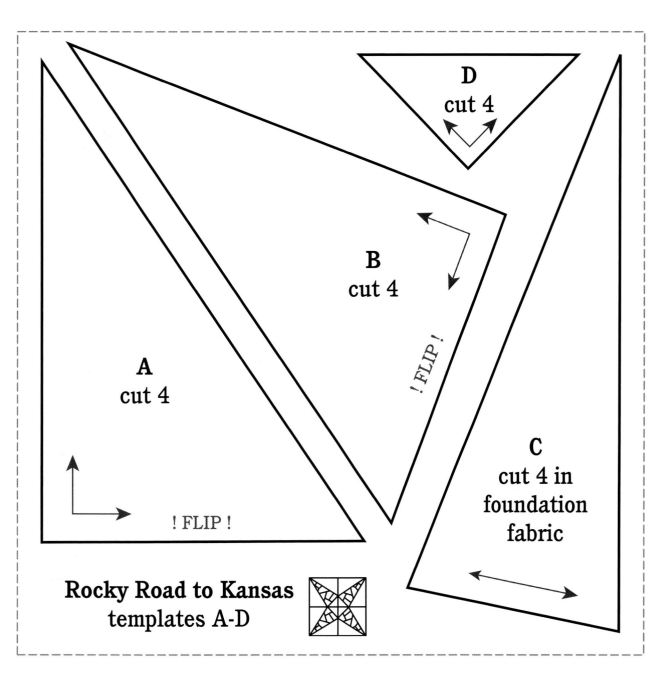

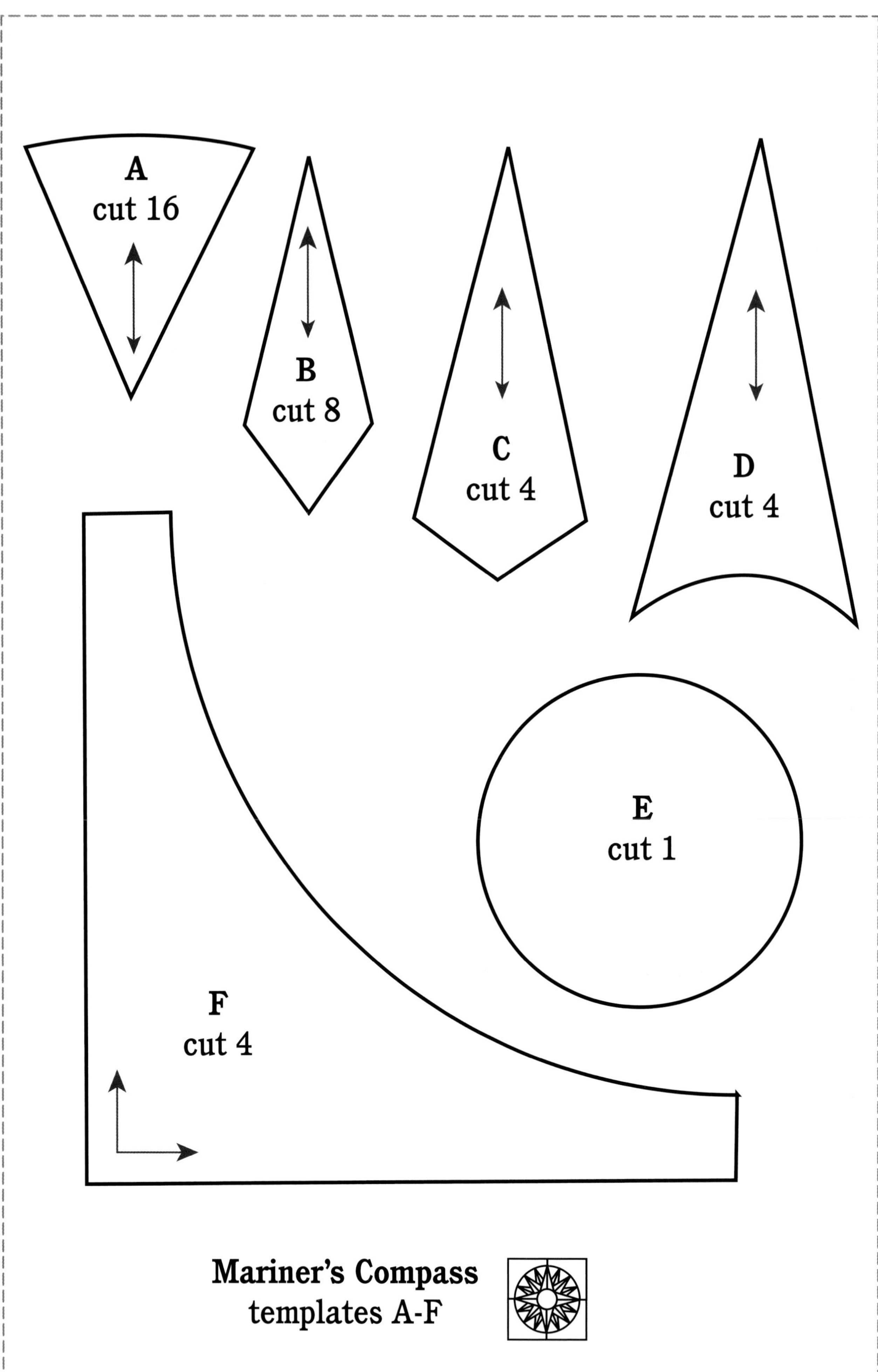

Mariner's Compass
templates A-F

A
cut 1

C
cut 4

D
cut 12
in total

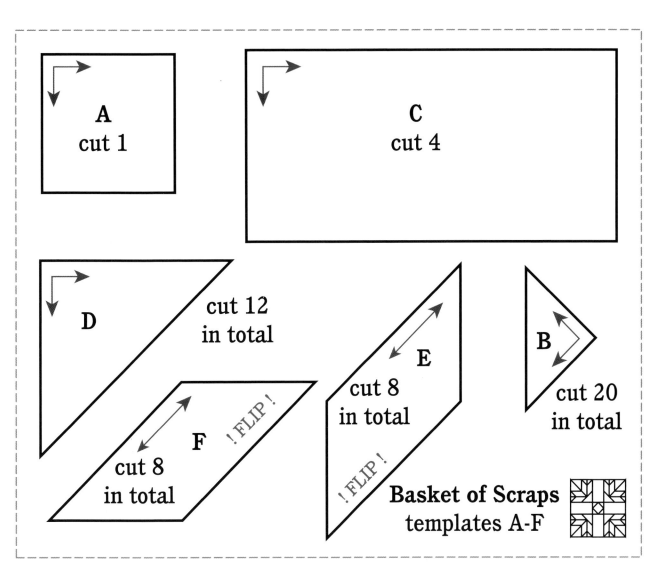

E
cut 8
in total
! FLIP !

B
cut 20
in total

F
! FLIP !
cut 8
in total

Basket of Scraps
templates A-F

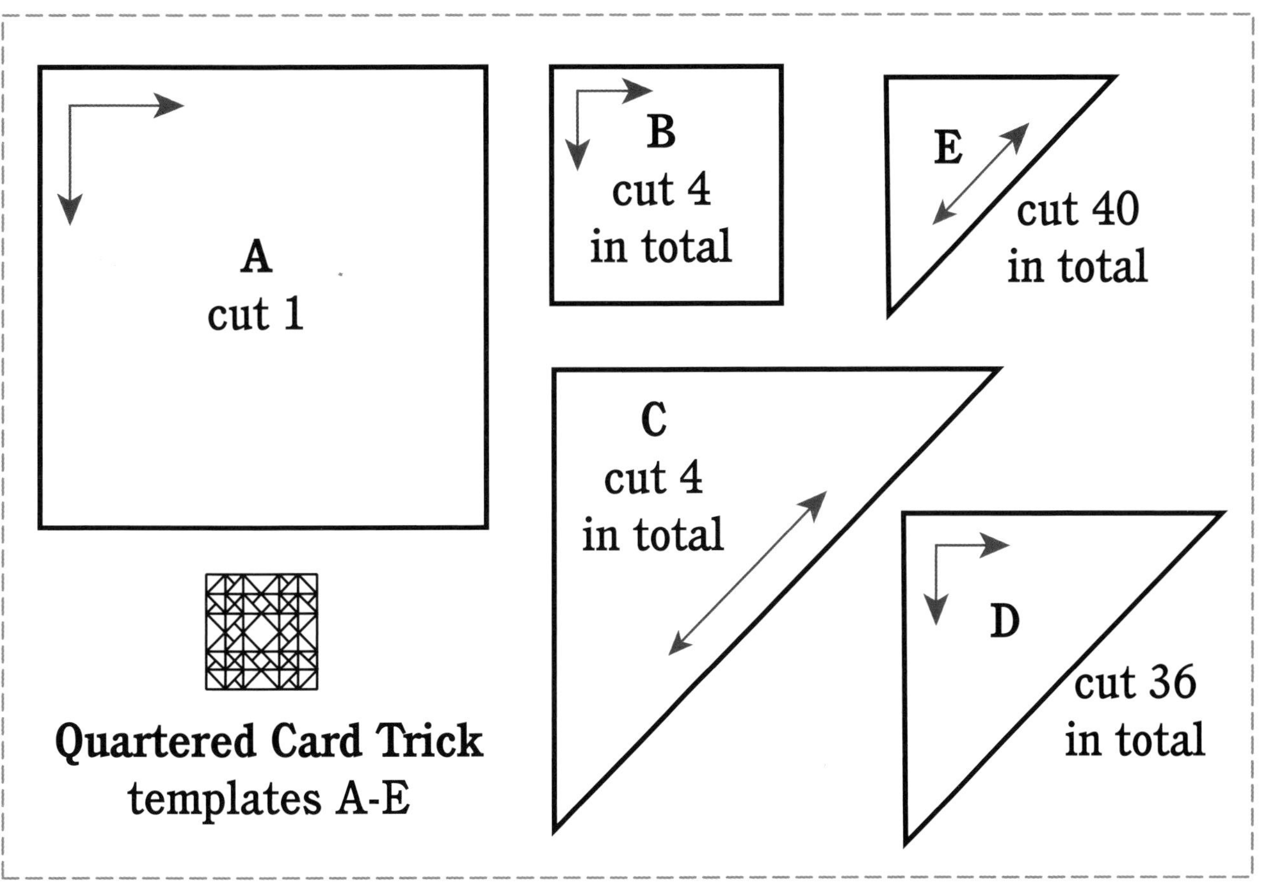

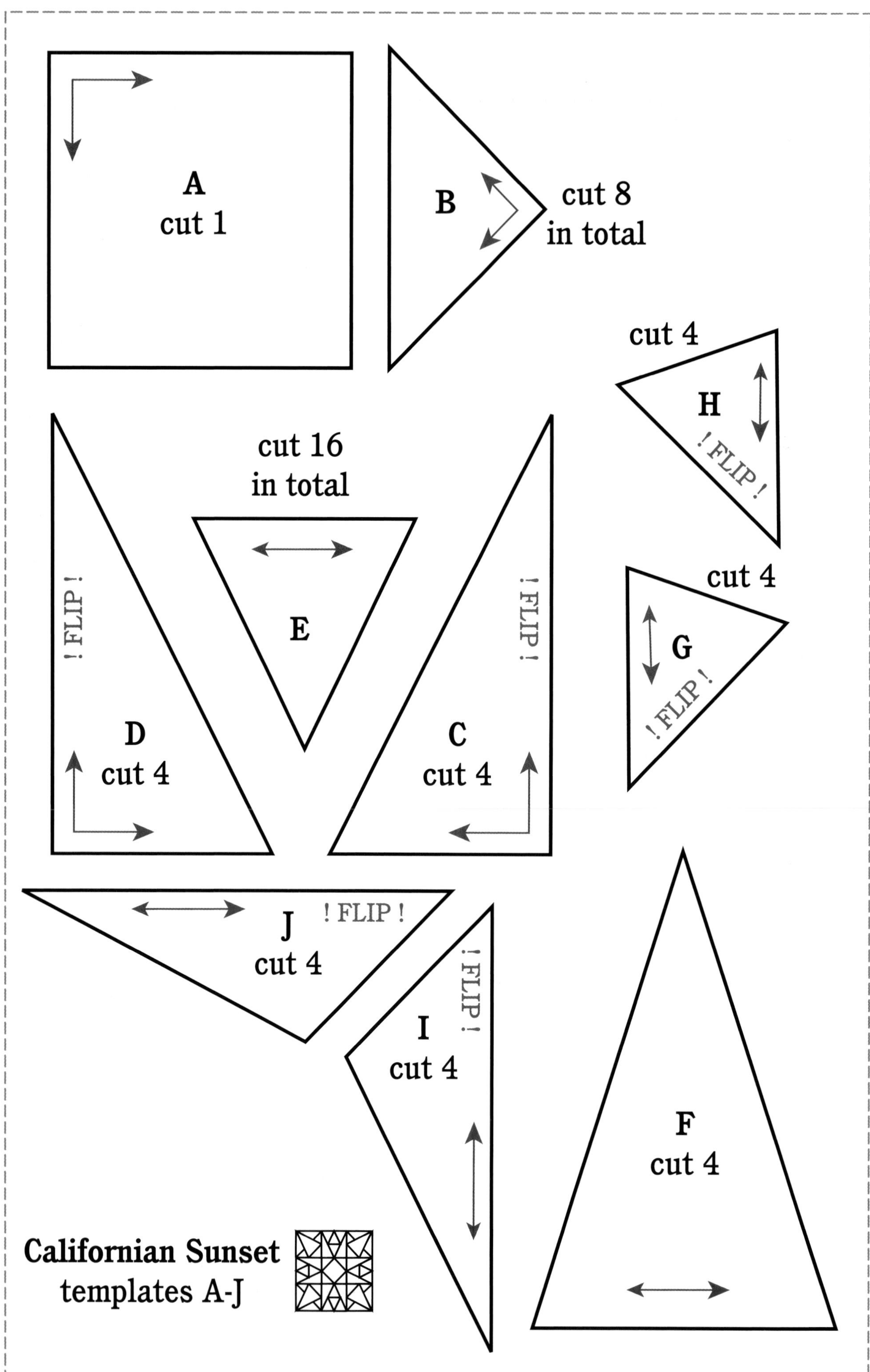
A
cut 1
B
cut 8
in total
cut 4
H
! FLIP !
cut 16
in total
E
! FLIP !
! FLIP !
cut 4
G
! FLIP !
D
cut 4
C
cut 4
J
! FLIP !
cut 4
! FLIP !
I
cut 4
F
cut 4
Californian Sunset
templates A-J

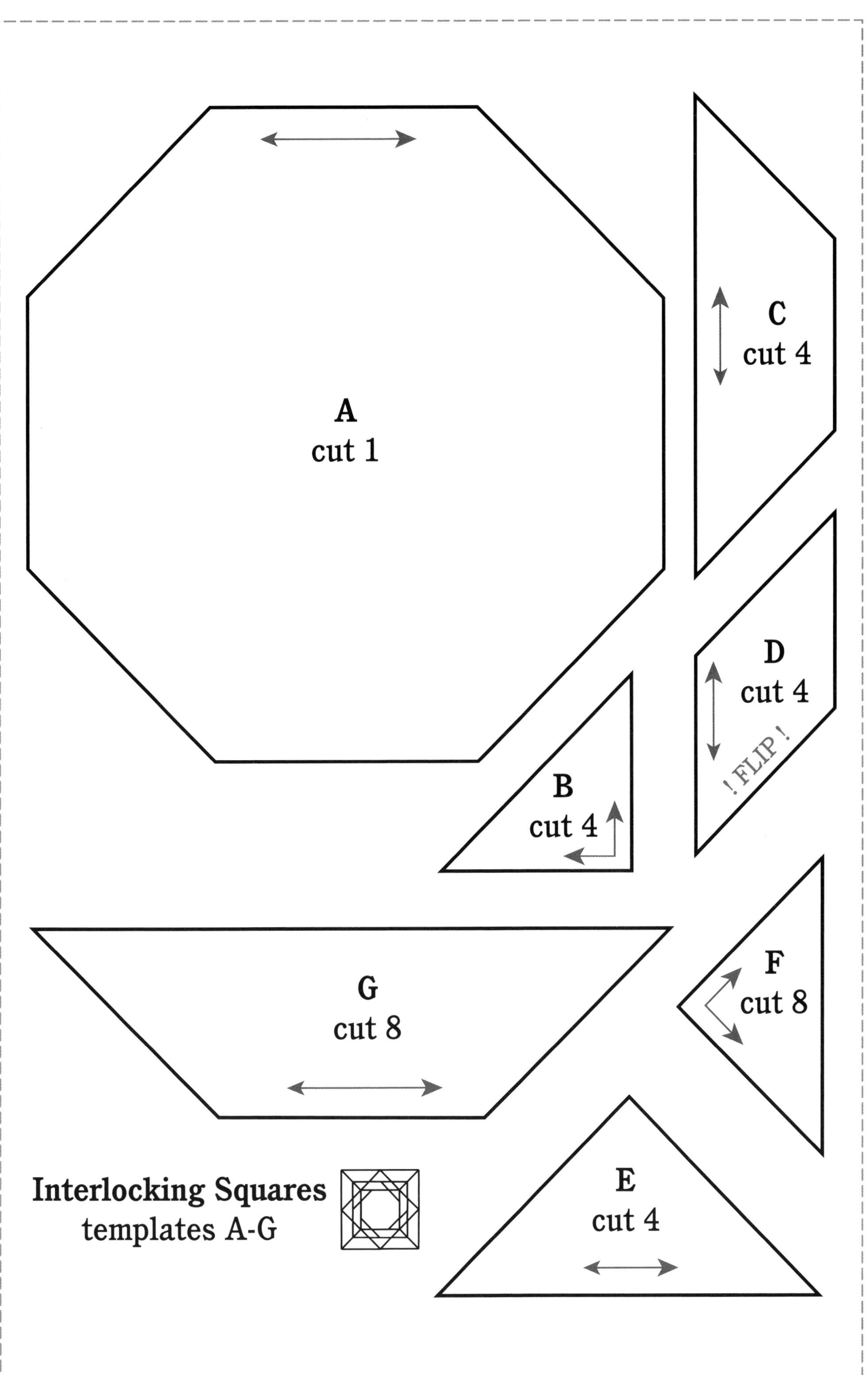
A
cut 1
C
cut 4
D
cut 4
! FLIP !
B
cut 4
G
cut 8
F
cut 8
E
cut 4
Interlocking Squares
templates A-G

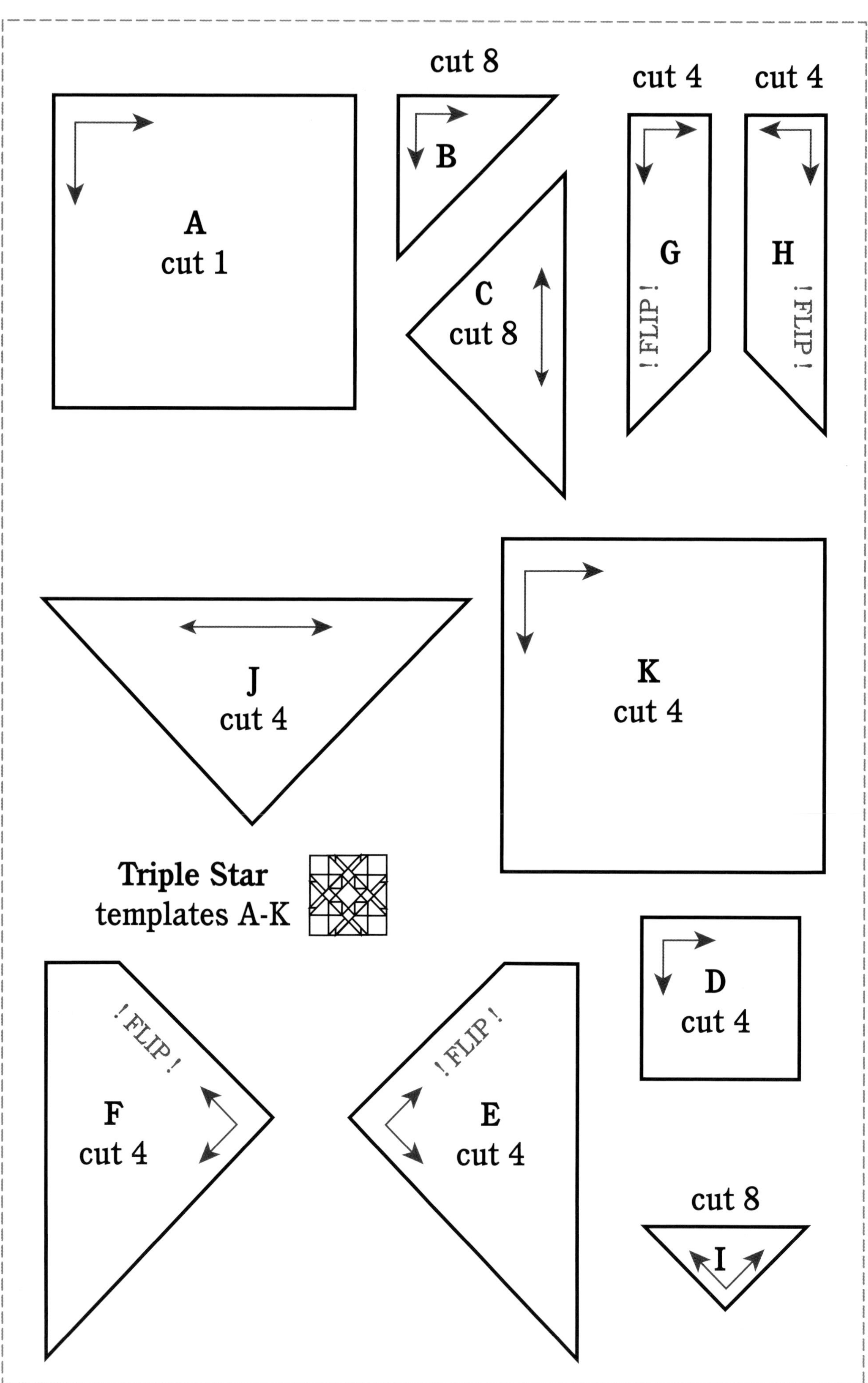
cut 8
cut 4
cut 4
B
A
cut 1
G
H
C
cut 8
! FLIP !
! FLIP !
J
cut 4
K
cut 4
Triple Star
templates A-K
D
cut 4
! FLIP !
! FLIP !
F
cut 4
E
cut 4
cut 8
I

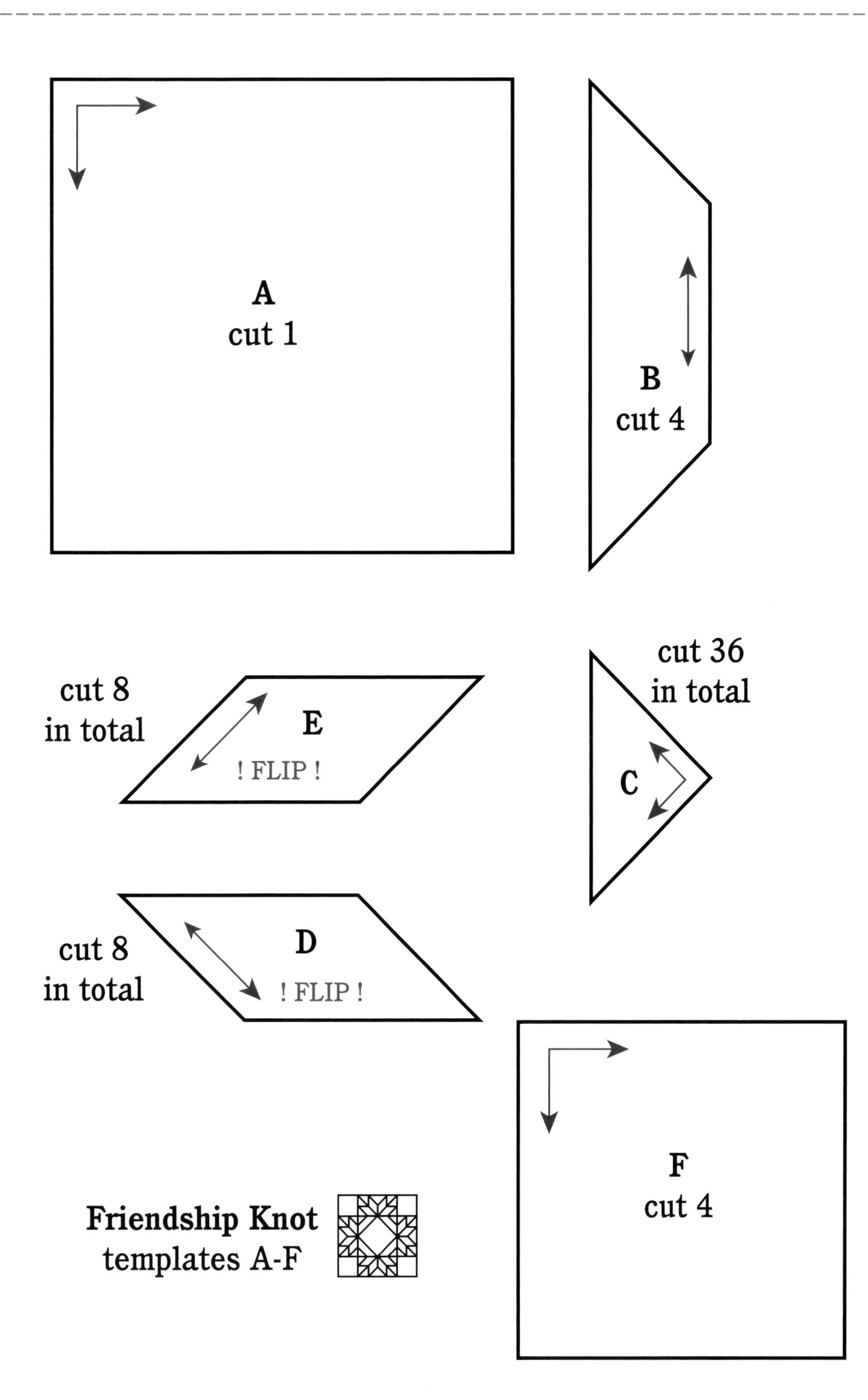
A
cut 1
B
cut 4
cut 36
in total
cut 8
in total
E
! FLIP !
C
D
cut 8
in total
! FLIP !
F
cut 4
Friendship Knot
templates A-F

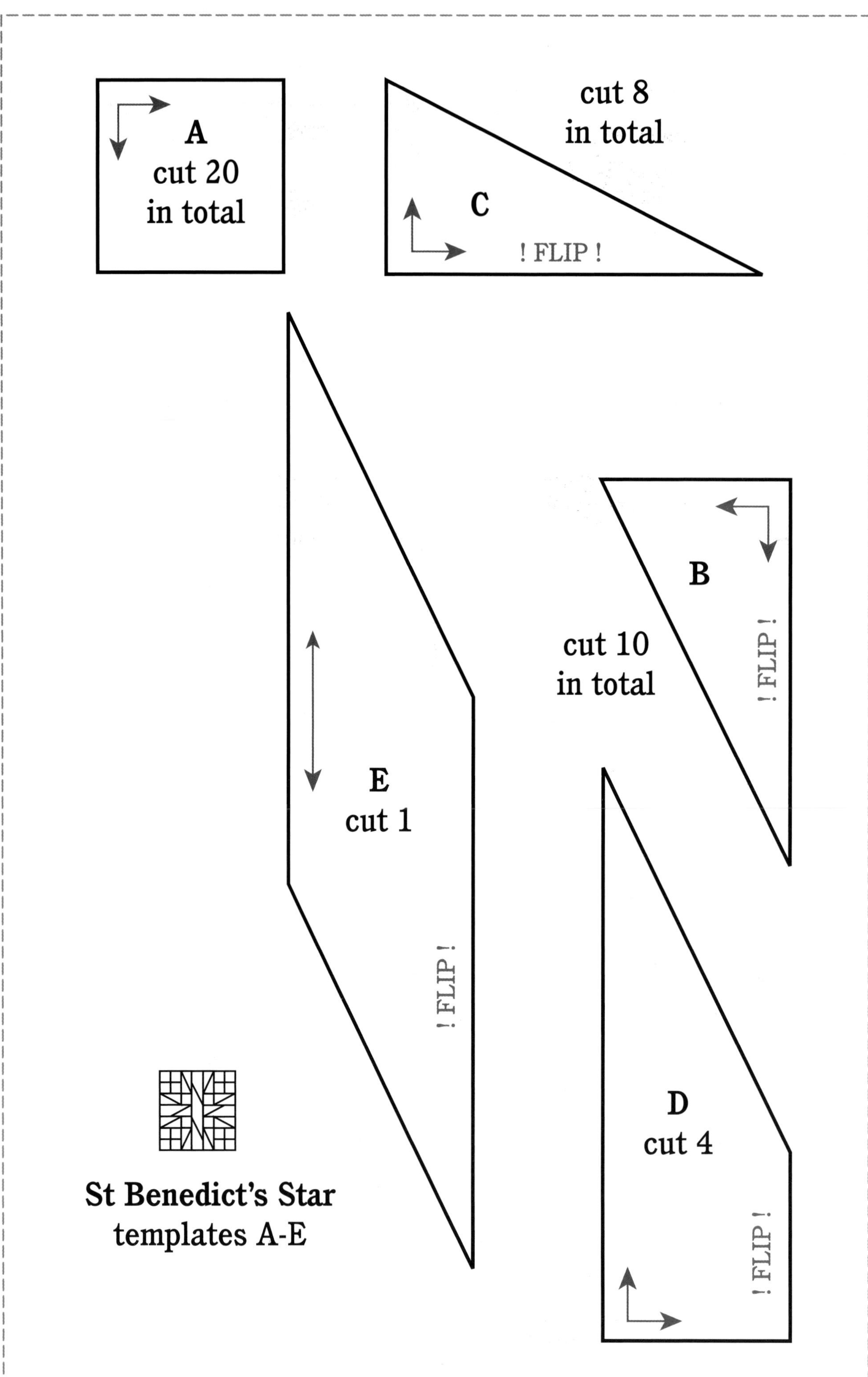
A
cut 20
in total
cut 8
in total
C
! FLIP !
E
cut 1
! FLIP !
B
cut 10
in total
! FLIP !
D
cut 4
! FLIP !
St Benedict's Star
templates A-E

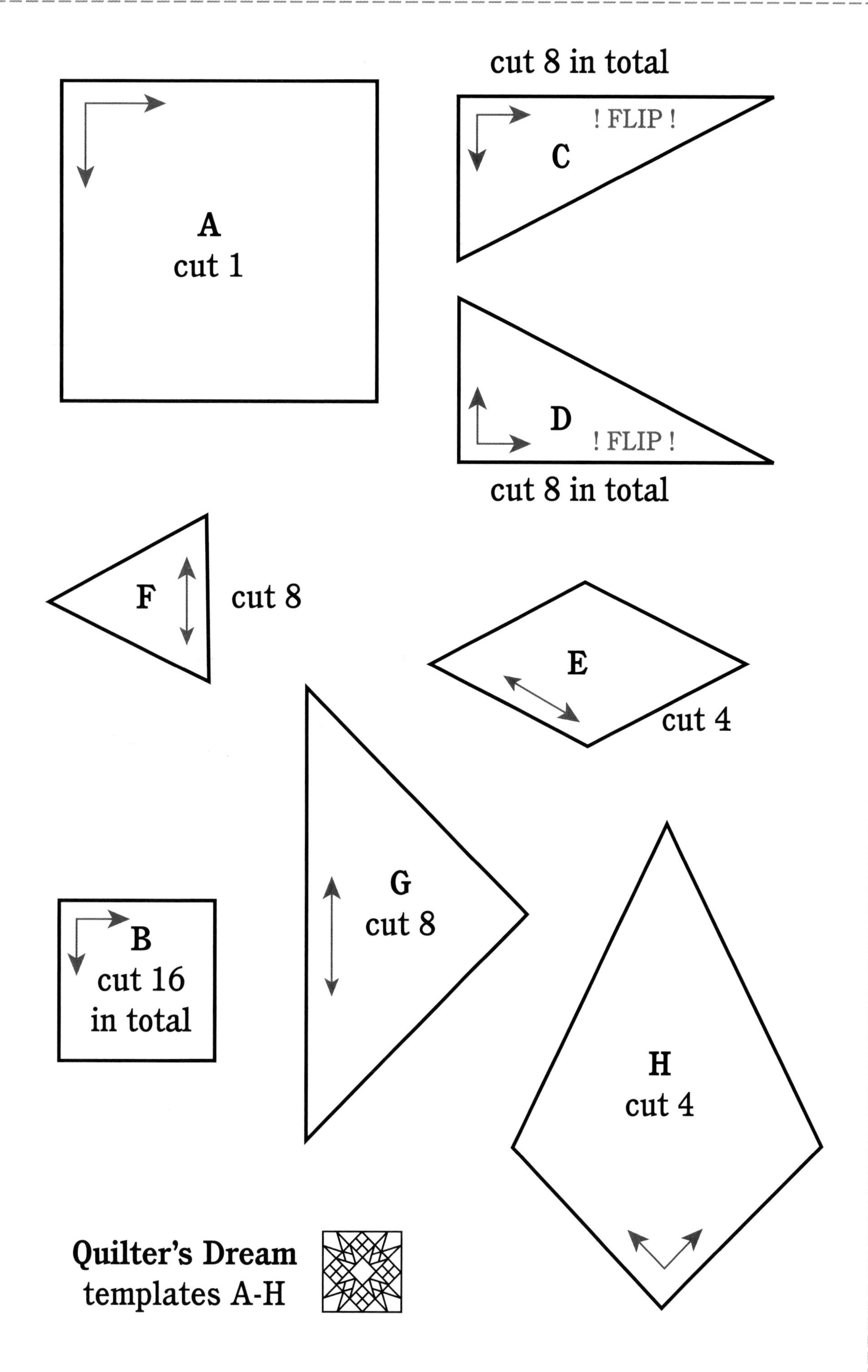
cut 8 in total
! FLIP !
C
A
cut 1
D
! FLIP !
cut 8 in total
F
cut 8
E
cut 4
G
cut 8
B
cut 16
in total
H
cut 4
Quilter's Dream
templates A-H

Drafting your own blocks

If you'd like to draft your own versions of the blocks to different sizes, this section will show you how to draw up each block that I've used in *Constant Inspiration*. When you're used to the technique, you'll find that you can work out how to draft many other blocks once you've studied the grids they're based on. For drafting your own blocks you'll need the following:

- A4 pad of 5mm squared paper
- sharp pencil
- pale crayons
- eraser
- pen (eg a fineliner)
- ruler measuring 18in (46cm), showing both inches and centimetres
- protractor
- pair of compasses

Each block begins with a basic underlying grid; using a crayon and ruler, draw the relevant grid at the correct size on a sheet of 5mm squared paper. Draw this underlying grid in pale crayon, then draw the construction lines necessary for each block in pencil. Once all the lines are in position, go over the ones that form the block in pen; look carefully at each block design, as not all the lines you use to construct it will necessarily become part of the finished design. The final diagram in each construction sequence shows you the templates you'll need to cut for your patches; refer to my full-size templates for each block (see pp75-95) to see the relevant SG (straight grain) arrows and any mirror-image markings. Make and cut your templates in the usual way (see p11).

Once you've learnt how to draft (or draw) the individual blocks on squared paper, cut a piece of card which measures the finished size of the block (remember: this can be any size you choose, you don't have to stick to my choice) and then reproduce your block within this square – then all you have to do is cut out the templates that you need.

On page 7 you'll find guidelines on calculating fabric and wadding requirements; once you've decided on the finished size of your blocks, you can use these guidelines to work out your requirements for quilts of different sizes.

Basic grids

To create a basic 2 x 2 (4-patch) grid, draw a square and mark the halfway points on each side. Join these to create four equal squares (**a**).

a

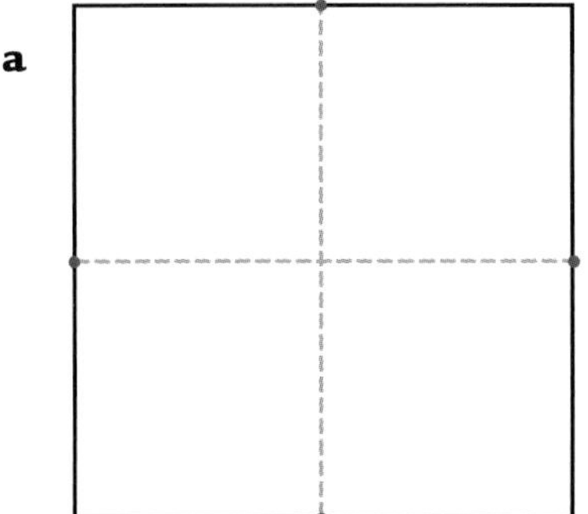

To create a basic 3 x 3 (9-patch) grid, draw a square and divide each side equally into three. Join these points to create nine equal squares (**b**).

b

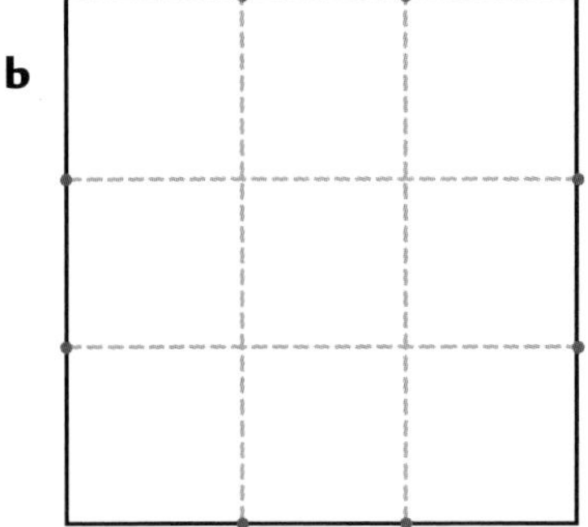

To create a basic 4 x 4 grid, draw a square and divide each side equally into four. Join these points to create 16 equal squares (**c**).

To create a basic 5 x 5 grid, draw a square and divide each side equally into five. Join these points to create 25 equal squares (**d**).

c

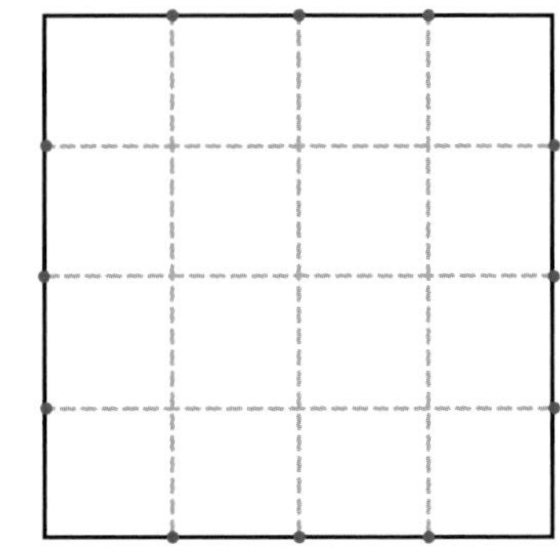

d

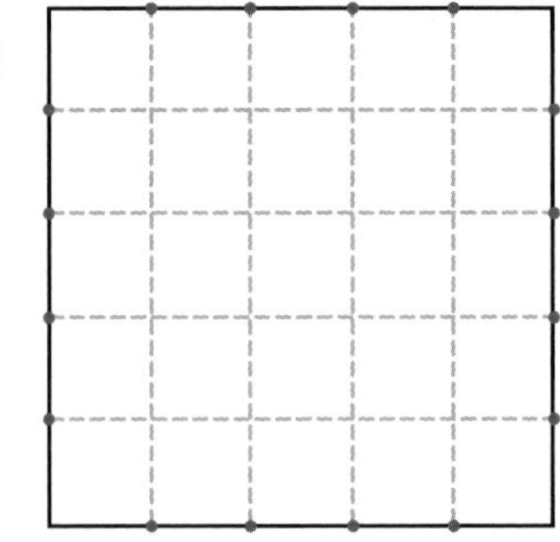

Use the same principle to create any other even grid that your design requires – for instance, a 6 x 6 grid (**e**), a 7 x 7 (**f**), an 11 x 11 grid (**g**) – used for Trip Around the World – and so on. Use a calculator to help you with trickier divisions (for instance 25cm ÷ 7, or 12 ÷ 5 etc).

e

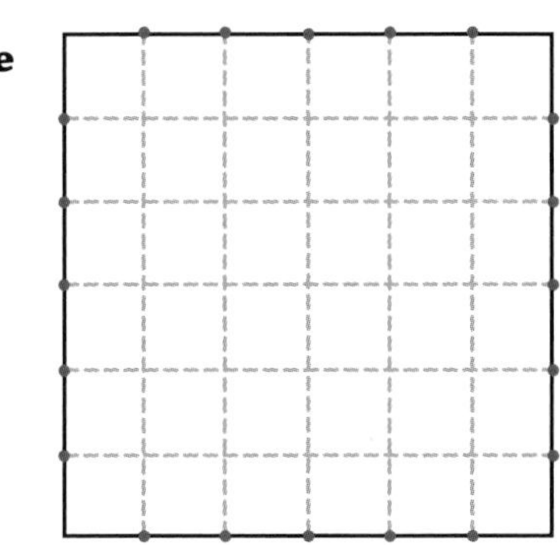

f

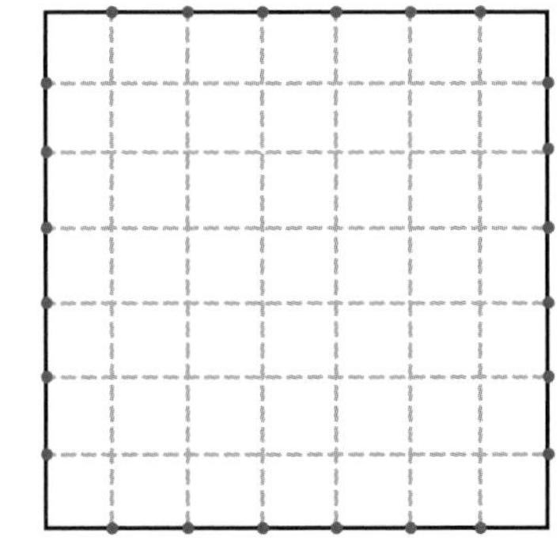

g

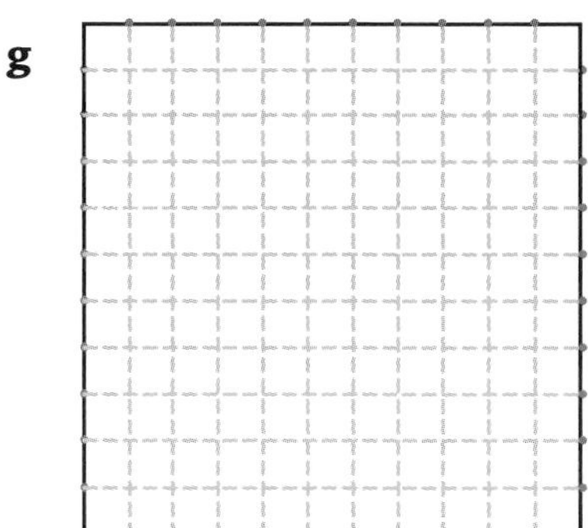

d

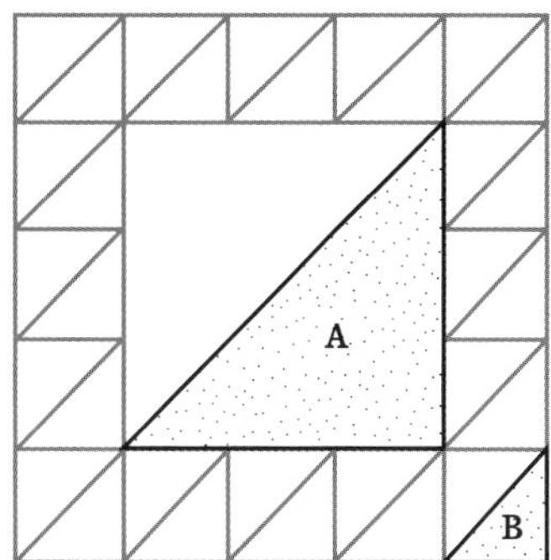

Lady of the Lake

Begin with a basic 5 x 5 grid (see p96). Draw a straight line from one corner of the square to the opposite one to mark the full diagonal (**a**).

a

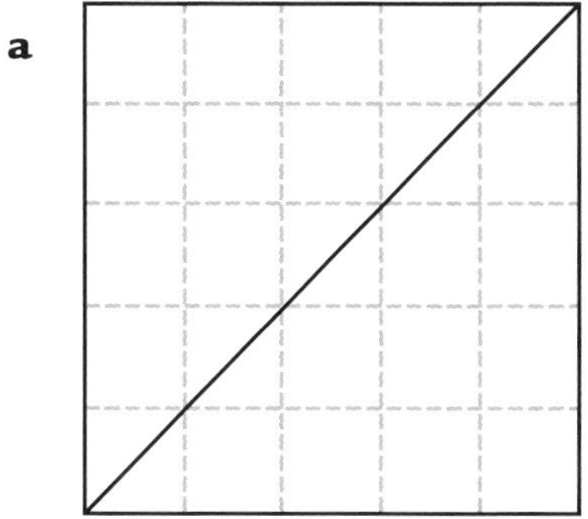

Use the division marks along each side to draw in horizontal and vertical lines as shown (**b**).

b

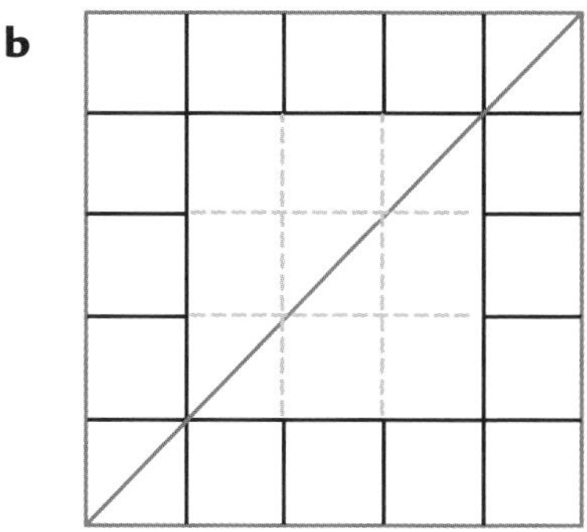

Using the ruler parallel with the main diagonal, draw in the diagonals of all the smaller squares (**c**). Diagram (**d**) shows the two templates required.

c

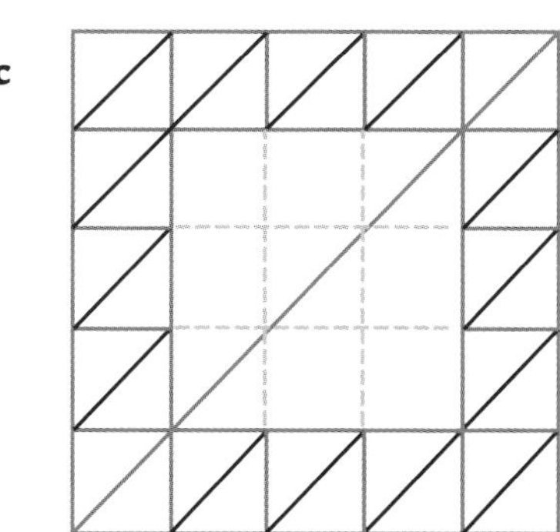

Dresden Plate

Begin with a basic 2 x 2 grid (see p96). Using a pair of compasses, draw two circles (**a**); the smaller one will become the centre of your plate, and the larger one the area covered by the petals. Remember to leave enough room outside the larger circle for the curved tops of the petals.

a

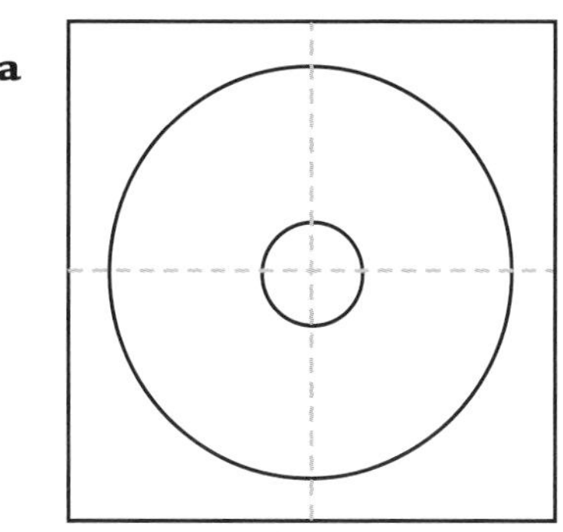

Using a protractor, divide each of the large quarter-circles into segments (**b**) as follows:

- for a 20-petal plate, each segment will be 18°
- for an 18-petal plate, each segment will be 20°
- for a 15-petal plate, each segment will be 24°
- for a 12-petal plate, each segment will be 30°

Using a ruler, draw in all the lines to divide the circle; make sure that each line goes right through the centre of the circle. The diagrams show the segments for 20 petals (**c**), 18 petals (**d**), 15 petals (**e**) and 12 petals (**f**).

b

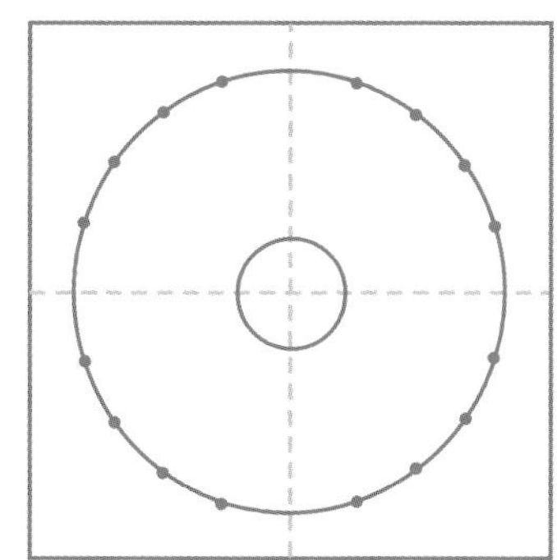

Add a smooth curve at the top of one segment to create the top of the petal (**g**).

c

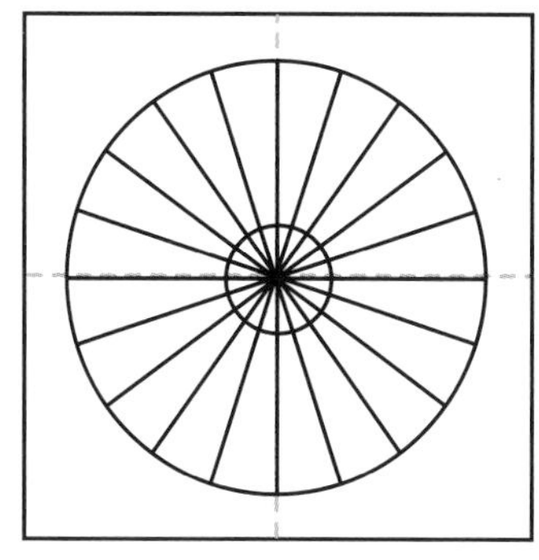

d

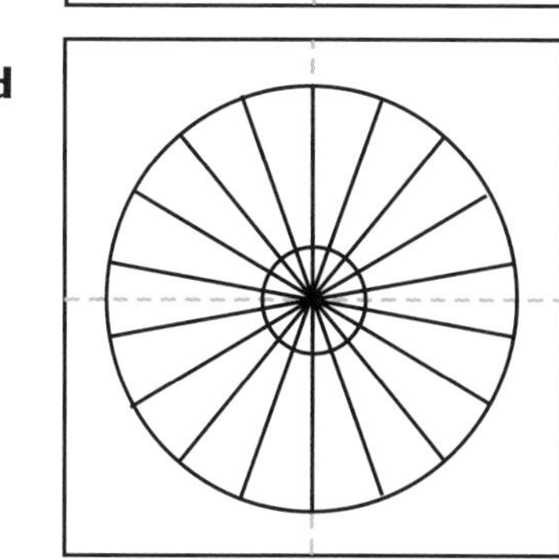

e

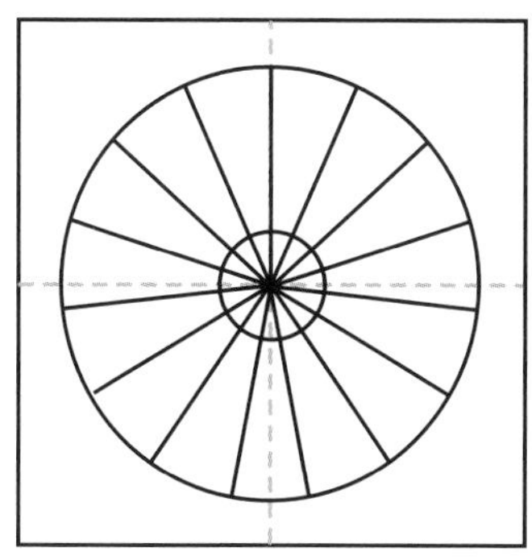

f

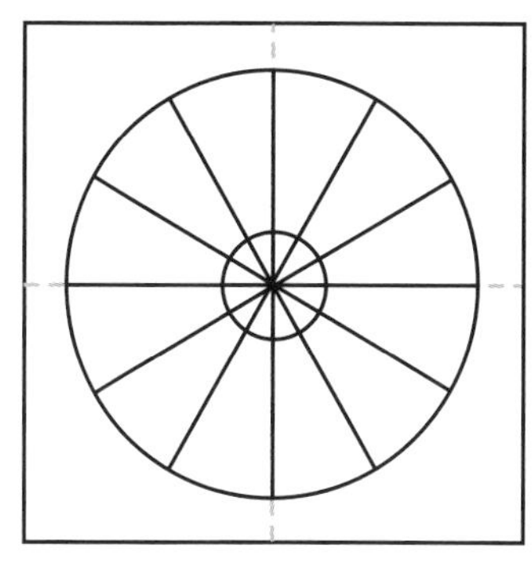

g

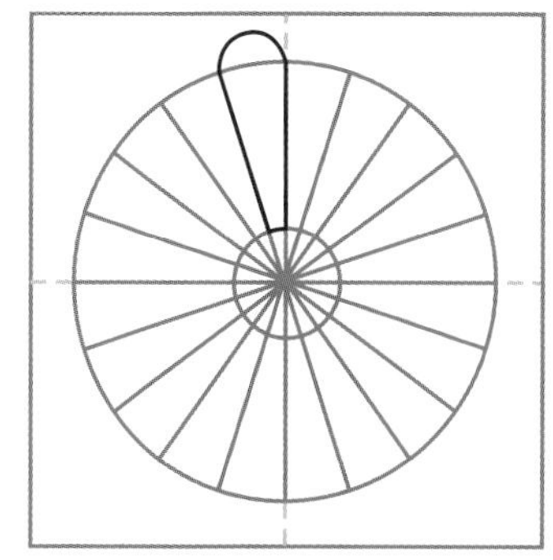

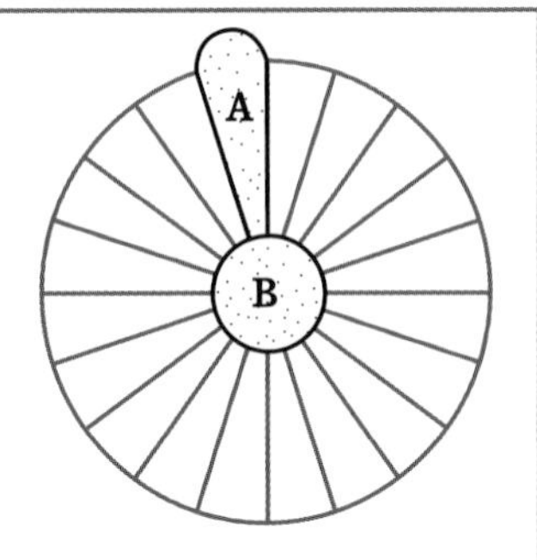

Diagram (**h**) shows the two templates required for a 20-petal plate.

Storm at Sea

Begin with a basic 4 x 4 grid (see p96). Draw in horizontal and vertical lines as shown (**a**).

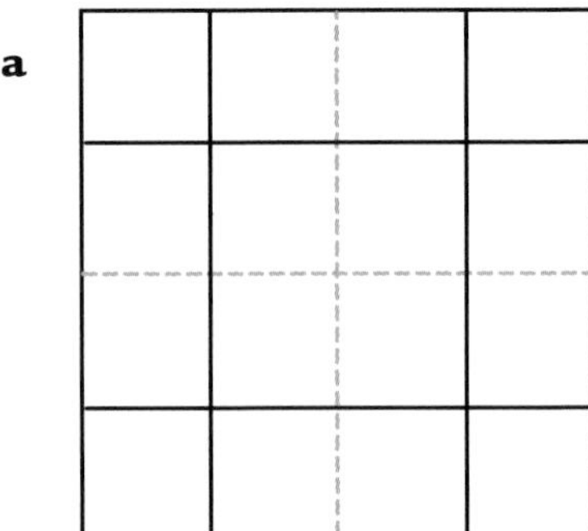

Mark the half-way point on each side of the central square and draw a square 'on point' within it; do the same with the four corner squares (**b**).

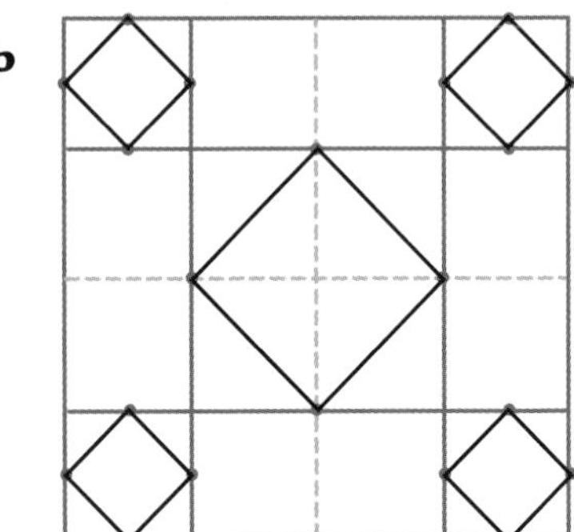

Mark the half-way points on the sides of each rectangle and draw a diamond within each one (**c**).

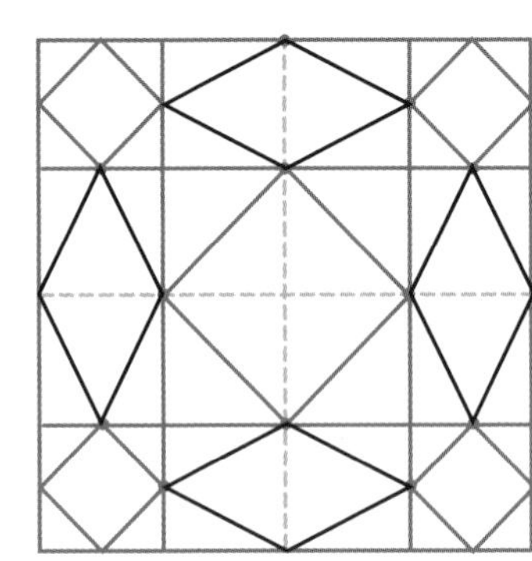

Diagram (**d**) shows the 7 templates required.

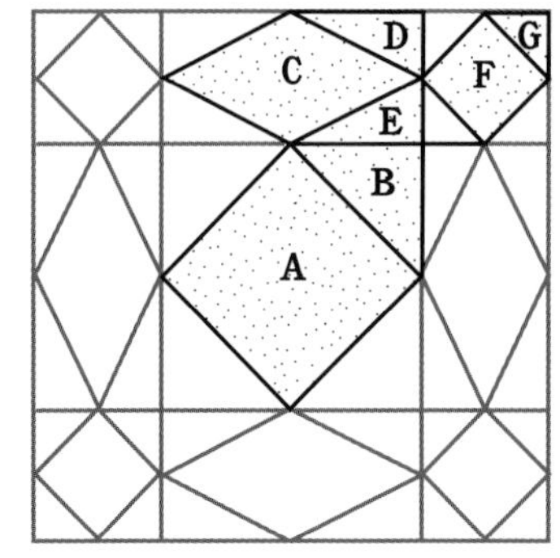

Basketweave

Begin with a basic 2 x 2 (4-patch) grid (see p96); draw in the horizontal and vertical half-way lines, and the full diagonals (**a**).

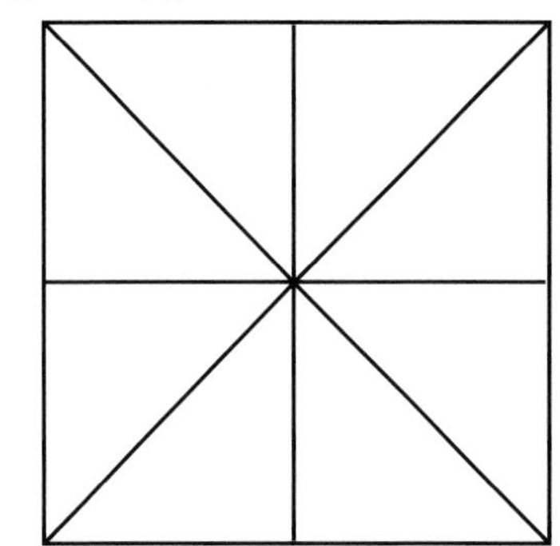

Using a protractor, mark the half-way point in each of the eight sections (22.5°); join these marks across the square with long lines (**b**) – make

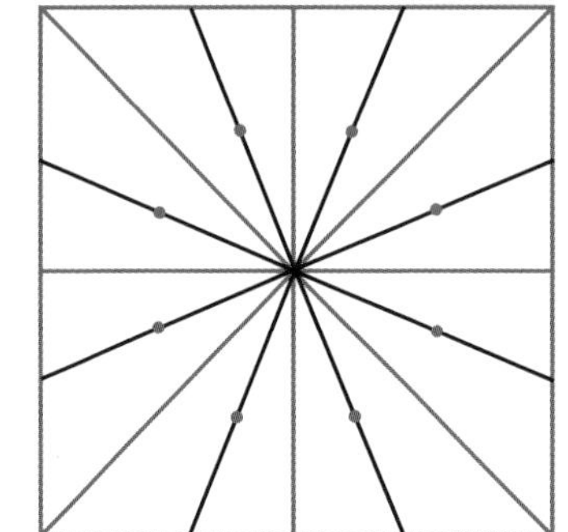

sure that each line passes through the centre of the design, otherwise your final templates won't be accurate.

Using the new points that these lines have created on the outside of the square, draw two vertical and two horizontal lines (**c**). Using the same marks, draw two rectangles diagonally across the design (**d**).

Diagram (**e**) shows the 3 templates required; note the shapes of the templates carefully, as not all the lines you've drawn appear on the final block design.

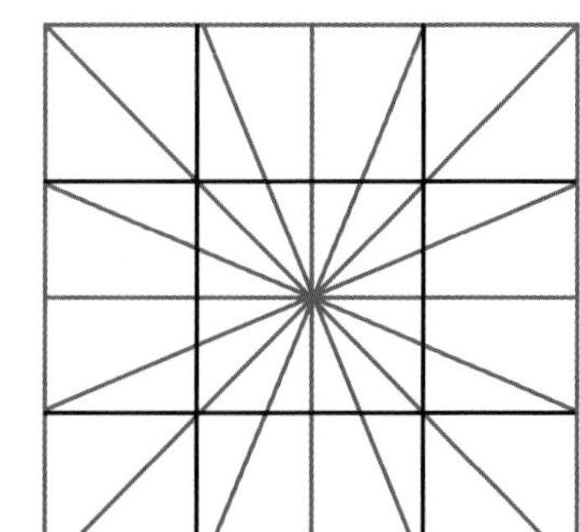

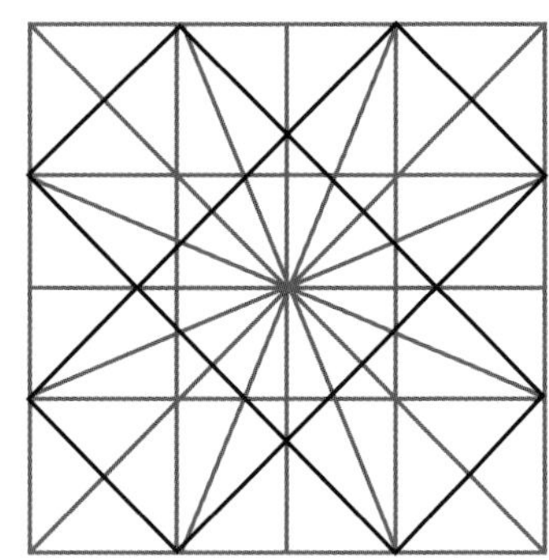

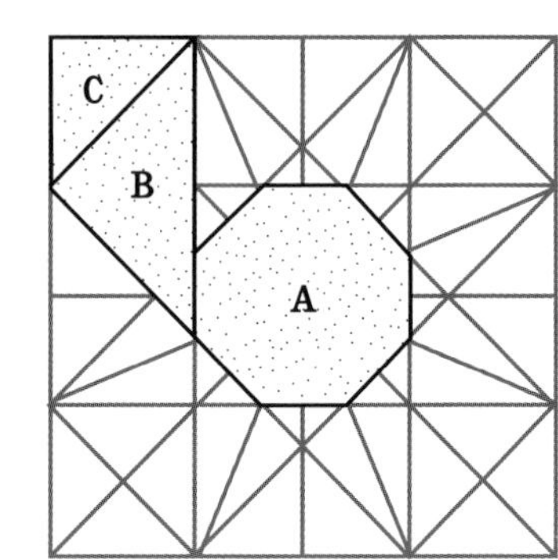

Bear's Paw

Begin with a basic 7 x 7 grid (see p96). Use the central division marks to position two parallel lines, one set vertically and one horizontally. Add the shorter lines shown to create five small squares in each corner of the design as shown (**a**).

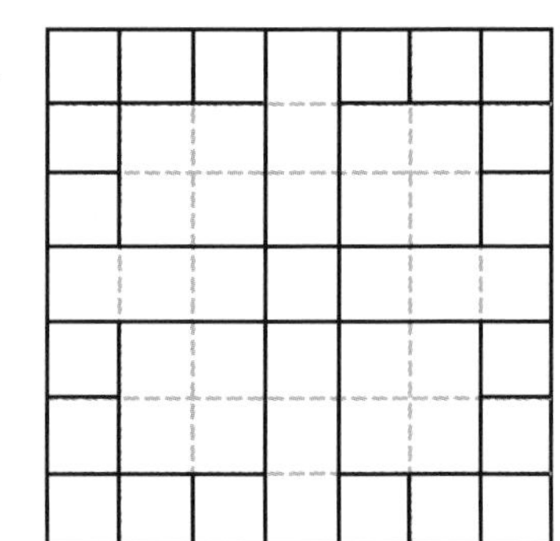

Draw a diagonal line across each small square (apart from the corner ones) as shown (**b**).

Diagram (**c**) shows the four templates required.

b

c

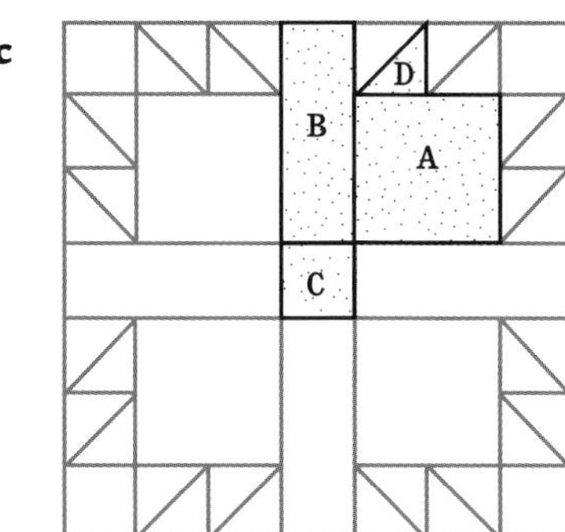

Celtic Knot

If you'd like to use my Celtic Knot design in a block of a different size, simply enlarge or reduce it on a photocopier until it's the required size. (Remember to leave at least ½in/1cm between the knot and the edge of the block all around the edge.) If you'd like to choose from a wider selection of Celtic knot patterns, see the Further Reading section on p109.

Snail Trail

Begin with a basic 2 x 2 grid (see p96). Join the half-way marks along each side to create a second square 'on point' (**a**).

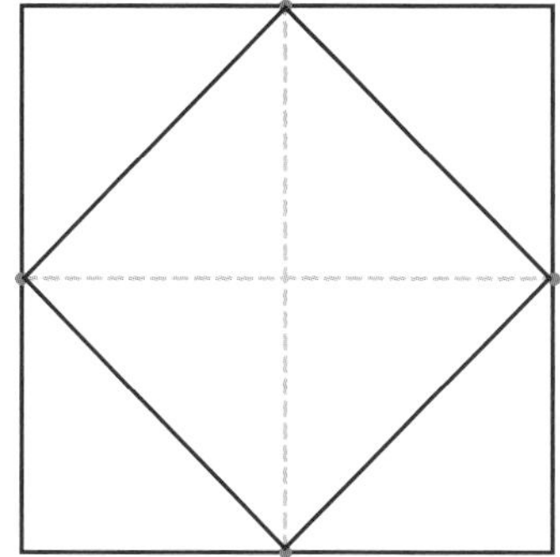

Mark the half-way points along the sides of the new square (the easiest way to do this is by placing your ruler across the full diagonal of the block); use these marks to draw a third square (**b**).

b

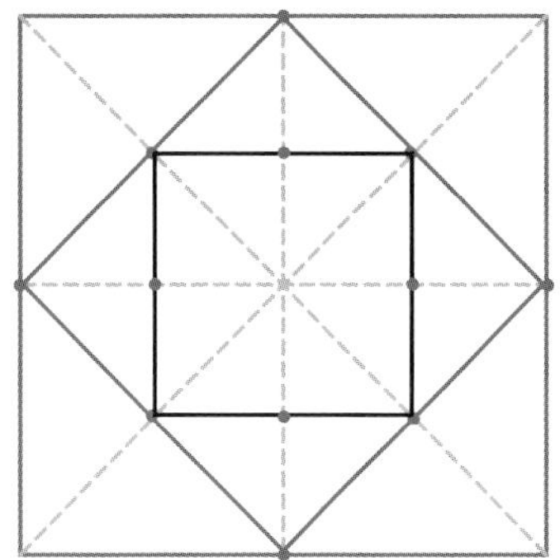

Join the half-way points along the sides of this next square to create a fourth square (**c**).

c

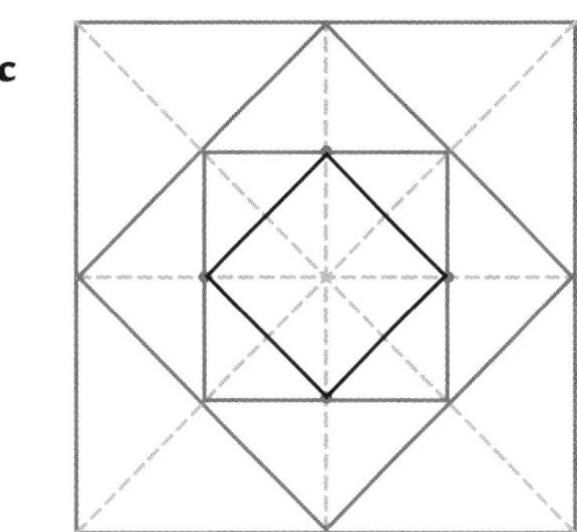

Once you've added as many squares as you want, divide the central square into four smaller squares (**d**); diagram (**e**) shows the 6 templates required for the version of the block I've used in my quilt.

d

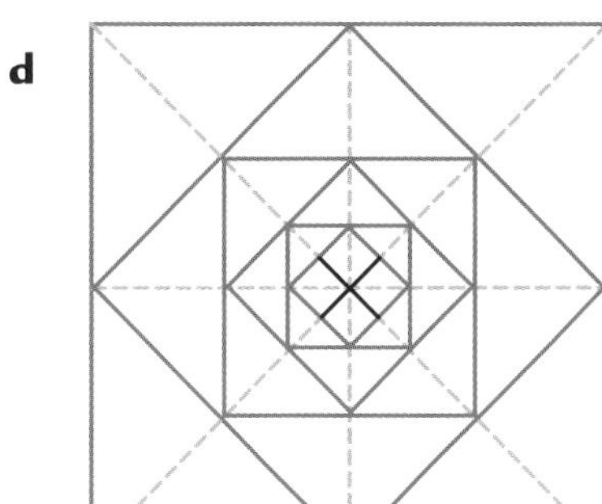

e

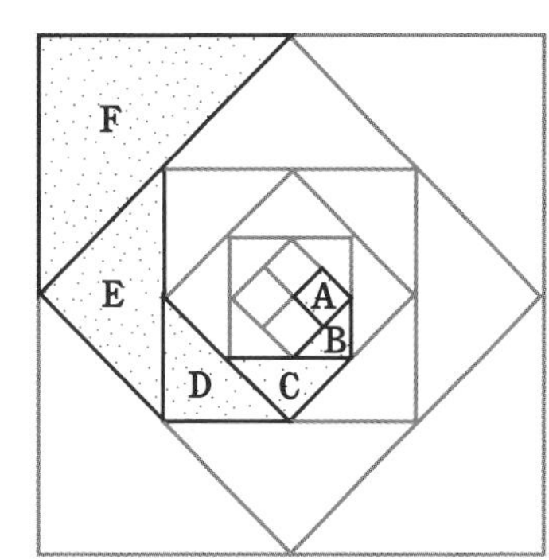

You can alter the block by using different numbers of squares; diagram (**f**) shows the effect of drawing three inner squares, (**g**) shows four, and (**h**) shows five.

f

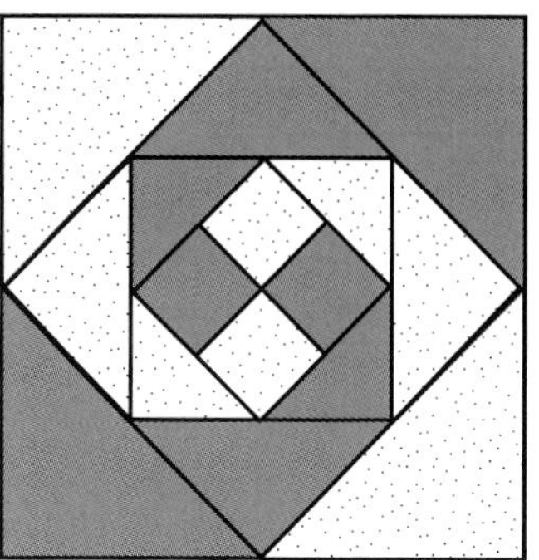

g

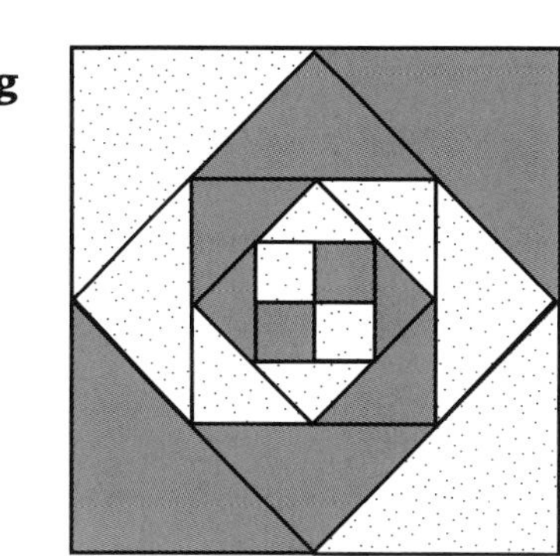

h

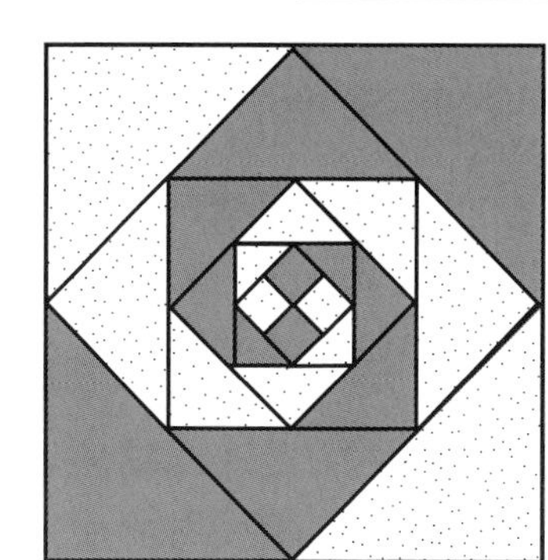

Trip Around the World

Begin with a square marked into an 11 x 11 grid (see p97). Draw in one horizontal and vertical line as shown (**a**); the square created in the corner is your template (**b**). If you want to draw in the other lines, you can then photostat the design and use it as a grid to try out your colour-schemes.

a

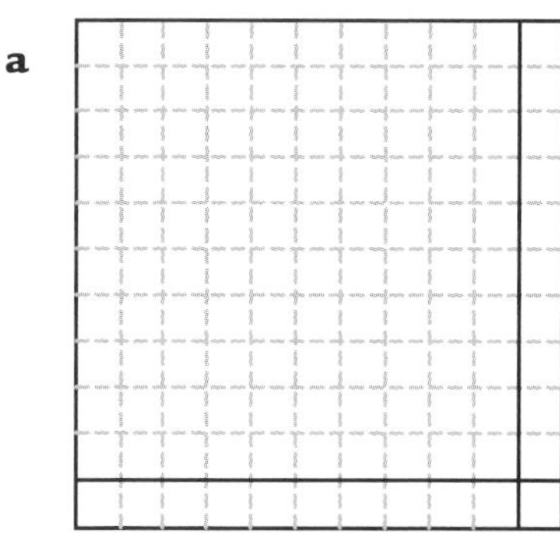

b

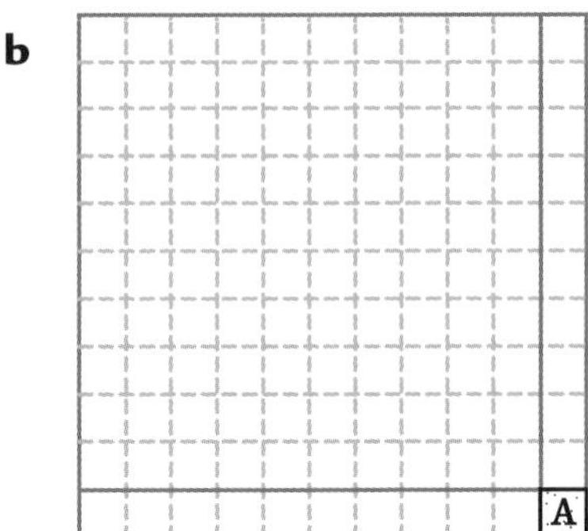

You can create a Trip Around the World grid with any odd number of squares in each direction; the diagrams show the effect of working with an 11 x 11 grid (**c**), a 9 x 9 grid (**d**), and a 7 x 7 grid (**e**).

c

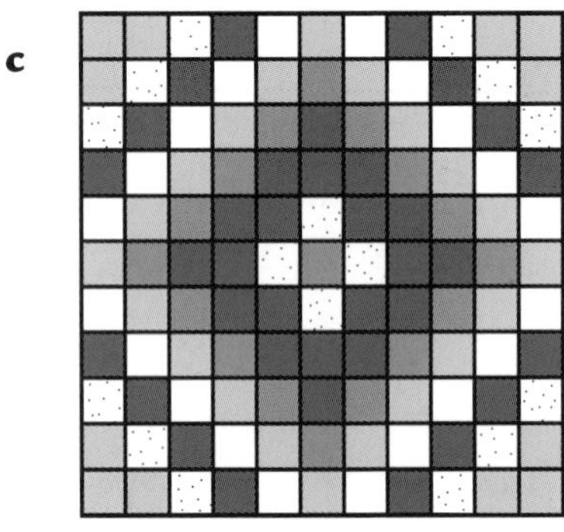

d

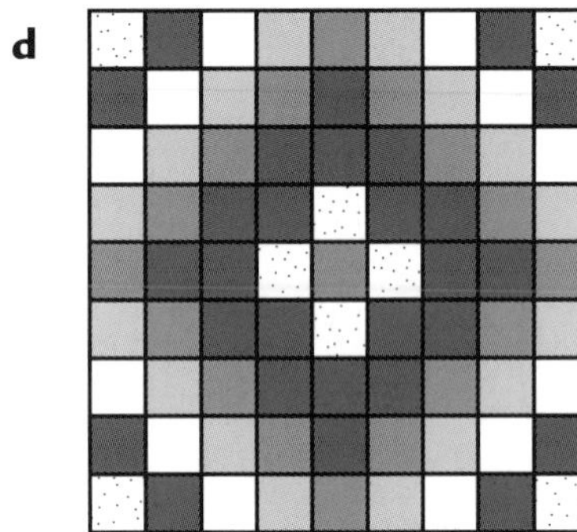

e

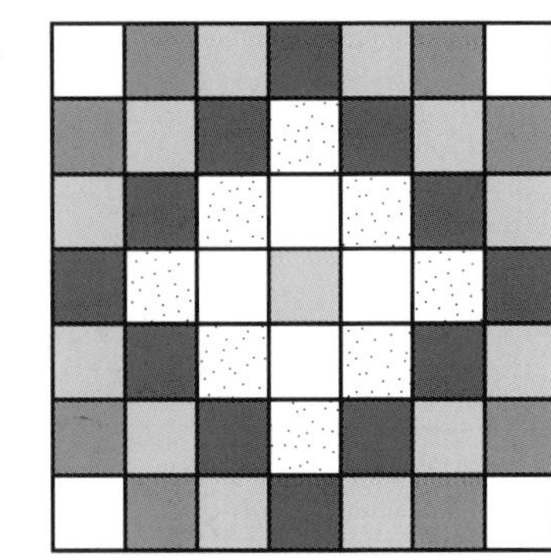

■ *Mohawk Trail* ■

Begin with a basic 4 x 4 grid (see p96); draw in long and short horizontal and vertical lines as shown (**a**).

a

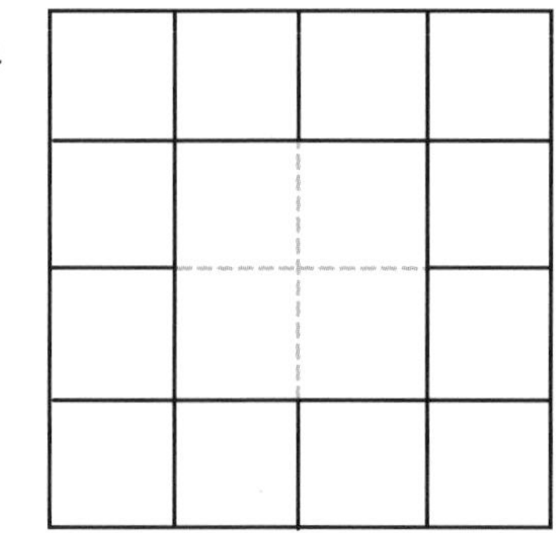

Use a pair of compasses to draw a quarter-circle in the corner of one small square; copy this curve into the four corners of the large central square (**b**).

b

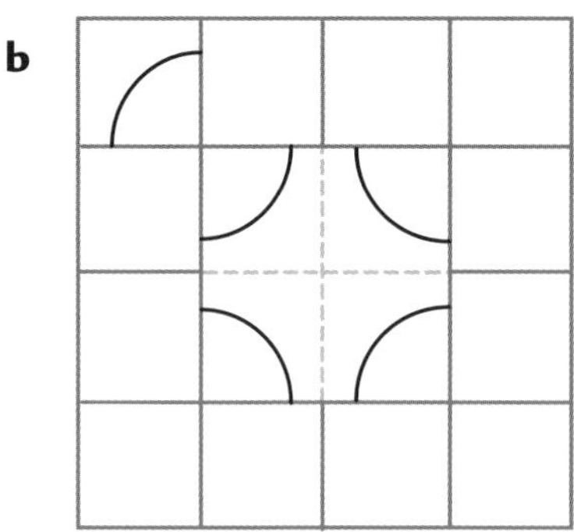

Use a protractor to divide the quarter-circle into 30° segments, then join these to the corner to create three wedge shapes (**c**).

c

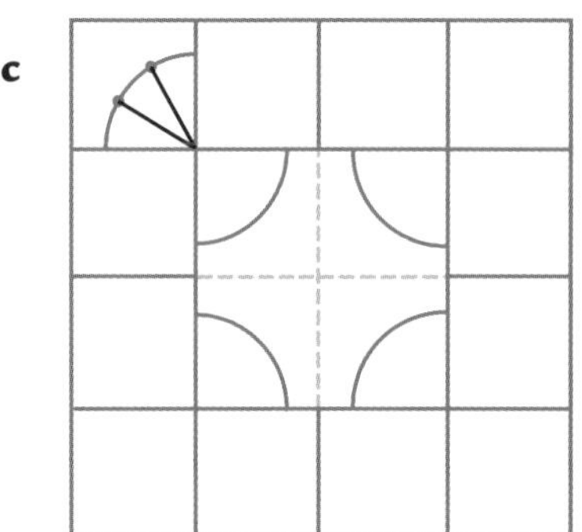

Diagram (**d**) shows the 3 templates required.

d

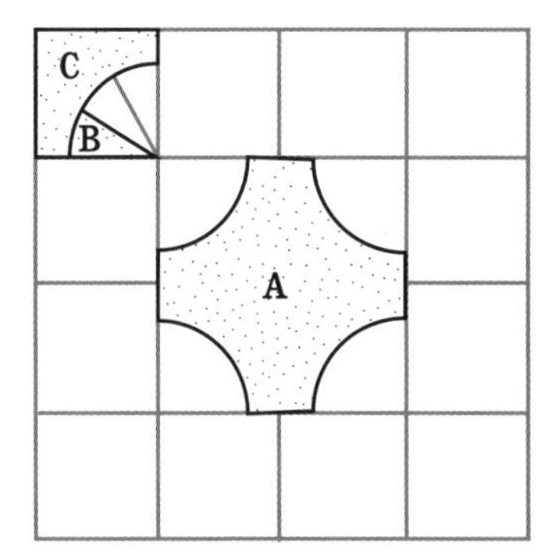

The basic block used for this design (a square with a quarter-circle patch) can be combined in many different arrangements; diagrams (**e**-**h**) show just four other options.

e

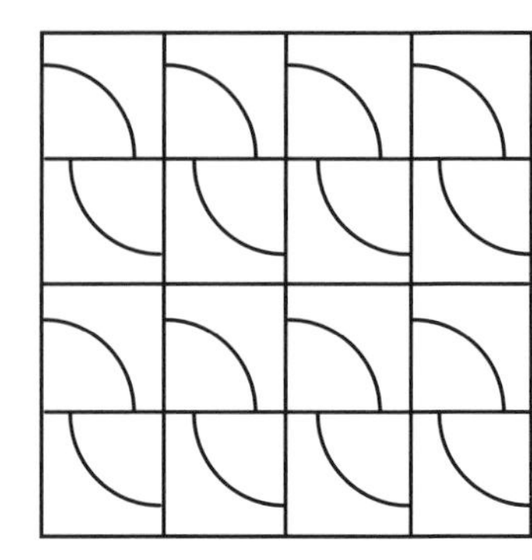

f

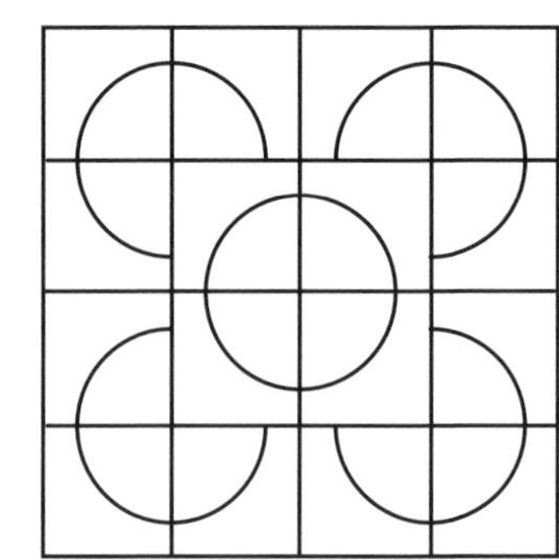

g

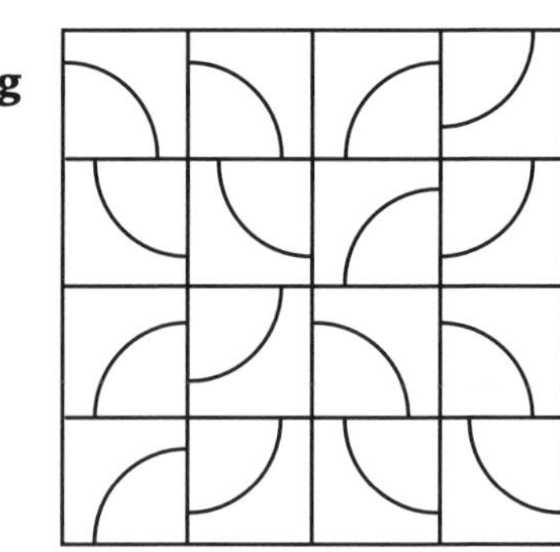

h

■ *Medallion Log Cabin* ■

Begin with a basic 2 x 2 (4-patch) grid (see p96); join the half-way points on each side of the square to create a second square 'on point' (**a**).

a

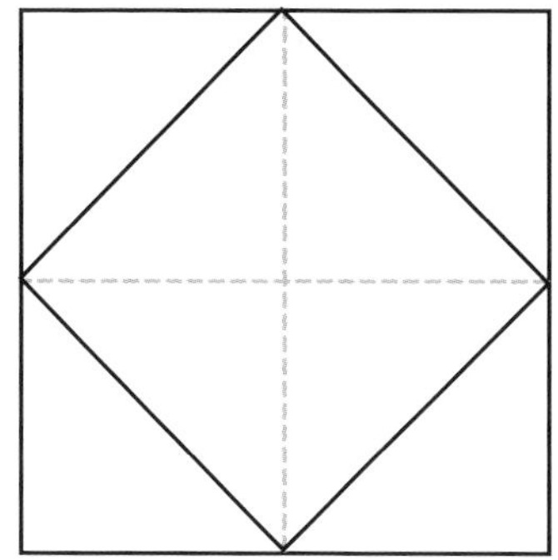

Decide on the width you would like the strips of fabric to be. See how many you can fit on either side of your square – you will need an equal number of strips coming in from the outer edges towards the middle, plus room for a central square. Draw a complete circuit of Log Cabin strips inside the inner square (**b**); begin with a strip across the whole width of the block, then work round in a circle drawing strips of the same width, always working within your previously-drawn lines. Carry on working round the block in the same way until you have the required number of strips (**c**).

b

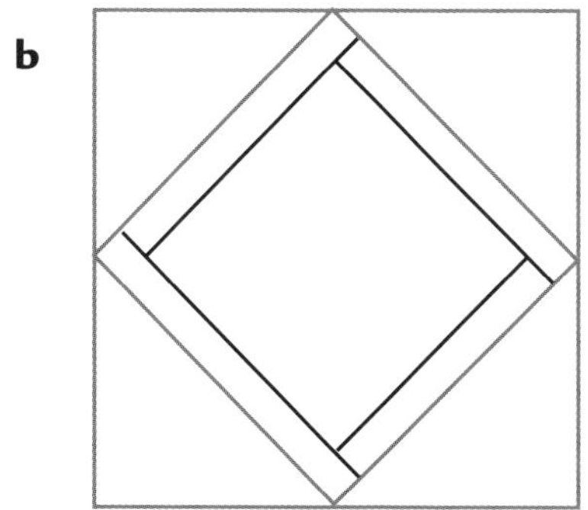

c

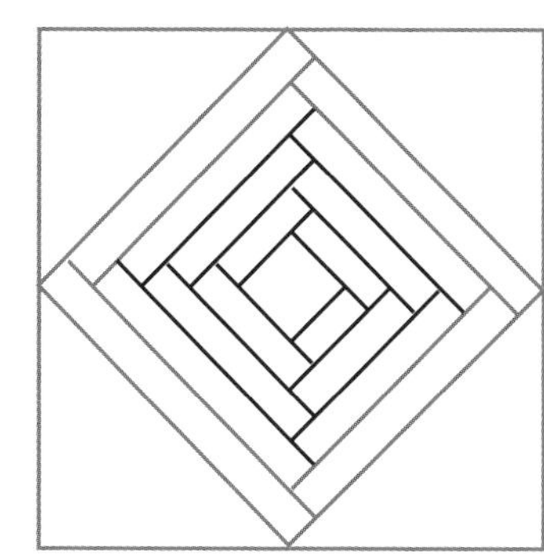

Draw a second Log Cabin design, working behind the first square so that the design appears in the corners of the block (**d**). (At this stage, three corners will be identical and one slightly different. Use the same set of templates for each corner: the illusion will work just as well, looking as though there's a second, complete Log Cabin behind the first.)

d

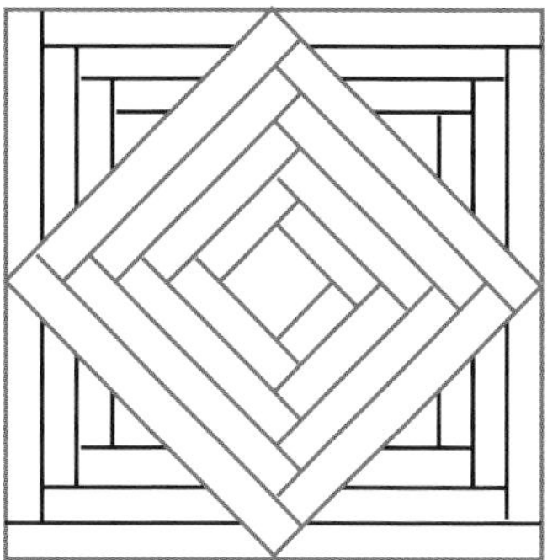

e

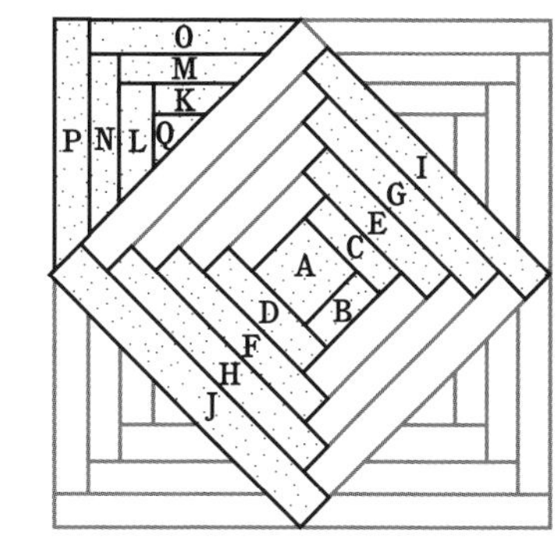

Diagram (**e**) shows the 17 templates required.

Altering the width and number of the Log Cabin strips creates a marked difference in the end design; diagrams (**f**) and (**g**) show two of many possible variations.

f

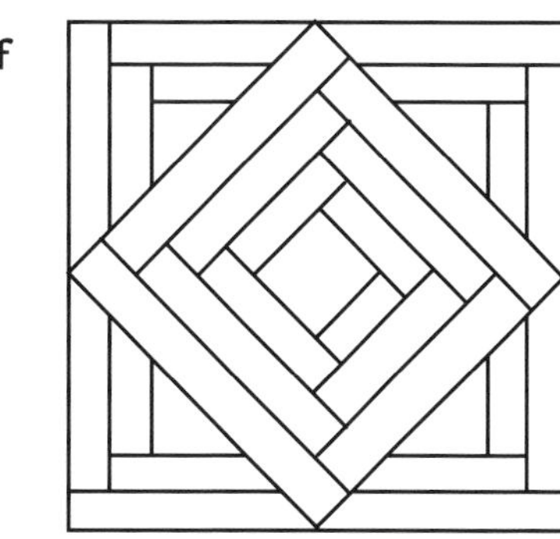

g

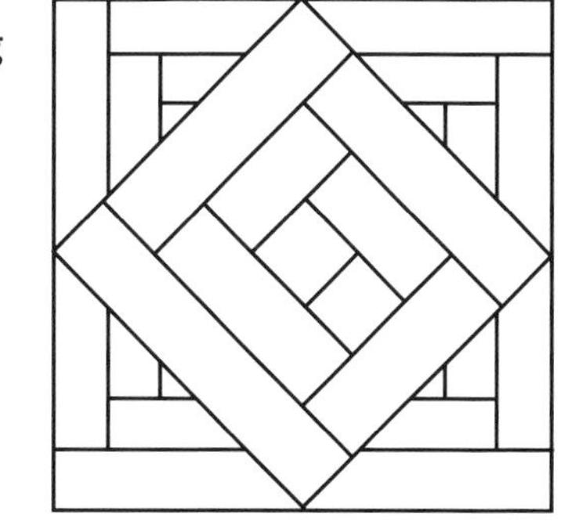

Hawaiian Hearts

If you'd like to use my Hawaiian-style appliqué design on a different-sized block, use a photocopier to enlarge or reduce the design that I've given (see p79), making sure that the complete design is ½in (1cm) smaller than your finished block.

If you'd prefer to create your own designs, cut several squares of paper the same size as your finished block. Fold each square into halves (**a**), then quarters (**b**), then diagonally into eighths (**c**).

a

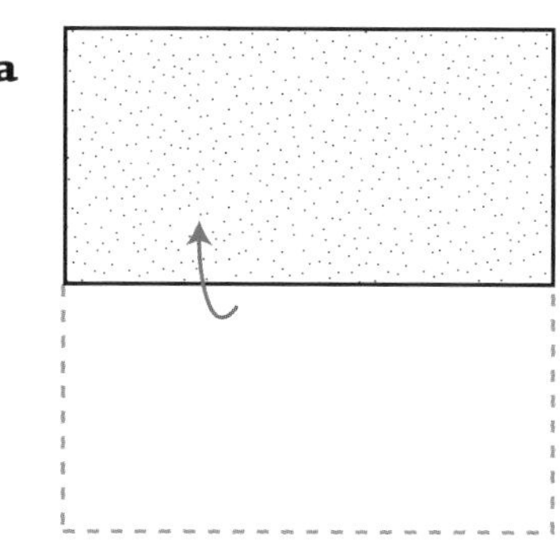

b

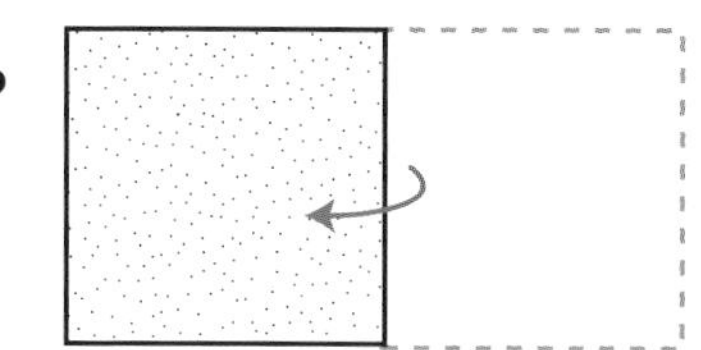

c

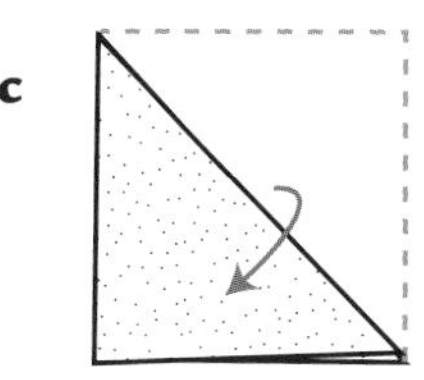

Draw a design (**d**) and cut round the edges and any inside sections (**e**). Unfold the design and see how it looks (**f**); if you're not happy with it, try another design or two. Once you have a good design, re-fold the paper, lay the design onto card and trace round it to create a card template.

d **e**

f

Castle Keep

Begin with a basic 2 x 2 (4-patch) grid (see p96); draw in the horizontal and vertical half-way lines, and the full diagonals (**a**).

a

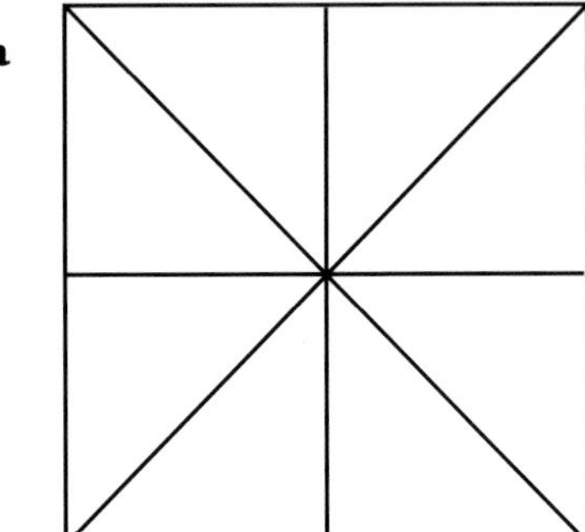

Using a protractor, mark the half-way point in each of the eight sections (22.5°); join these marks across the square with long lines (**b**) – make sure that each line passes through the centre of the design, otherwise your final templates won't be accurate.

b

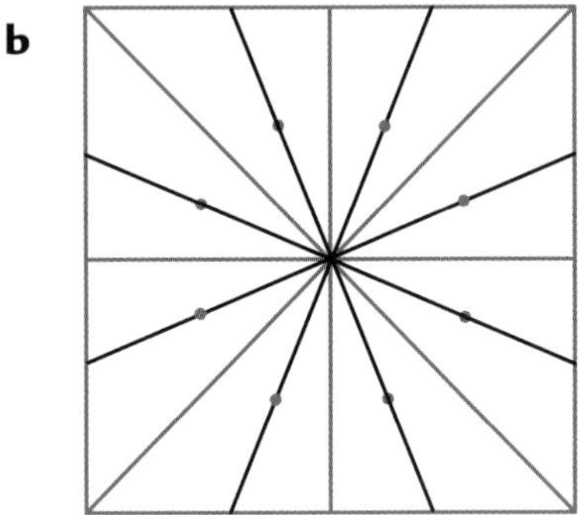

Using the new points that these lines have created on the outside of the square, draw two vertical and two horizontal lines (**c**).

c

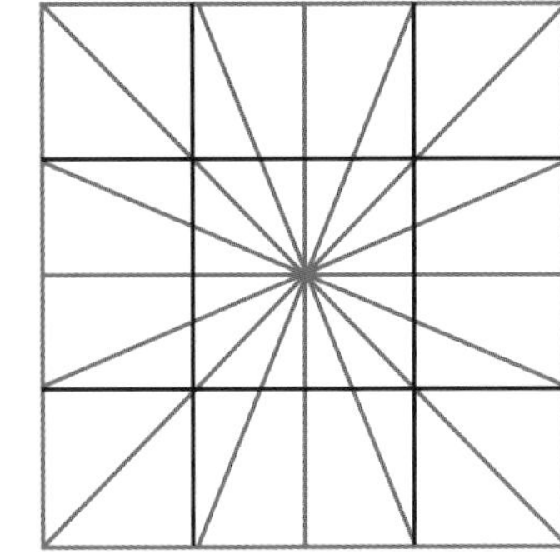

Using the same marks, draw two rectangles diagonally across the design (**d**).

Using the original half-way marks on the outer edge of the square as guides for your ruler, draw a short diagonal line in each corner.

d

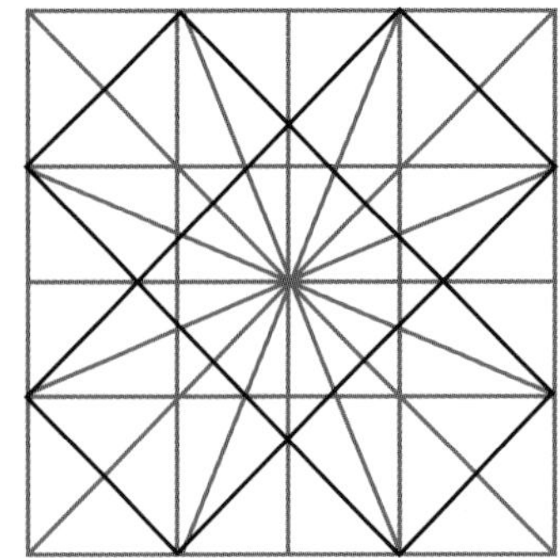

Mark the half-way points of the four corner squares, and use these as ruler guides to draw in two short horizontal lines and two vertical ones as shown (**e**).

e

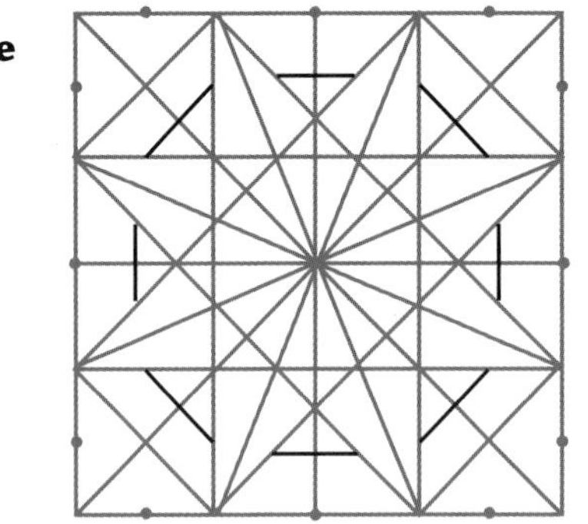

Highlight the template lines. Disregard or erase the construction lines in pencil that are NOT template lines.

Diagram (**f**) shows the 7 templates required; note the shapes of the templates carefully, as not all the lines you've drawn appear on the final block design.

f

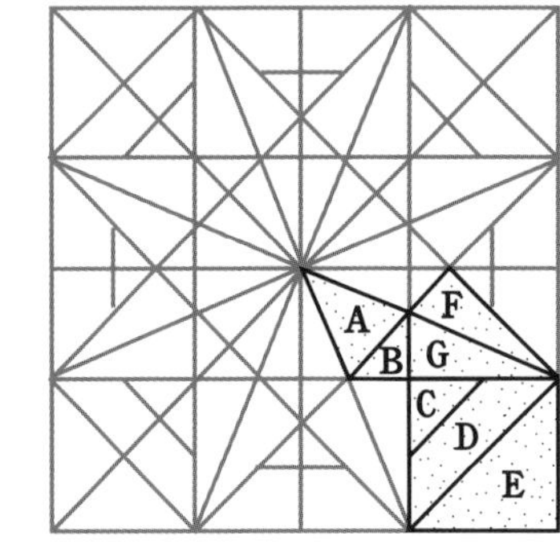

Eccentric Star

Begin with a basic 9-patch grid (see p96). Draw in diagonal lines as shown (**a**), working first in one direction, and then in the opposite direction.

Add the extra diagonal lines as shown (**b**).

a

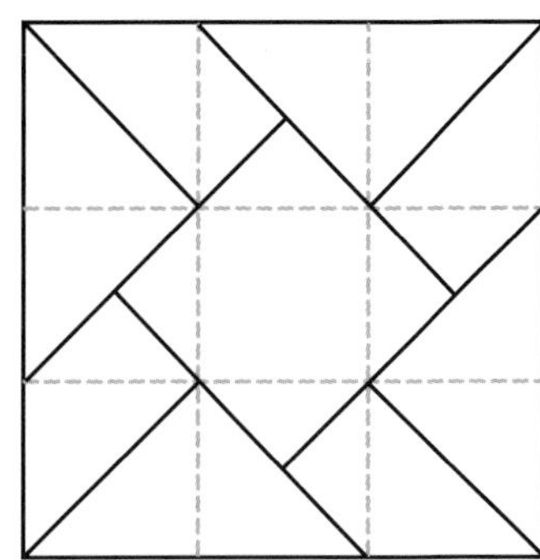

b

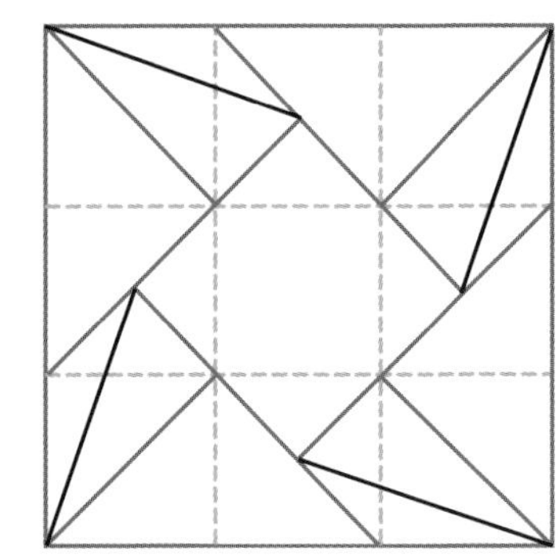

Draw round the central square of the grid, then mark the half-way point on each side and join these marks to draw a square 'on point' (**c**).

Diagram (**d**) shows the 6 templates required.

c

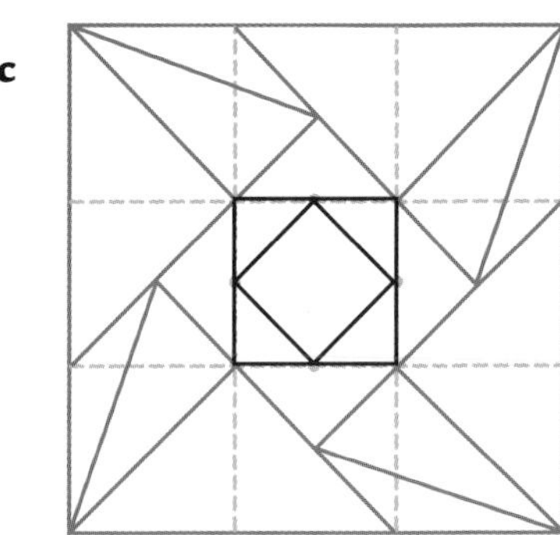

d

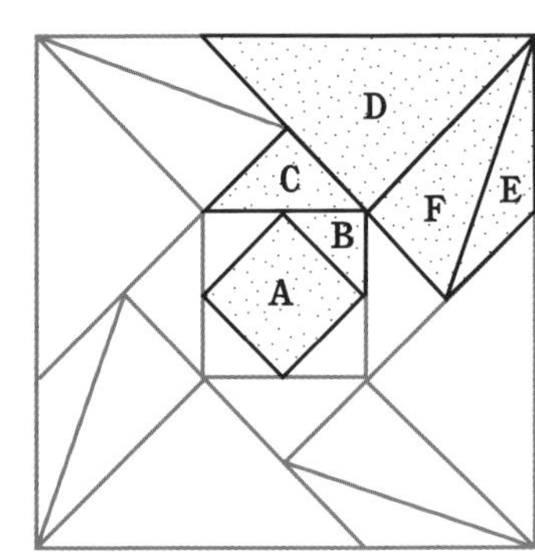

Indian Wedding Ring

Begin with a basic 2 x 2 (4-patch) grid (see p96), and draw in the horizontal and vertical lines. Draw a small square in each corner of one quarter (**a**) – the size of your squares

a

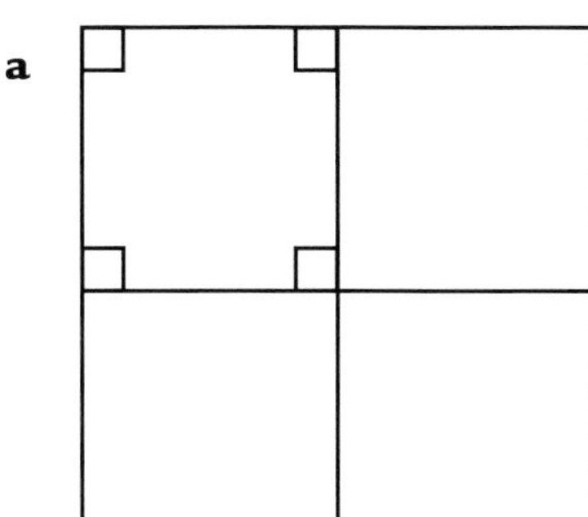

will determine the width of the arcs on the design (see diagram **g**).

Place the pin of a pair of compasses on the inner corner of the square at the centre, and position the pencil point on the upper outer corner of the left-hand square (marked with an asterisk); carefully draw an arc. Move the pencil point only to the upper inner corner of the left-hand square (marked with a black dot) and draw a second arc inside the first (**b**).

b

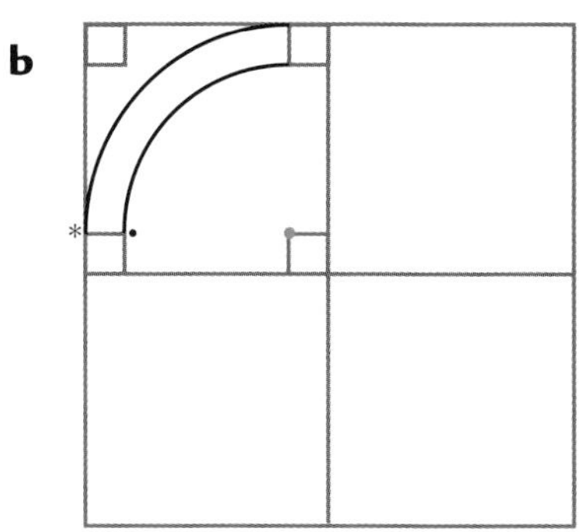

If you're happy with the width of the arc, use the outer corner square to draw its mirror-image in the same way (**c**).

c

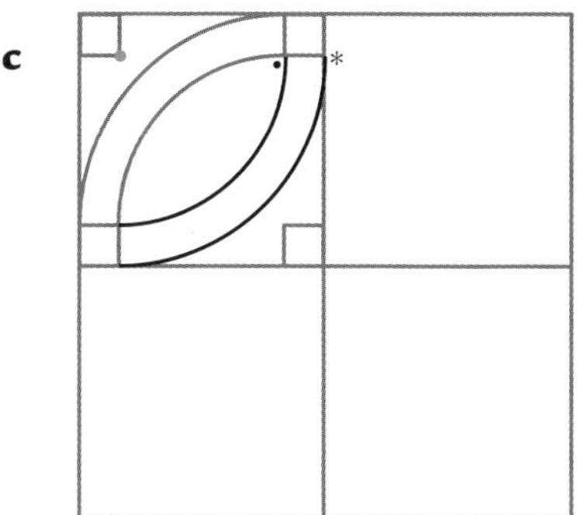

Use a protractor to divide the arc into 15° sections and use these marks to draw in guidelines across the arc (**d**). Use these guides to draw in the pattern of diagonal lines shown (**e**).

Diagram **f** shows the 7 templates (A-G) required. If you prefer to use a solid arc rather than a pieced one, use template H instead of templates D-G.

d

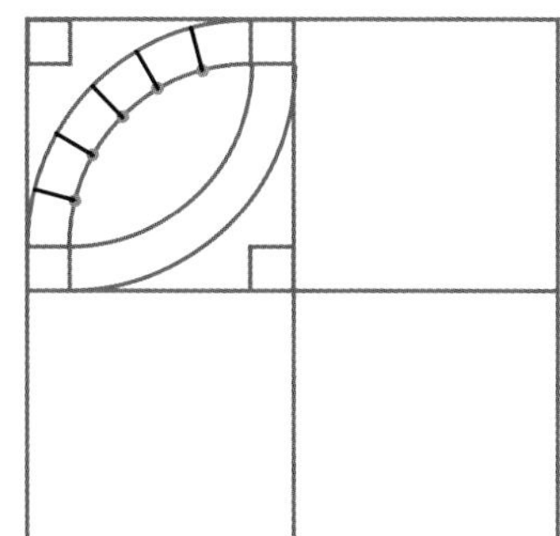

e

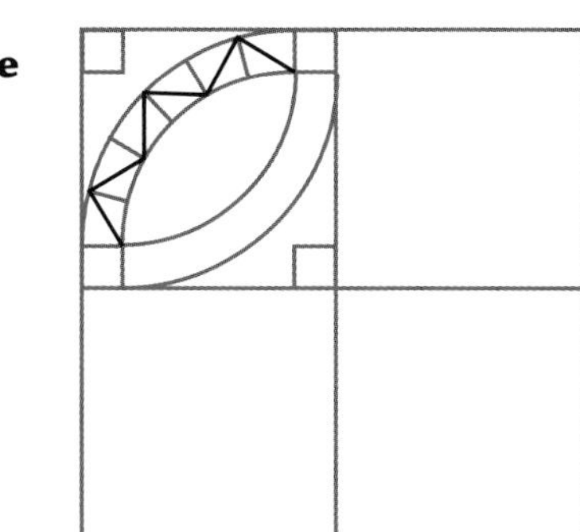

f

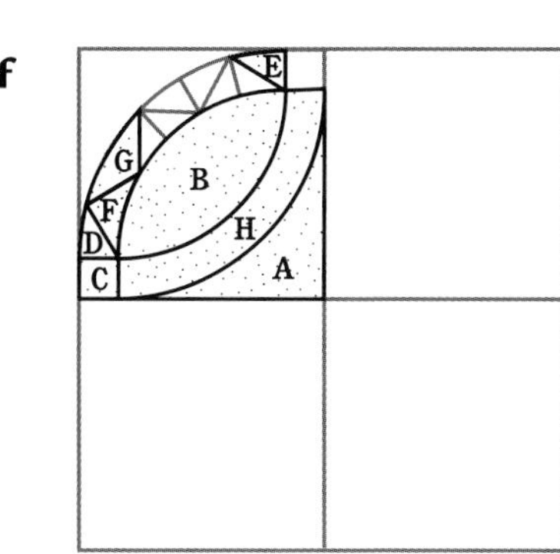

To create a design with a wider or narrower arc, alter the size of the small corner squares accordingly; diagram (**g**) shows various options.

g

Rocky Road to Kansas

Begin with a basic 2 x 2 (4-patch) grid (see p96), and mark in the horizontal and vertical half-way lines.

Decide on the rough size and proportions of your main triangle, and mark appropriate points for the bottom corners; these should be an equal distance from the centre of the square, along the horizontal and vertical grid lines (**a**).

a

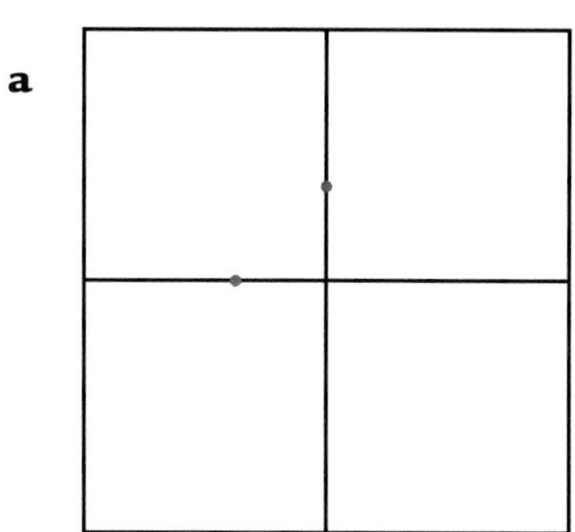

Join these points and the corner of the square to create a triangle (**b**).

b

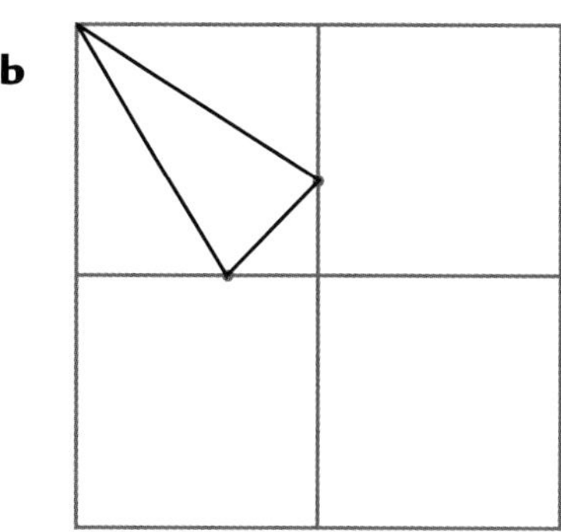

Diagram (**c**) shows the 4 templates required.

Using triangles of different proportions will make your block look completely different; try marking out different triangles and see which one you prefer (**d**). Or, if you want a really unusual block, use a different-sized triangle within each quarter.

c

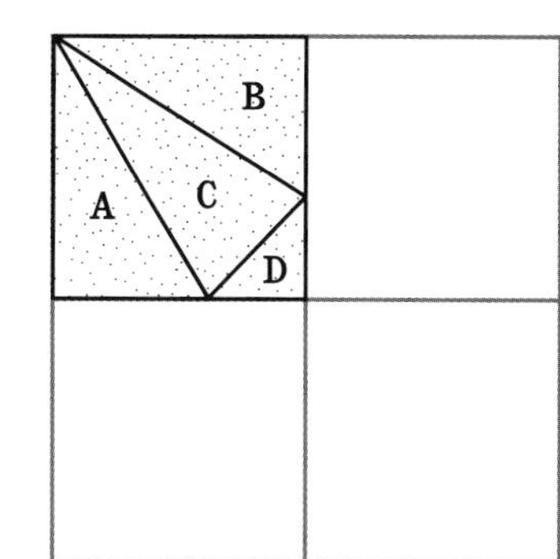

d

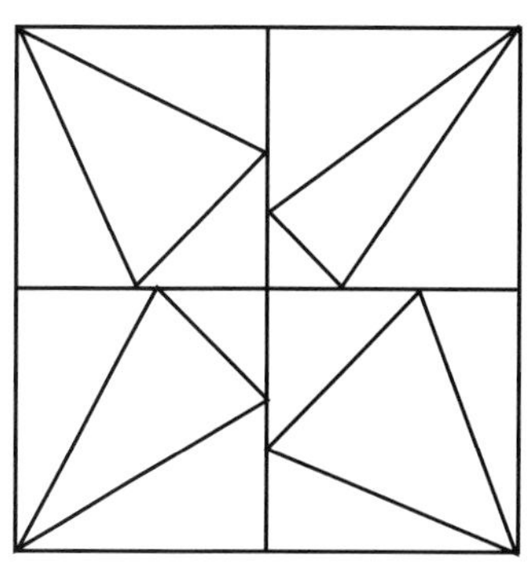

Goose in the Pond

Begin with a basic 5 x 5 grid (see p96), and draw in all the horizontal and straight lines (**a**).

a

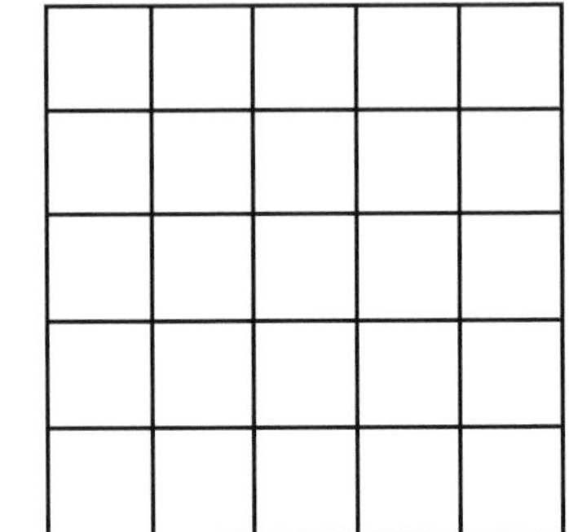

Working in one direction, and then in the opposite direction, draw in diagonal lines as shown (**b**).

b

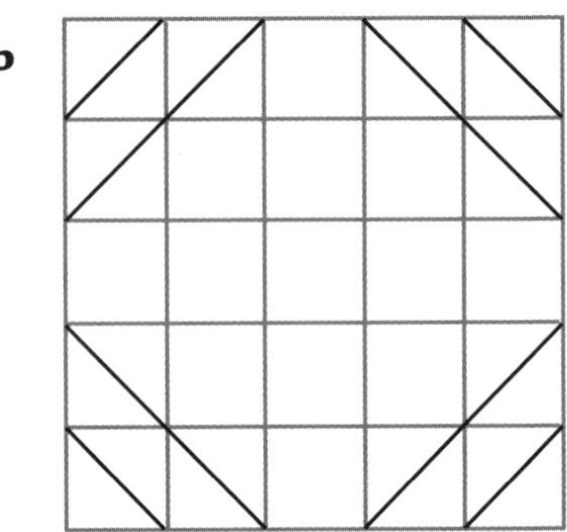

Divide the measurement of one individual square evenly into three and position the next set of marker points as shown. Use these as guidelines to rule in the last lines (**c**).

c

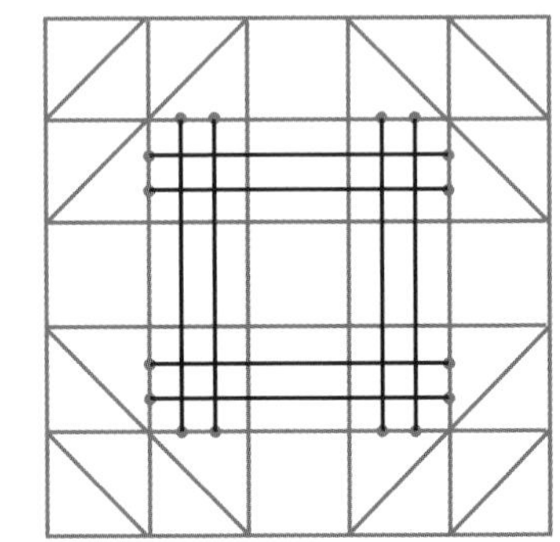

Diagram (**d**) shows the four templates required.

d

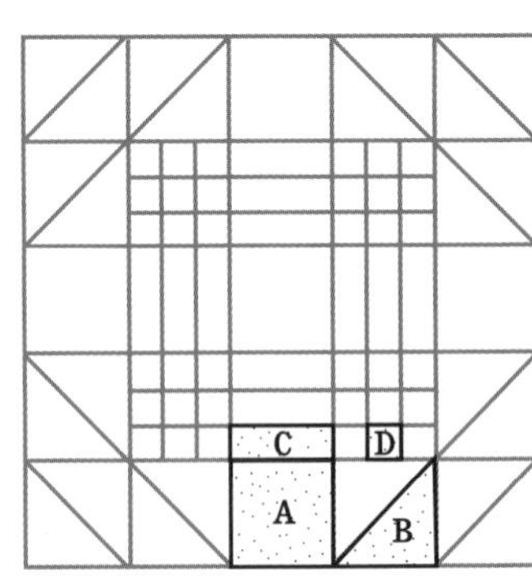

Mariner's Compass

Begin with a basic 2 x 2 (4-patch) grid (see p96); draw in the vertical and horizontal lines and the full diagonals (**a**).

a

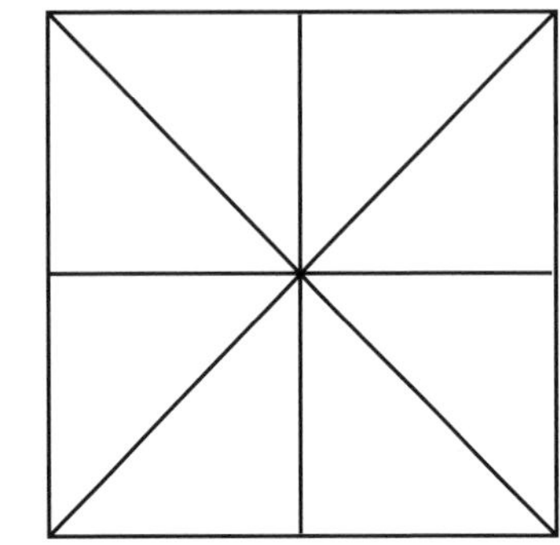

Draw a smaller inner circle and a larger outer one (**b**). Using the diagonal cross-grid lines as guides, and working between the two circles only, draw the first 'spikes' at the north, south, east and west positions (**c**).

b

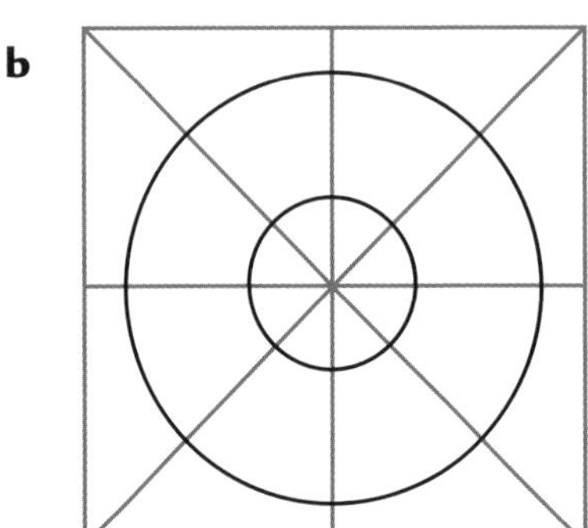

c

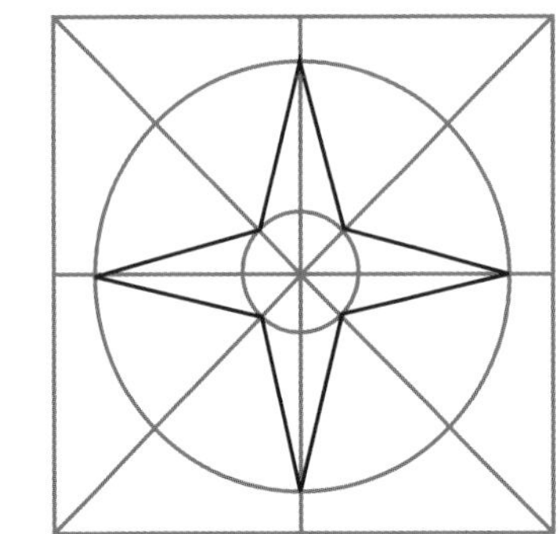

Still working between the circles, use the diagonal and cross-grid lines as guides for drawing in the second set of spikes behind the first (**d**).

d

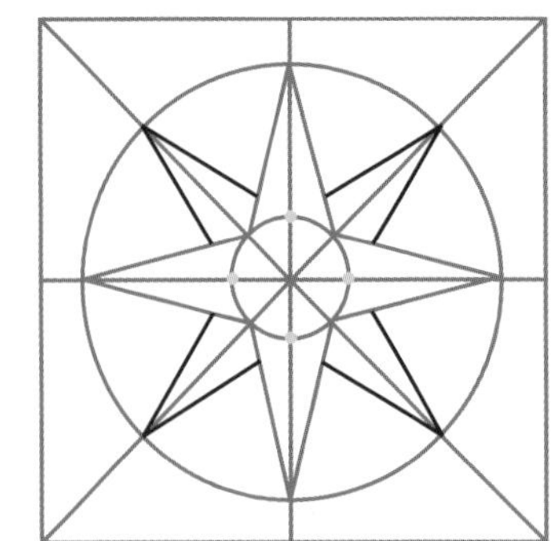

To add further spikes, mark the valleys or intersections between the spikes, then lay your ruler between these and use them as guides to draw a new set of construction lines (use a coloured pencil to distinguish these from the previous lines). Each new line passes through the centre and through two opposite valleys or intersections (**e**). Draw in the next layer of spikes behind the first two layers (**f**).

Diagram (**g**) shows the 6 templates required.

e

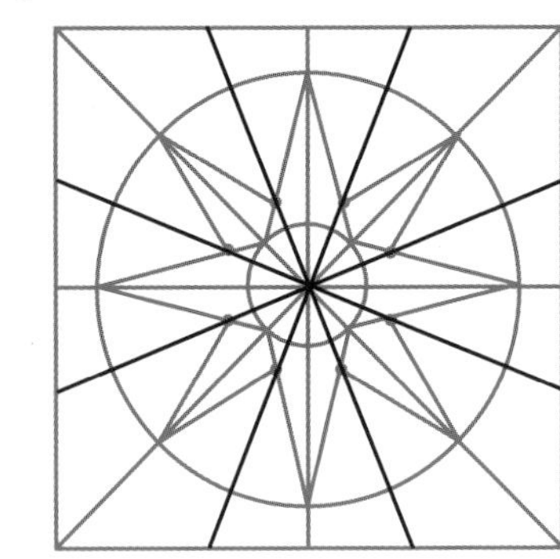

f

g

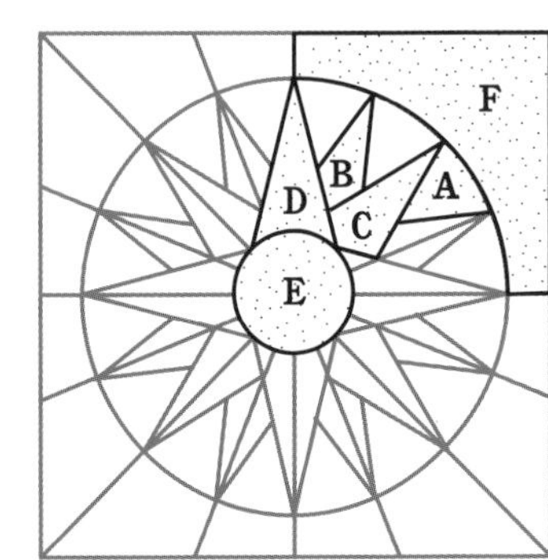

The measurement of your circles will determine the length and width of the spikes – try alternative measurements to find a size that you prefer. Diagrams (**h**) and (**i**) show the effects of using the same-sized outer circle and a larger or smaller central circle.

h

i

Quartered Card Trick

Begin with a basic 6 x 6 grid (see p96). Working methodically, row by row, draw in diagonal lines as shown (**a**).

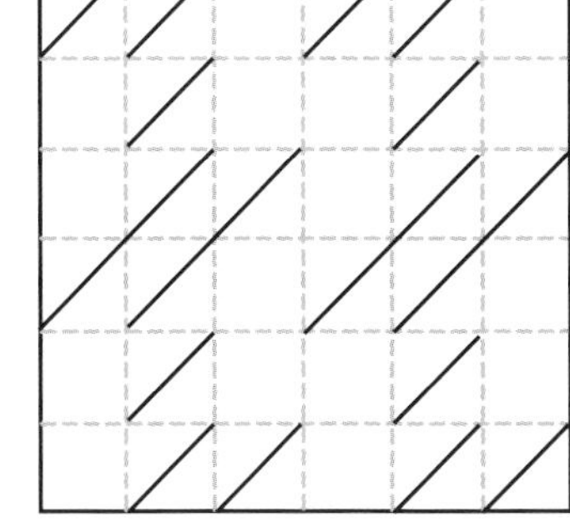

Again working row by row, mark diagonal lines in the opposite direction as shown (**b**).

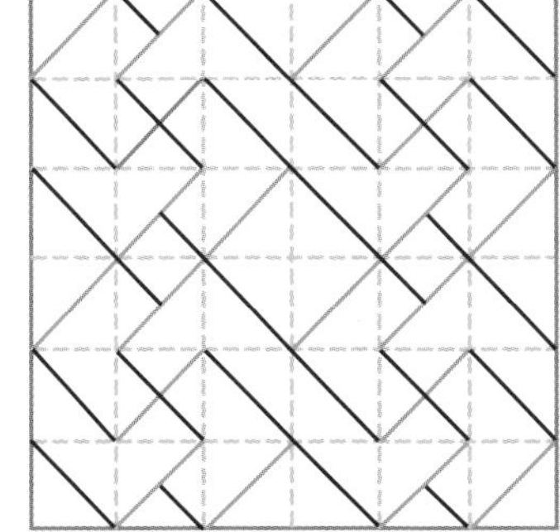

Complete the design with 8 short diagonal lines in the positions marked (**c**).

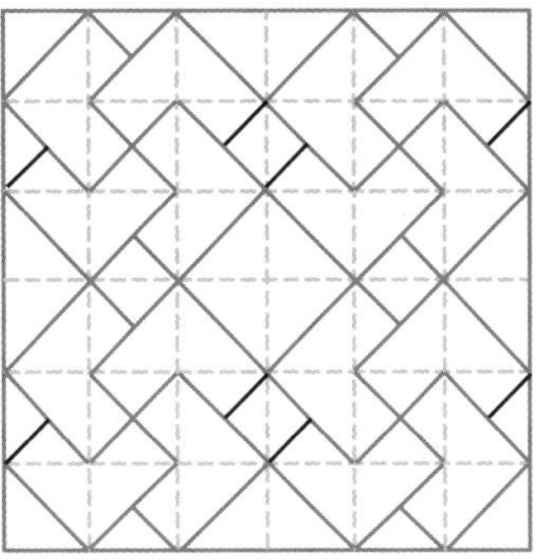

Diagram (**d**) shows the 5 templates required; note the shapes of the templates carefully, as not all the lines you've drawn appear on the final block design.

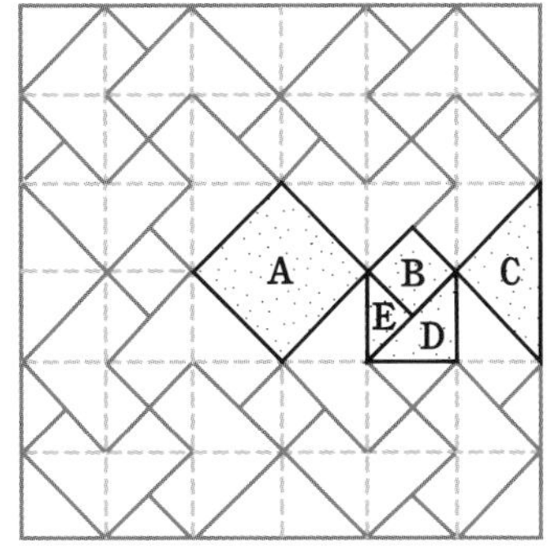

Basket of Scraps

Begin with a basic 5 x 5 grid (see p96). Use the central divisions to draw one pair of parallel lines vertically, and one pair horizontally. Mark the half-way point on each side of the central square and use these points to draw a smaller square 'on point' (**a**).

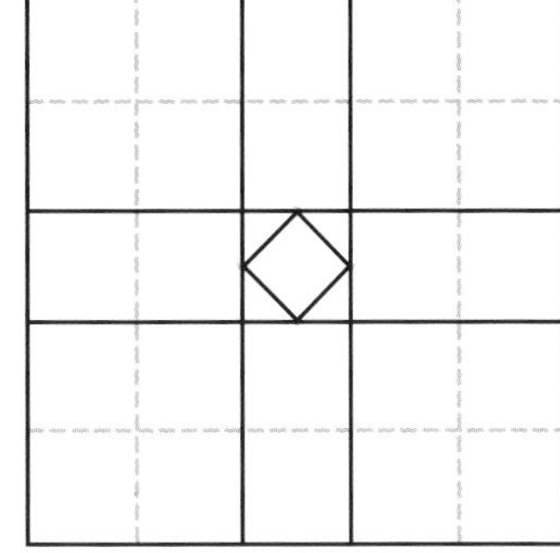

Draw in the short diagonal lines as shown, then lay your ruler across the full diagonal of the square and draw diagonal lines at the corners in each direction in turn (**b**).

Draw a double L shape in each corner as shown (**c**); the outer L in each corner is on the grid lines, and the marker points for the second L are half-way along the next grid squares.

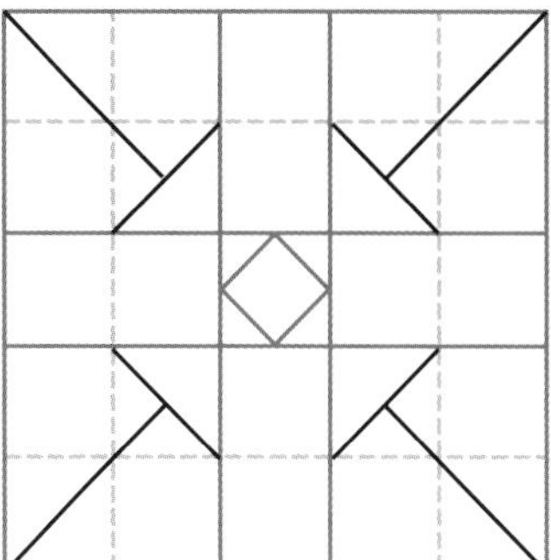

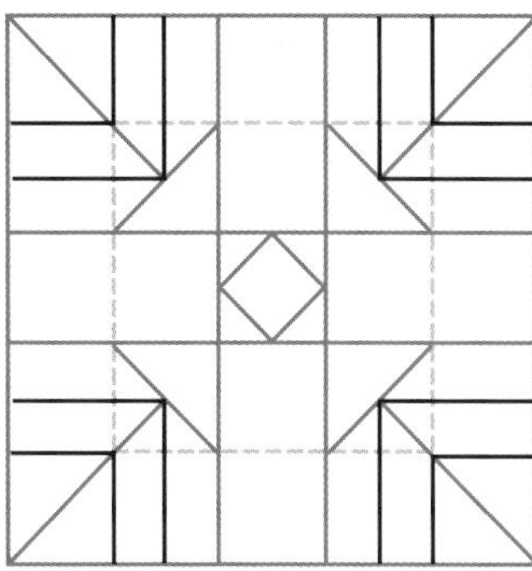

Add the remaining diagonal lines as shown (**d**), working first in one direction and then in the opposite direction, to complete the pattern.

Diagram (**e**) shows the 6 templates required.

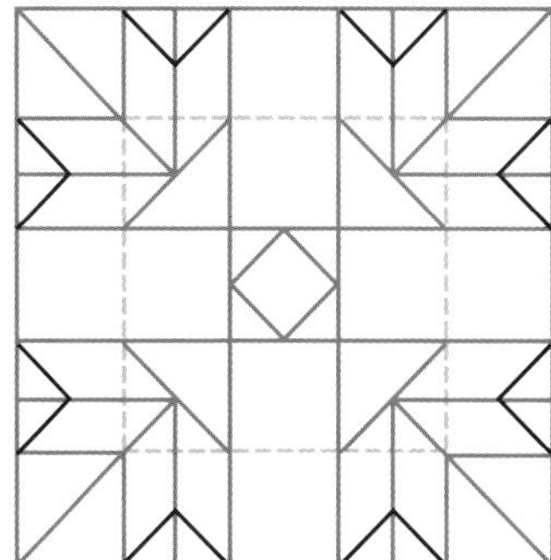

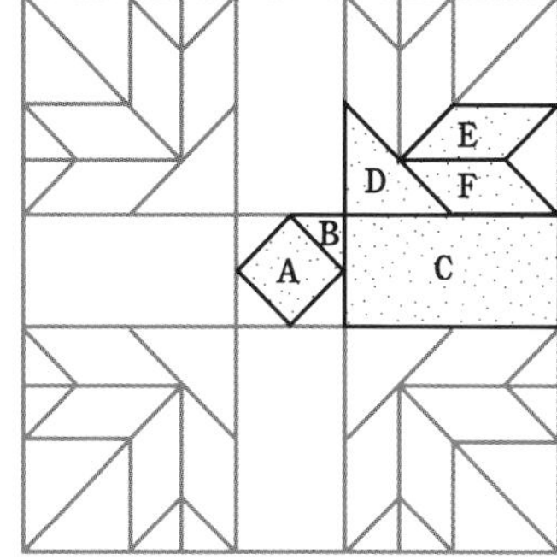

Californian Sunset

Begin with a basic 3 x 3 (9-patch) grid (see p96). Mark the half-way point on each side of the central square and use these to draw a small central square 'on point' (**a**).

a

Use the same marks to draw a large V in each side block as shown (**b**); these Vs create the 'spikes' of the first star.

b

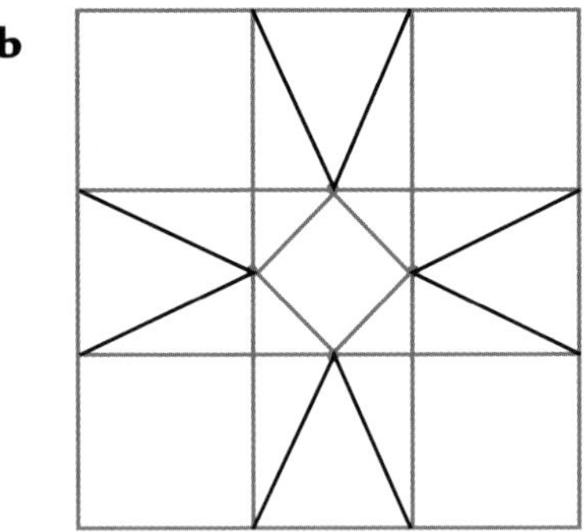

Mark the half-way points on each of the corner squares and use these to draw the second batch of spikes as shown (**c**).

c

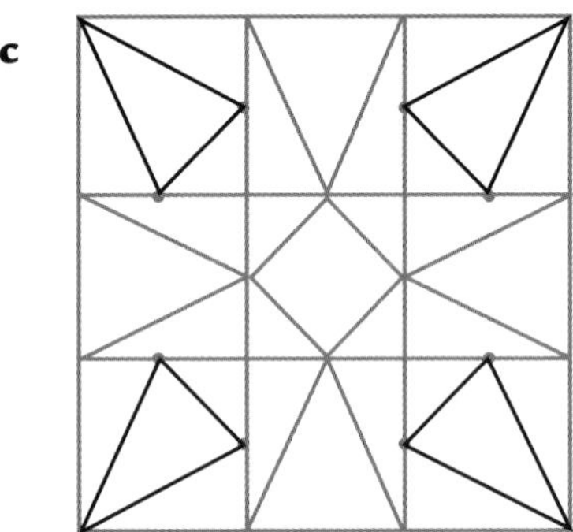

Mark the half-way points on each side of each large V (these points will be level with the ones you used to create the corner spikes), and mark in the half-way points along each outer edge of the block. Join these sets of points to create small triangles (**d**).

d

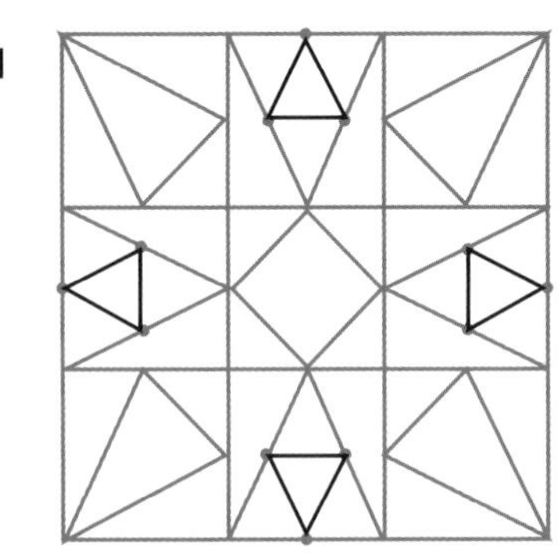

Lay your ruler diagonally across each corner square; use it as a guide to draw in the short diagonal lines at each side of the corner spikes (**e**).

Diagram (**f**) shows the 10 templates required.

e

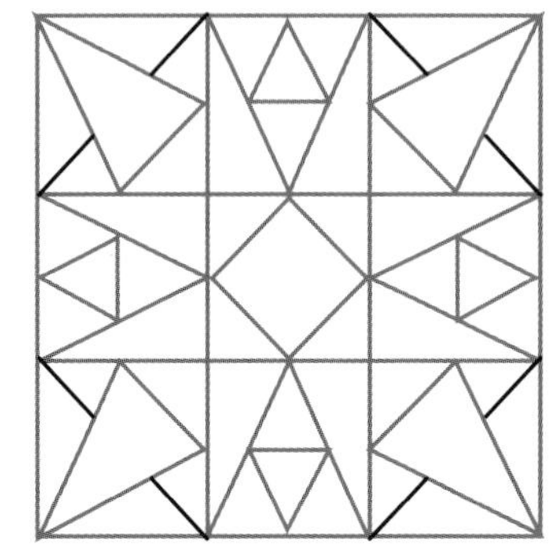

f

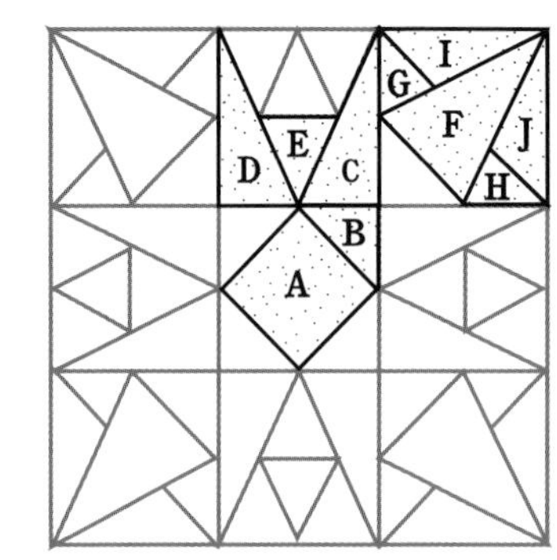

Interlocking Squares

Begin with a 2 x 2 (four-patch) grid (see p96); draw in the horizontal and vertical half-way lines, and add the full diagonal line in each direction (**a**).

a

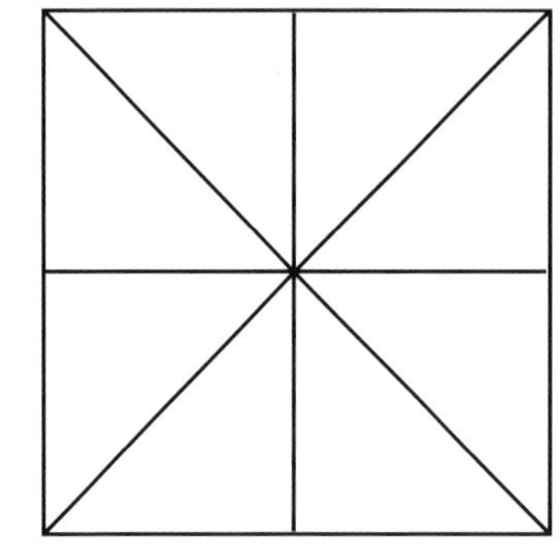

Note the measurement of half of your main (ie largest) square; measure this distance outward from the centre along each diagonal, and mark the spots. Join these marks to make an inner square, and join the centre marks along each side of the main square to create another square 'on point' (**b**).

b

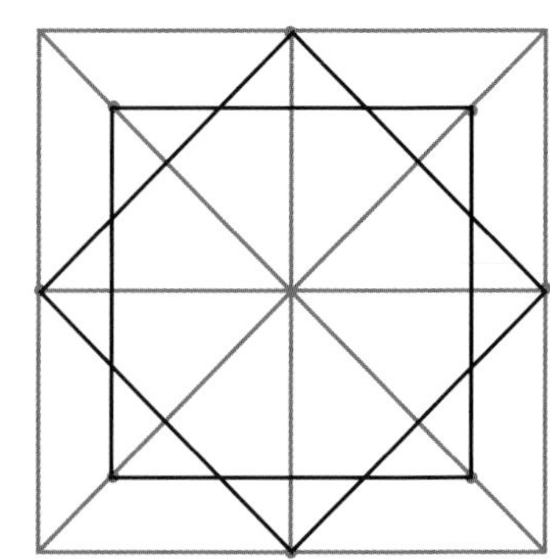

Mark the points where the diamond shape intersects with the diagonals, then join these points to create a further square (**c**). Mark the points where the first inner straight square intersects with the horizontal and vertical lines, and join these points to create the final square (**d**).

c

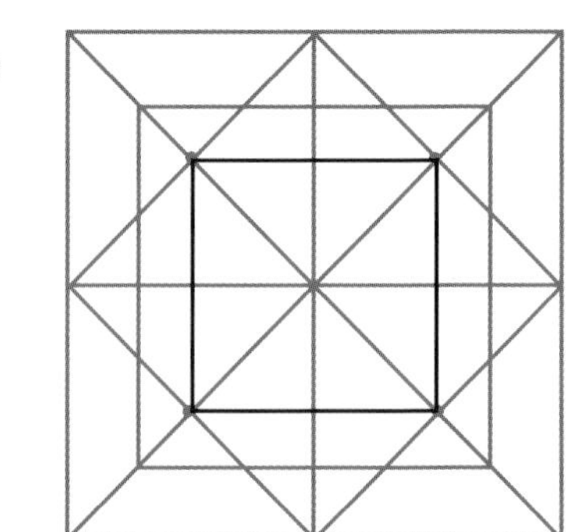

d

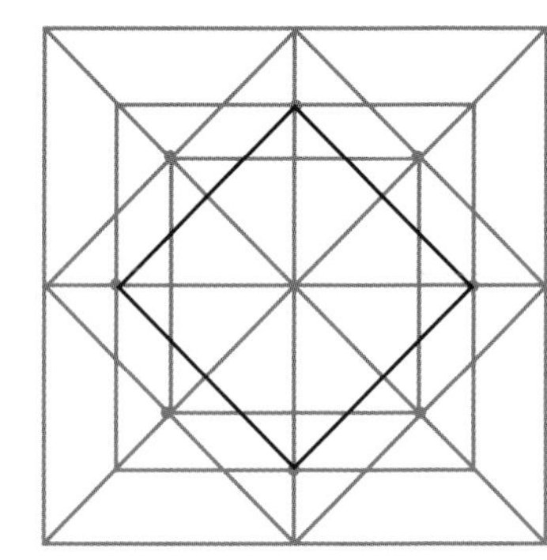

Diagram (**e**) shows the 7 templates required; note the shapes of the templates carefully, as not all the lines you've drawn appear on the final block design.

e

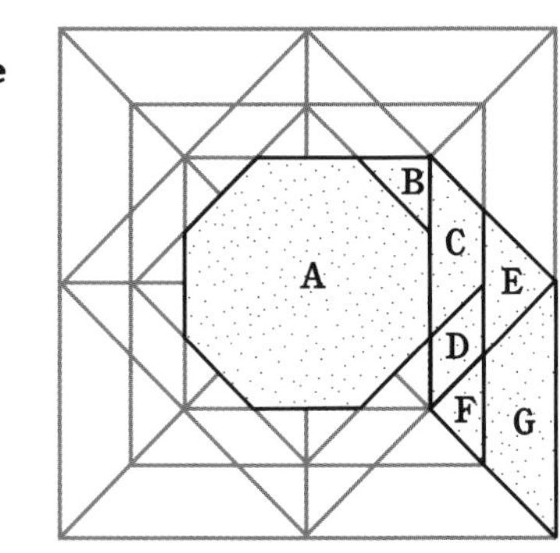

Triple Star

Begin with a basic 3 x 3 (9-patch) grid (see p96). Draw in the horizontal and vertical lines of the grid, then join the ends of these lines with diagonals as shown (**a**).

a

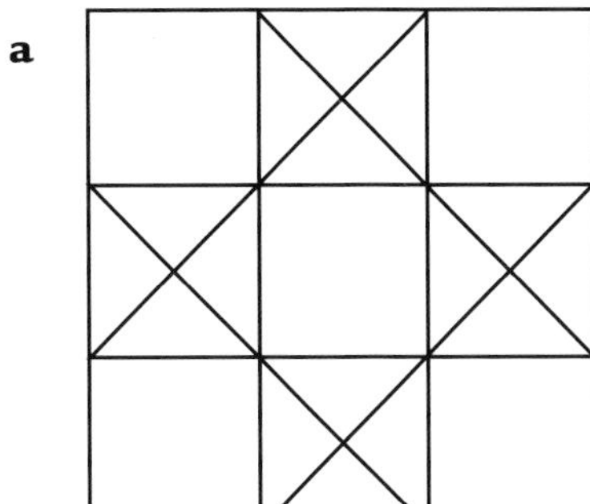

Mark the half-way point on each side of the central square and join these to create a smaller square 'on point' (**b**). Mark the halfway points on this new square, then draw in horizontal and vertical lines to create L-shapes as shown (**c**); the Ls extend to the diagonal lines.

b

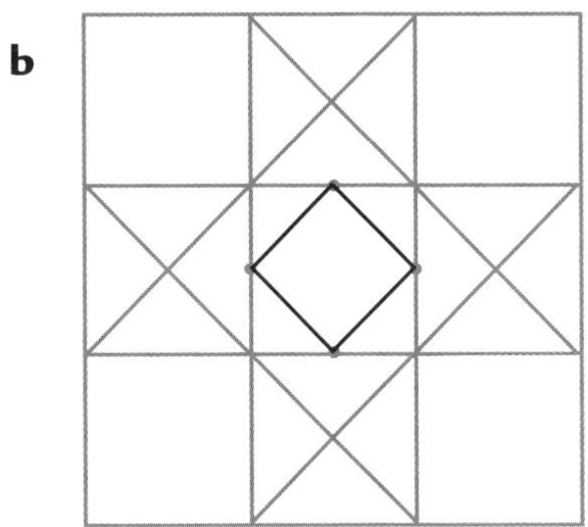

c

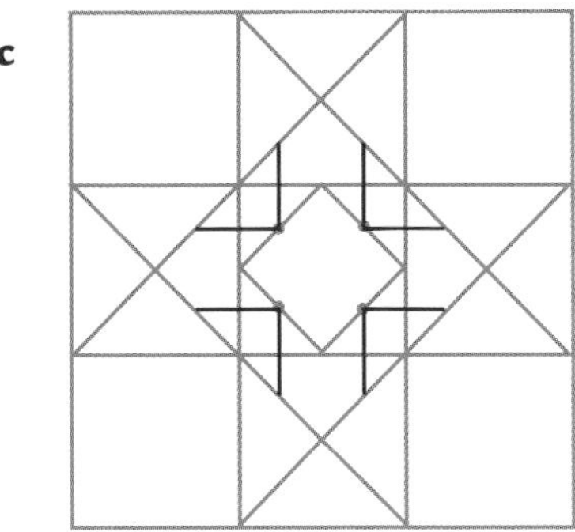

Using the ends of the arms of the Ls as guides for your ruler, draw in horizontal and vertical parallel lines as shown (**d**).

Use these new outer edge marker points to draw diagonal lines as shown, then extend the lines of the central diamond shape to create small V-shapes (**e**).

d

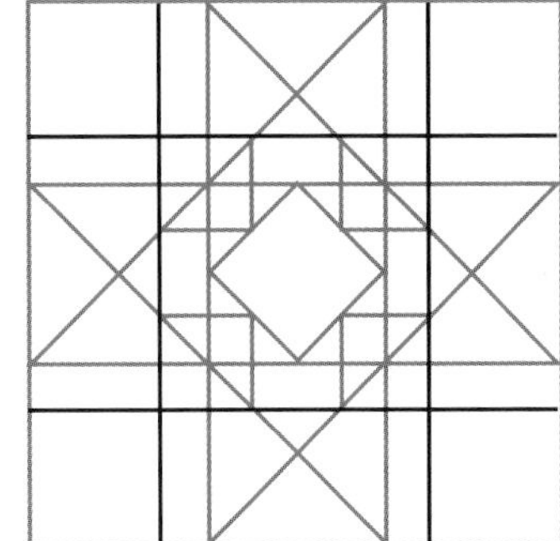

e

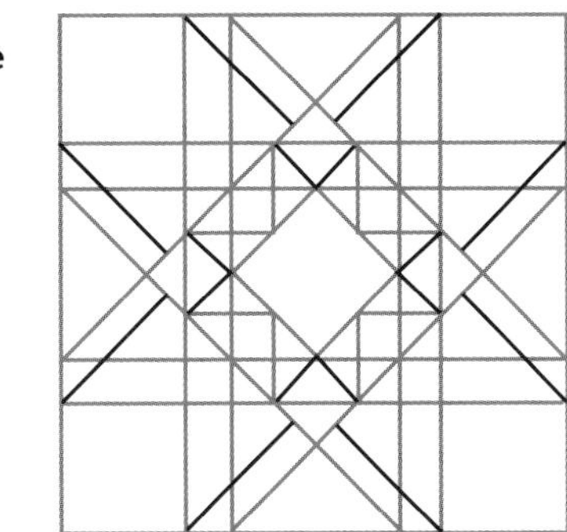

f

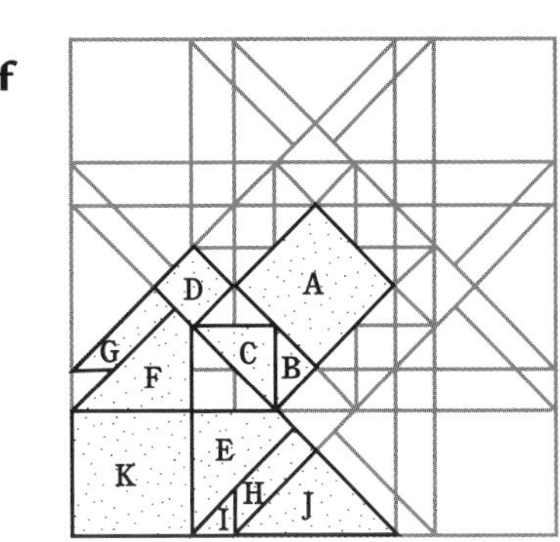

Diagram (**f**) shows the 11 templates required; note the shapes of the templates carefully, as not all the lines you've drawn appear on the final block design.

Friendship Knot

Begin with a basic 4 x 4 grid (see p96); draw in long and short horizontal and vertical lines as shown (**a**).

a

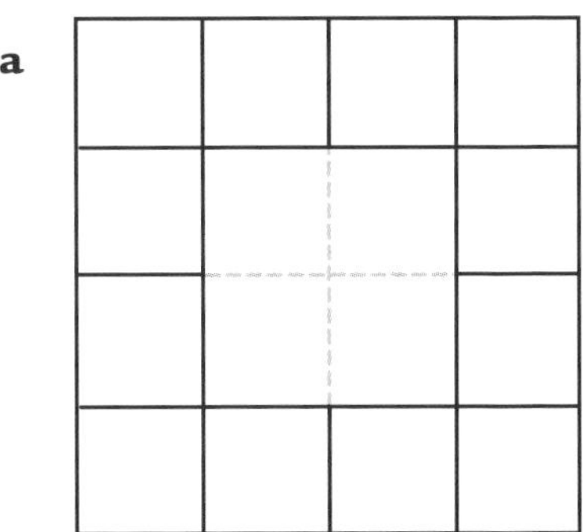

Placing your ruler on the diagonal, draw a pair of parallel lines in one direction; do the same in the opposite direction (**b**).

b

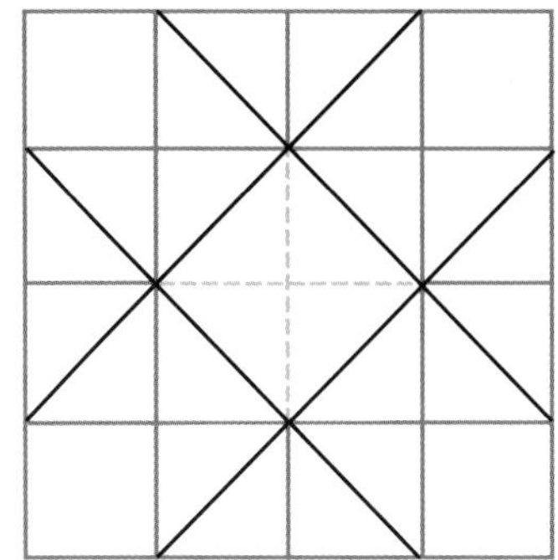

On the outline of the block, mark the half-way point of each small square. Use these new marker points to draw L-shaped lines as shown (**c**); draw all the horizontal lines first, then all the vertical ones.

c

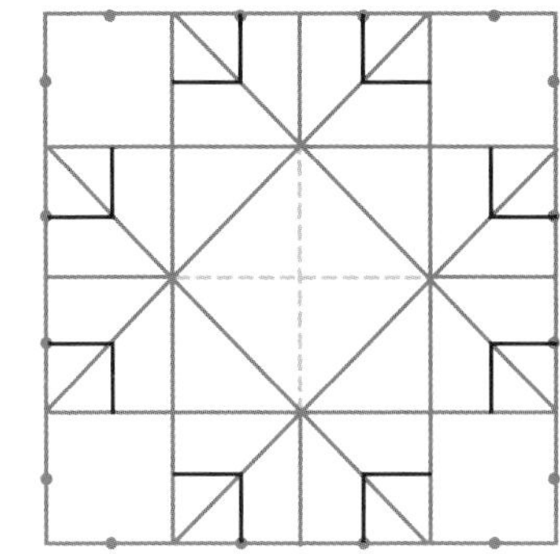

Use the marker points shown as guides for your ruler, and draw in a series of short diagonal lines as indicated (**d**). Complete the pattern with small diagonal lines in the opposite direction as shown (**e**).

d

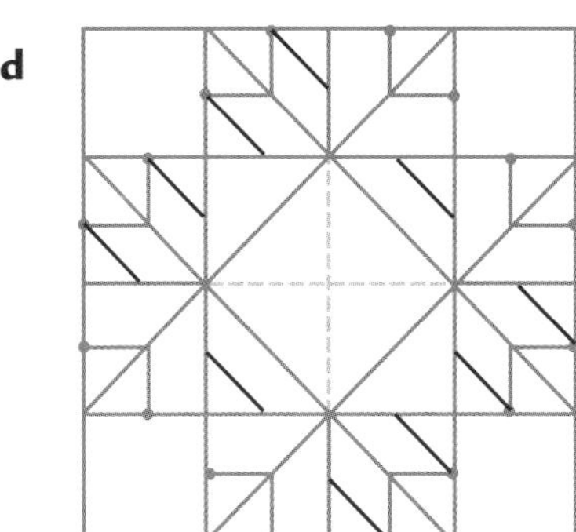

e

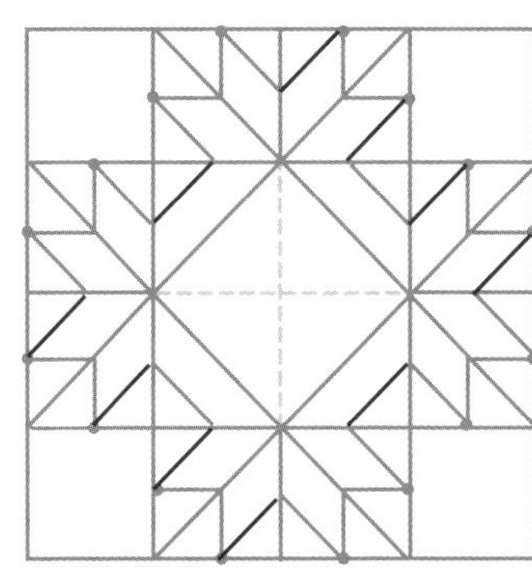

Diagram (**f**) shows the 6 templates required.

f

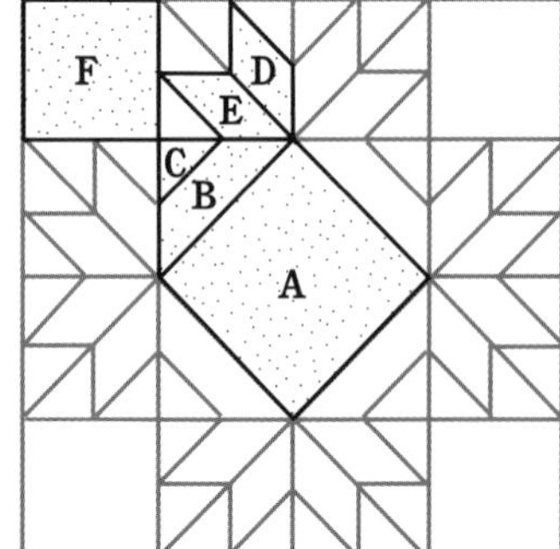

St Benedict's Star

Begin with a basic 7 x 7 grid (see p96). Draw in the two central vertical lines, then a pair of shorter horizontal lines at the sides of the vertical ones as shown (**a**).

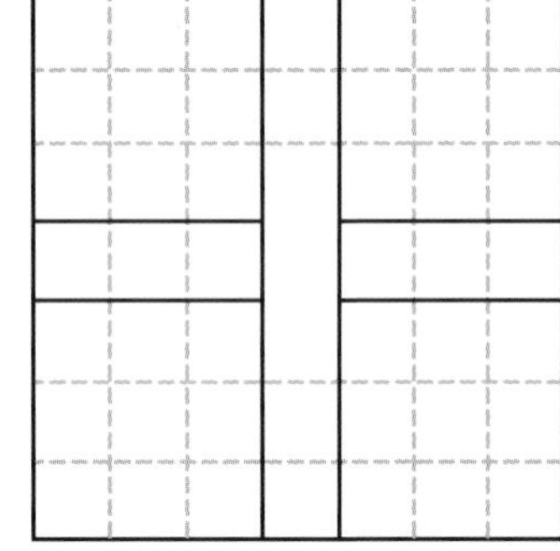

In each corner of the design, use the gridlines to draw in the pattern of horizontal and vertical lines shown (**b**), starting with the longer lines, then following these with the shorter lines.

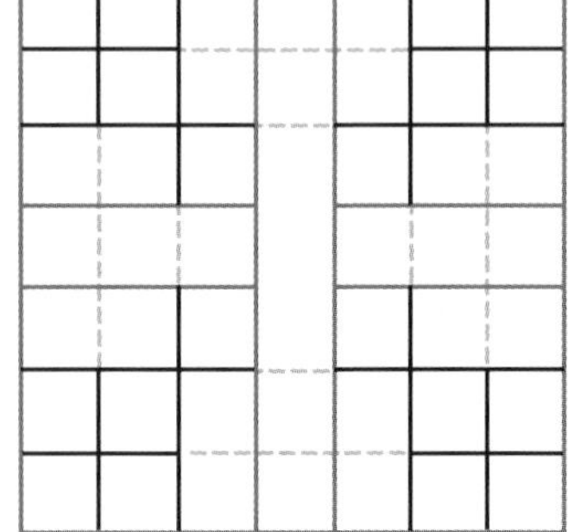

Join appropriate junctions on the grid to create a series of diagonal lines at various angles as shown (**c**).

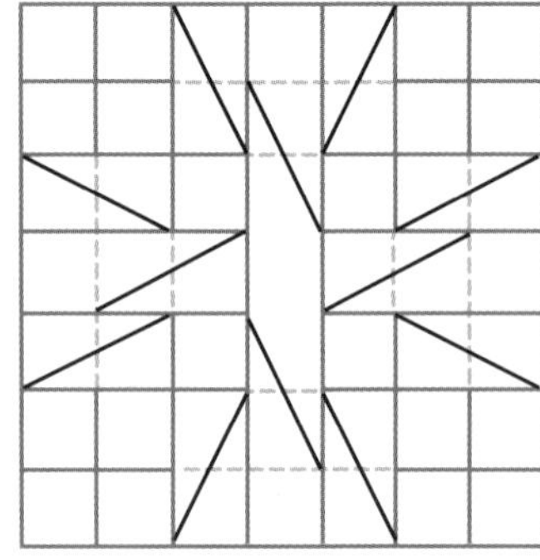

Diagram (**d**) shows the 5 templates required.

d

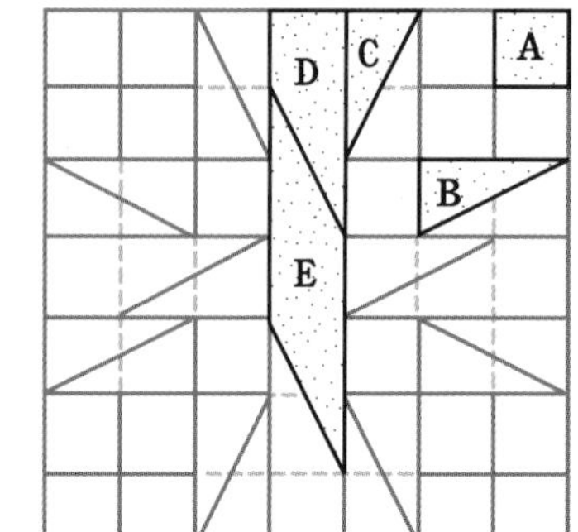

Quilter's Dream

Begin with a 2 x 2 (4-patch) grid (see p96), and mark the full diagonals (**a**).

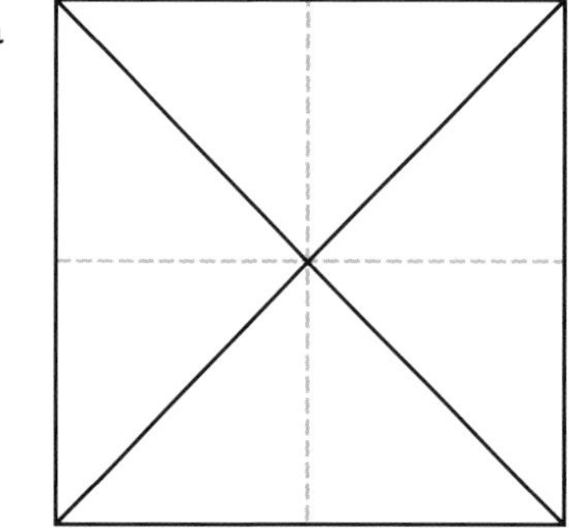

Join the half-way marker points to draw a second square 'on point' (**b**). Measure this second square, then divide each side into three equal sections and mark the points.

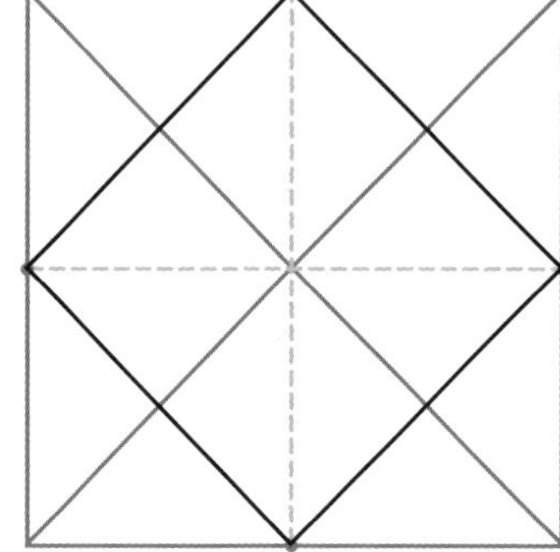

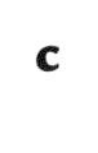

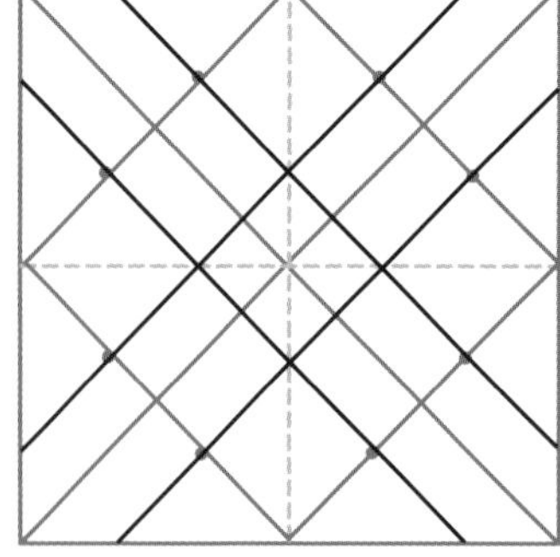

Use these marker points to draw a 9-patch (3 x 3) grid on the inner square, at the same time extending the lines out to the edges of the design (**c**).

On each corner square of the central 9-patch, mark the half-way points and join them to divide the squares into four (**d**).

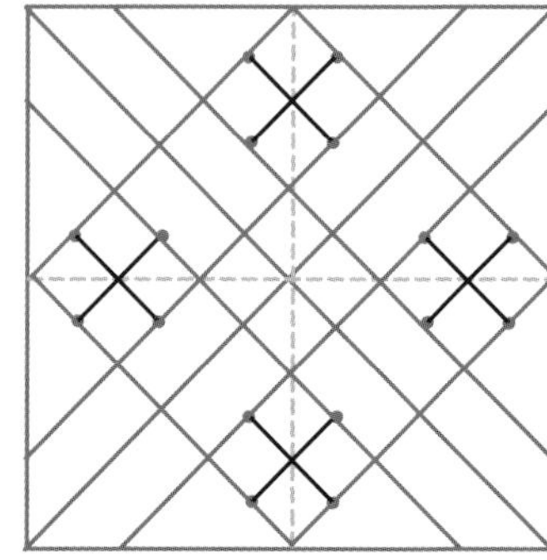

Use marker points on the diagonals to help you draw a large V shape within each central side square of the 9-patch design. Now do the same in each corner of the main block – but on these Vs, extend the lines so that they cross and meet the inner V shapes (**e**).

Diagram (**f**) shows the 8 templates required.

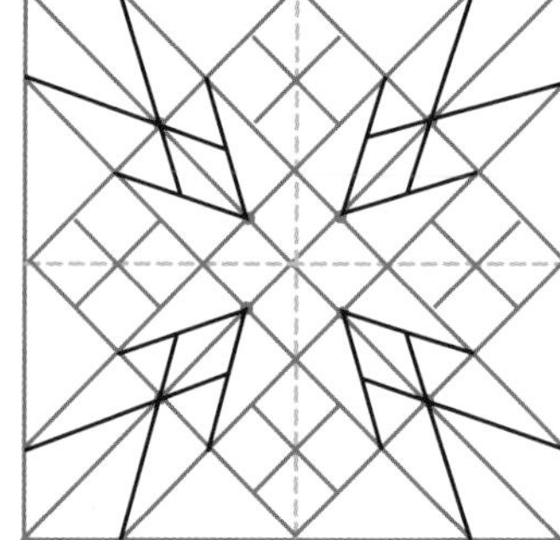

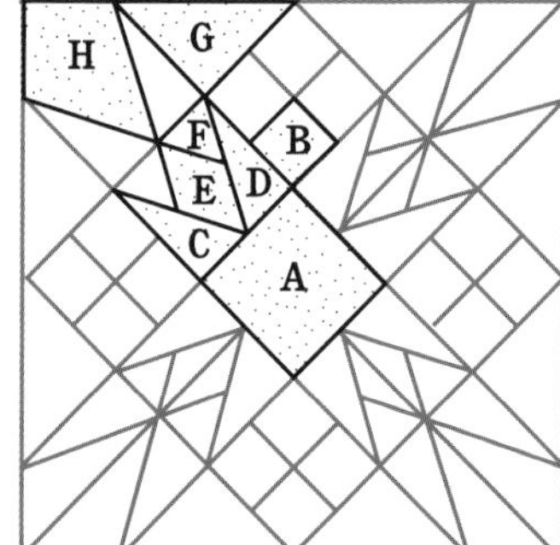

Further reading

Books

The Sampler Quilt Workbook
Dinah Travis

The Complete Book of Patchwork, Quilting and Appliqué
Linda Seward

The Complete Quilting Course
Gail Lawther

The Encyclopaedia of Quilting and Patchwork
Katharine Guerrier

Quilting Masterclass
Katharine Guerrier

Patchwork and Quilting: a step-by-step guide
Gail Lawther and Angela Besley

Big Book of Quilting
M Harer, M Michler, K Wood, L Farson

Star Studded Quilts
Roxanne Carter

Quilting With A Difference
Nikki Tinkler

Old Patchwork Quilts
Ruth E Finley

Quilts: the American Story
Susan Jenkins and Linda Seward

Quilter's Block Bible
Celia Eddy

Quiltmaking by Hand
Jinny Beyer

Once More Around The Block
Judy Hopkins

Loving Stitches, Guide to Fine Hand Quilting
Jeana Kimball

Guide to Machine Quilting
Diane Gaudynski

Drafting and Design Simplified Rodale

Pieced Borders
J Martin and M McCloskey

Borders, Bindings & Edges
S Collins

Celtic Quilting and *More Celtic Quilting*
Gail Lawther

UK patchwork and quilting publications

Popular Patchwork

British Patchwork & Quilting

Fabrications

Magic Patch

Suppliers

The Quilt Room
20 West Street, Dorking,
Surrey RH4 1BL
shop phone: 01306 740739
mail order phone: 01306 877307
e-mail: info@quiltroom.co.uk
website: www.quiltroom.co.uk
specialist quilt shop and mail order

House of Patchwork
Unit 30/32 Tower Centre,
Hoddesdon, Herts EN11 8UD
phone: 01992 447544
fax: 01992 446892
website: www.houseofpatchwork.co.uk
specialist quilt shop

Sew Creative
Wroxham Barns, Tunstead Road,
Hoveton, Norfolk NR12 8QU
phone: 01603 781665
e-mail: sewcreative@sylvia79.fsbusiness.co.uk
specialist quilt shop

Puddleducks
116 St John's Hill, Sevenoaks,
Kent TN13 3PD
phone: 01732 743642
specialist quilt shop

The Cotton Patch
1285 Stratford Road, Hall Green,
Birmingham B28 9AJ
phone: 0121 702 2840
e-mail: mailorder@cottonpatch.net
website: www.cottonpatch.net
specialist quilt shop and mail order

Patchwork Corner
51 Belswains Lane, Hemel
Hempstead, Herts HP3 9PW
phone: 01442 259000
fax: 01442 402982
e-mail: jenny@patchworkcorner.co.uk
website: www.patchworkcorner.co.uk
specialist quilt shop

Creative Grids (UK) Ltd
Unit 5, Swannington Road,
Broughton Astley, Leicester LE9 6TU
phone: 0845 450 7722 or 7733
fax: 01455 285323
e-mail: sales@creativegrids.com
website: www.creativegrids.com
mail order: patchwork and quilting products

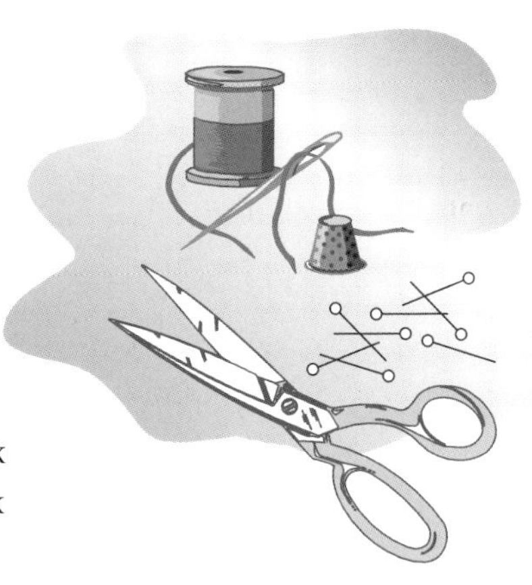

Acknowledgements

Writing a book is not easy: it involves a lot of hard work, concentration, hours of time and – in the case of a quilt book generally – mathematics. However, it's also immensely enjoyable, a lot of fun and completely rewarding. I'd like to say thankyou here to my husband, Jim, and my (now grown-up) children, Stephen and Jade, for their support, encouragement and help – without which I wouldn't have even made the quilt in the first place, let alone written the book and seen it through to fruition.

Enormous thanks wing their way to Gail and Chris Lawther who helped me make sense of what was, in essence, a pile of paper with copious notes and diagrams. Special thanks go to Jacqui Vallis for her knowledge, motivation and encouragement. Thanks too to all the ladies (where were all the men?) who came to my classes to learn how to make their very own 'heirloom sampler quilt' based on this one, while letting me share in both the process and the progress.

I hope your own quilts have given you all just as much pleasure as mine has given me. My daughter Jade worked magic with her camera: a huge thankyou for all the photography.

Quotations on the inside front cover and below are from *The Persian Pickle Club* by Sandra Dallas, reproduced by kind permission of The Random House Group.

A small fraction of the 'thanks' received by the author over the years of teaching:

☺ *Thankyou so much for starting me on what feels like a 'rest of my life' hobby!*

☺ *I consider myself lucky to have had such an inspiring teacher.*

☺ *Thankyou for a terrific workshop. We all had a lovely time and learned lots.*

☺ *I'm really fired with enthusiasm! Absolutely tremendous.*

☺ *I feel you have put me on a path of learning and discovery that will last a lifetime.*

☺ *Thankyou for all the teaching and inspiration that you have given me over the last couple of years.*

☺ *It was lovely to share your knowledge.*

☺ *Thankyou for being so patient and for all your encouragement.*

☺ *I have received several thankyou notes all saying how much they enjoyed the day. We all went home with our minds buzzing. Thankyou.*

Contact details

Nikki Tinkler
22 Aperfield Road,
Biggin Hill,
Kent TN16 3LU
phone: 01959 574604
e-mail:
nikkitinkler@ntlworld.com
website:
www.nikkitinkler.com
workshops and talks

'I look across the land, and all I see are quilts.'

From *The Persian Pickle Club* by Sandra Dallas

Nikki has exhibited her own quilt work widely since the early 1990s. She regularly travels to visit quilt groups and patchwork shops to pass on her knowledge and enjoyment of quilting through a variety of workshops offering diverse techniques. Nikki takes an equal interest in all quilt work she sees on her travels, including both traditional and contemporary work, from 'family quilts' through to progressive and experimental quilt art – and all those exciting things that happen in between. She contributes to patchwork and quilting publications on a regular basis and is an active member of the Quilters' Guild of the British Isles; she was one of the first qualified UK Quilt Judges to be accredited by the Guild.

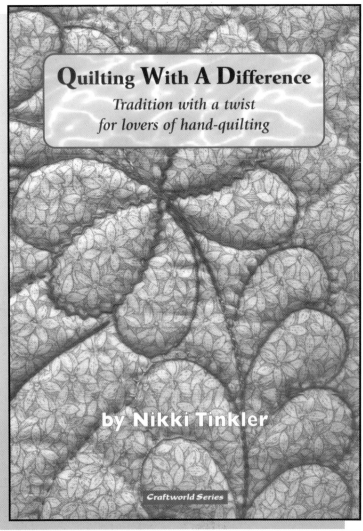

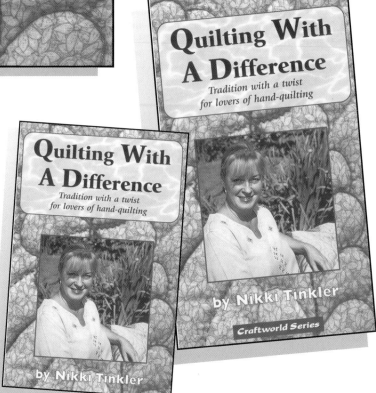